OXFORD WORLD'S CLASSICS

THE REPUBLIC AND THE LAWS

MARCUS TULLIUS CICERO (106–43 BC) was the son of a Roman knight from Arpinum, some 70 miles (112 km.) south-east of Rome. He rose to prominence through his eloquence at the bar and in the Senate; but, without hereditary connections or military achievements, he lacked a solid power-base; and so, in spite of strenuous manœuvres, he failed to reconcile Pompey and later Octavian (Augustus) to the Senate. He could have joined Caesar, but he refused and was eventually murdered at the insistence of Antony, whom he had castigated in his *Philippics*. But although Cicero was ultimately a political failure, he became for long periods of Europe's history a symbol not only of constitutional government but also of literary style. More important still, he is recognized as the main vehicle for the transmission of Hellenistic philosophy to the West. As a historian of thought, his lack of personal commitment in the main served him well. But in his political theory, where he purported to be describing a constitution or framing laws, his conservatism tended to outweigh his intellectual open-mindedness. Hence, in his vision of political life, he remained above all an old-fashioned Roman.

JONATHAN POWELL is Professor of Latin, Royal Holloway, University of London. He has published commentaries on Cicero's *De Senectute* (1988) and *De Amicitia* and *Somnium Scipionis* (1990) and has edited a volume of papers on Cicero's philosophy (*Cicero the Philosopher*, Oxford University Press, 1995). He is preparing a new text of *De Republica* and *De Legibus* for the Oxford Classical Texts series.

NIALL RUDD is Emeritus Professor of Latin, Bristol University. His books include an edition of Horace, *Epistles 2* and *Ars Poetica* (Cambridge, 1989), a verse translation of Juvenal's *Satires* (Oxford, World's Classics 1992), and a study of certain English poems and their Latin forerunners, entitled *The Classical Tradition in Operation* (Toronto and London, 1994).

OXFORD WORLD'S CLASSICS

*For over 100 years Oxford World's Classics have brought
readers closer to the world's great literature. Now with over 700
titles—from the 4,000-year-old myths of Mesopotamia to the
twentieth century's greatest novels—the series makes available
lesser-known as well as celebrated writing.*

*The pocket-sized hardbacks of the early years contained
introductions by Virginia Woolf, T. S. Eliot, Graham Greene,
and other literary figures which enriched the experience of reading.
Today the series is recognized for its fine scholarship and
reliability in texts that span world literature, drama and poetry,
religion, philosophy and politics. Each edition includes perceptive
commentary and essential background information to meet the
changing needs of readers.*

OXFORD WORLD'S CLASSICS
CICERO

The Republic
and
The Laws

Translated by
NIALL RUDD

With an Introduction and Notes by
JONATHAN POWELL
and
NIALL RUDD

OXFORD
UNIVERSITY PRESS

OXFORD

UNIVERSITY PRESS

Great Clarendon Street, Oxford OX2 6DP

Oxford University Press is a department of the University of Oxford.
It furthers the University's objective of excellence in research, scholarship,
and education by publishing worldwide in

Oxford New York

Athens Auckland Bangkok Bogotá Buenos Aires Cape Town
Chennai Dar es Salaam Delhi Florence Hong Kong Istanbul Karachi
Kolkata Kuala Lumpur Madrid Melbourne Mexico City Mumbai Nairobi
Paris São Paulo Shanghai Singapore Taipei Tokyo Toronto Warsaw

with associated companies in Berlin Ibadan

Oxford is a registered trade mark of Oxford University Press
in the UK and in certain other countries

Published in the United States
by Oxford University Press Inc., New York

British Library Cataloguing in Publication Data

Data available

Library of Congress Cataloging in Publication Data

Cicero, Marcus Tullius.
[De republica. English]
The republic; and, The laws/Cicero; translated by Niall Rudd;
with an introduction and notes by Jonathan Powell and Niall Rudd.
(Oxford world's classics)
Includes bibliographical references and index.
1. Political science—Early works to 1800. 2. State, The—Early
works to 1800. 3. Rome—Politics and government—265–30 B.C.
I. Rudd, Nial. II. Powell, J. G. F. III. Cicero, Marcus Tullius,
De legibus, English. IV. Title: Laws. V. Series.
JC81.C613 1998 320.1—dc21 97–23394

ISBN–13: 978–0–19–283236–8
ISBN–10: 0–19–283236–0

9

Typeset by Best-set Typesetter Ltd., Hong Kong
Printed in Great Britain by
Clays Ltd, St Ives plc

CONTENTS

PREFACE

Although parts of the *Republic* have been translated fairly
recently, and a full version has been published by Bréguet in the
Budé series, this is the first English translation of the whole work
since that of Sabine and Smith (1929). It is also the first English
translation of the *Laws* since Keyes's Loeb edition (1928). Students of Latin have Zetzel's commentary on selections from the
Republic (1995) and the elementary edition of *Laws* 1 by Rudd
and Wiedemann (1987). But most of the scholarship on these two
works has come from the Continent, especially Germany, as may
be seen from the bibliographies of Schmidt (1973) and Suerbaum
(1978). A particularly relevant example is Büchner's edition of the
Republic.

This translation is based on an eclectic text, but special mention
should be made of Ziegler's text of the *Republic* (5th edn. 1960)
and Ziegler and Görler's text of the *Laws* (1979). Where other
readings have been adopted their sources can usually be found
in the apparatus criticus supplied by those editors. In addition,
several of Professor Watt's conjectures have been gratefully
accepted. Many of the decisions taken will be reflected in the
Oxford Classical Text which Jonathan Powell is preparing. In the
present work the division of labour has been roughly as follows:
J.P. wrote the introduction to the *Republic*, the section on the text
of both works, and the notes on the *Republic*. He also helped with
the revision of the volume as a whole, including the translation.
The rest of the work is by N.R.

As we are dealing with incomplete texts, the sequence of ideas
is not always clear. Headings have therefore been supplied to the
main sections, and where possible some indication has been given
of the contents of the lost passages.

J.P.; N.R.

January 1997

ABBREVIATIONS

Cicero:

L   *The Laws*
R   *The Republic*

Cicero's letters:

Fam.   *Ad Familiares* (to his friends)
Att.   *Ad Atticum* (to Atticus)
Q. fr.   *Ad Quintum Fratrem* (to his brother Quintus)

Other abbreviations are as follows:

ANRW   *Aufstieg und Niedergang der römischen Welt*
CP   *Classical Philology*
D.L.   Diogenes Laertius, *Lives of Eminent Philosophers*, tr. R. D. Hicks, 2 vols. (Loeb Classical Library: Cambridge, Mass., repr. 1959)
Festus   Sextus Pompeius Festus (late second cent. AD). His partly extant abridgement of Verrius Flaccus' *De Verborum Significatu* was edited by W. M. Lindsay (Teubner, 1913)
JHI   *Journal of the History of Ideas*
JRS   *Journal of Roman Studies*
Nonius   Nonius Marcellus (early fourth cent. AD?). His dictionary was edited by W. M. Lindsay, 3 vols. (repr. Hildesheim, 1964)
OCD   *Oxford Classical Dictionary*, 2nd edn.
OLD   *Oxford Latin Dictionary*
P–A   S. E. Platner and T. Ashby, *A Topographical Dictionary of Ancient Rome* (London, 1929)
REL   *Revue des Études Latines*
ROL   *Remains of Old Latin*, tr. E. H. Warmington, Loeb Classical Library, 4 vols. (Cambridge, Mass., repr. 1961)
SIFC   *Studi italiani di filologia classica*
SVF   *Stoicorum Veterum Fragmenta*, ed. H. von Arnim, 3 vols. (Leipzig, 1903–5)

INTRODUCTION

The Importance of Cicero's *Republic* and *Laws*

The two works of Cicero translated in this volume have suffered much damage in transit to the modern world, and on this account have usually been regarded as the preserve of specialists, largely inaccessible to the public or even to classics students. Yet they offer considerable rewards to the modern reader, and especially to the student of the history of political thought. Despite the gaps and problems in the text, it is still possible to appreciate something of their literary qualities, and the ideas discussed in them are in many ways as relevant to the modern world as they were to their original historical context. The lasting merit of these works is that they concentrate on first principles. The concepts of legitimacy, justice, and responsibility in government; the nature of liberty and equality, and the conflict of these ideals with the need for directed policy; the evils of tyranny and unjust government in general; the question of the character and qualifications of those who are to be politicians; the nature of law and its relationship to morality—all these are matters which cannot be ignored as long as the human race continues to have any kind of political organization.

Both the *Republic* (*De Republica*) and the *Laws* (*De Legibus*) have had considerable and varied influence over the centuries. There is little evidence for the latter's circulation in antiquity, but there are indications that the former enjoyed great popularity both immediately on publication (as a letter to Cicero from one of his friends testified[1]) and later during the first century AD.[2] Tacitus shows signs of engagement with the ideas of the *Republic*, but takes a cynical and pessimistic line far removed from Cicero's, and directly rebuts Cicero's view that the mixed constitution is especially durable.[3] For the Christian writers of late antiquity, to whom we owe such knowledge as we have of some parts of the lost text,

---

[1] Caelius to Cicero, *Fam.* 8. 1. 4 (51 BC): 'Your books on the *Republic* are well received on all sides.'
[2] Seneca, *Epistles* 108. 30 ff. implies that it was well known.
[3] Tacitus, *Annals* 4. 33; cf. ibid. 3. 26–7.

Cicero's *Republic* represented the culmination of pagan thinking about political theory and about the Roman state in particular, and this naturally served as a foil for their own reflections on these matters. At approximately the same period, the Neoplatonist Macrobius picked out the concluding passage of the dialogue for detailed commentary,[4] and may therefore have been responsible for setting the so-called *Dream of Scipio* on its way as a separate literary entity. The *Dream*, thus torn out of its context, was the only part of the text known in the Middle Ages, and, as a vision of the cosmos and of life in the hereafter, it became a highly formative influence on medieval and Renaissance views of the world.[5]

The fragments of the rest of the *Republic* were collected in the sixteenth century,[6] but could give little idea of the overall shape of the work. With the discovery of the Vatican manuscript in 1820, it became possible again to speculate more fruitfully about Cicero's political message, although the mutilated state of the text has allowed more latitude for debate than is the case with many classical works. Victorian Englishmen could see the *De Republica* as a prophecy of British parliamentary democracy,[7] while one influential view at the beginning of this century interpreted Cicero's ideal statesman as a kind of saviour-dictator.[8] Ronald Syme's dismissal of the *Republic*, on the brink of the Second World War, as 'a book about which too much has been written',[9] doubtless reflects more on Cicero's interpreters than on Cicero himself. Subsequently the work suffered some neglect, particularly in the English-speaking world. However, scholarly interest in it has recently started to revive, and it appears that the time may now be ripe to take a fresh look at the *Republic* and at its companion,

[4] Macrobius, tr. Stahl.

[5] See Lewis 23–8. (Full details of modern sources are given in the Bibliography.)

[6] See Heck 270–81 for the 16th-cent. editions.

[7] See the edition of G. G. Hardingham (London, 1884).

[8] This view was first put forward in 1917 by Reitzenstein, who (probably incorrectly) regarded the *Republic* as a foreshadowing of, and possibly an inspiration for, the Augustan principate. The debate on this issue has continued ever since; for a convenient summary of its progress, see MacKendrick 64. The question largely depends on the meaning of the phrase *rector rei publicae*, for which see n. 34 below.

[9] Syme 144 n. 1.

the *Laws*, which has been less prominent in modern debates, but was influential in informing Renaissance and early modern theories of natural law.

The Background to the Composition of the *Republic* and *Laws*: Cicero's Career to 54 BC

In May 54 BC Cicero wrote from his villa at Cumae to his brother Quintus: 'I am writing the *political* treatise I mentioned. It's a pretty heavy and laborious work. But if it goes according to plan, the effort will have been well spent. Otherwise I shall throw it into the sea on which I am looking out as I write, and I shall start on other things, since I can't stay idle.'[10]

The word *political*, here italicized, is in Greek. It refers not primarily to practical politics, but to a branch of philosophy, the theory of the *polis* or city-state; this was regarded as a part of the larger study of 'ethics', the theory of human character and behaviour. Cicero, in other words, was writing a work in the tradition of Plato and Aristotle (as far as we know, the first of its kind in Latin) which would cover not only the theory of constitutions and laws, but also matters such as the moral education and training of citizens, the place of culture and the arts in a well-run society, the character of the kind of individual best equipped to take part in government, and (perhaps more surprisingly for a modern reader) the place of well-run states in the cosmic order.

Marcus Tullius Cicero had made his own way to the top in Roman politics, as a 'new man' from an Italian country town, the first of his family to seek office in the capital.[11] His father had been on companionable terms with Roman aristocrats, but had forgone a political career owing to uncertain health. Cicero himself, however, was ambitious to succeed not only in the political sphere but also in cultural and intellectual activities: he had studied philosophy with enthusiasm in his youth (see the following section) and also fancied himself, not without some justification, as a Latin poet. He was highly accomplished in Greek as well as in Latin; his balanced, rhythmical style owed much to the great Greek

[10] *Q. fr.* 2. 12. 1; cf. nn. 26 and 27 below.
[11] For a more detailed account of his career and its historical circumstances, see e.g. E. Rawson (3); Griffin.

orators, especially Demosthenes and Isocrates, but also to the current fashions of the Greek East. This mastery of style could be turned to advantage in literary activity as well as in political or legal oratory. When the political situation went against him Cicero easily cast himself in an alternative role of thinker, writer, and educator of his fellow-citizens, presenting to them the critical spirit and high-minded values of Greek philosophy while at the same time affirming the patriotic duty owed to the Roman state and its empire.[12]

In his year as consul in 63 BC, he had defeated the conspiracy of Catiline (Lucius Sergius Catilina). The importance of this episode has been variously assessed by historians, but at the very least it was a threat to stability and a symptom of recurrent problems. Cicero claimed to stand for reconciliation of factional interests for the sake of the common good: his catchwords were *concordia ordinum* (i.e. that all social classes should work together), *consensio omnium bonorum* (consensus of all good citizens), *otium cum dignitate* (peace with honour). The Catilinarians, to him, represented only an extreme and criminal minority; once they had been flushed out, the state could return to normal. Cicero did apparently succeed in uniting the Roman people behind him for a short time. But by his high-handed action in executing the conspirators without proper trial (even though he did so on the advice of the Senate), he offered a handle to his political enemies, one which was seized a few years later by the tribune P. Clodius Pulcher. Cicero incurred his enmity in 61 by testifying against him in the curious case of the profanation of the rites of the Bona Dea (see note on *L.* 2. 36). Now Clodius had his revenge by passing a law which enacted that anyone who had put Roman citizens to death without trial was to be outlawed. Cicero, as Clodius intended, withdrew into exile rather than face trial under this law (cf. *R.* 1. 6, *L.* 2. 42).

Some fourteen months later Cicero was recalled, largely at the instance of Pompey, who had himself begun to suffer harassment at Clodius' hands. Cicero's orthodox progression up the *cursus*

---

[12] The prefaces to the later philosophical works present the writing of philosophy as a patriotic service to Rome. See in general Douglas 135–70.

honorum had led him to identify himself more and more with the interests of the senatorial aristocracy. After his consulship he had attempted to keep on good terms both with Pompey, whom he admired and whose influence he valued,[13] and with the so-called 'optimates',[14] aristocratic senators who were protective of the Senate's role in government, and jealously obstructive of anyone who tried to circumvent it. But one of the chief targets of optimate obstruction was Pompey, and Cicero found himself in an impossible position, especially after the 'Conference of Luca' in 56 when Pompey, Crassus and Caesar reinforced their informal alliance and gained effective control of Roman politics. Cicero's political debt to Pompey obliged him to move away from the 'optimates', in whose eyes he consequently lost all credibility, and he confessed privately to Atticus that he had been a prize ass.[15] Thereafter Cicero could no longer play a leading part in senatorial politics. Although he continued to attend the Senate from time to time and was continually occupied in the lawcourts (not least in defending various friends of Pompey whom he had previously opposed), he sought distraction from the turbulent political situation about which he could do nothing, and turned to writing.

Cicero's Philosophical Education and Affiliations

In his youth, Cicero had spent time in the company of Greek philosophers, both in Rome and in Athens. After a brief flirtation with Epicureanism, he became a follower of the Academic philosopher Philo of Larissa, who attracted him partly because of his interests in rhetoric. Philo was the latest representative of the sceptical turn taken by the Academy since Arcesilaus in the third century BC. Later, Cicero attended the lectures of another Academic, Antiochus of Ascalon, who had been a pupil of Philo but had abandoned scepticism, claiming to restore the authentic doctrines of the 'Old Academy' (i.e. of Plato's

---

[13] On the course of Cicero's relations with Pompey, cf. B. Rawson.

[14] The word *optimates* originally meant simply 'aristocrats' and is so used in the *Republic*, regardless of its current use as a political catchword (see Note on the Translation).

[15] *Att.* 4. 5.

immediate successors) as opposed to the sceptical 'New Academy'. Antiochus argued not only that the true Platonic tradition did after all allow certain knowledge, but also that there was no difference other than in terminology between the doctrines of the Academy (as interpreted by himself), those of Aristotle and those of the Stoics.[16]

In the later series of philosophical works,[17] written in 45–44 BC, Cicero proclaims himself as an adherent of the sceptical methods of the New Academy. His version of scepticism, owed presumably to Philo, was a moderate one; far from insisting on absolute suspension of judgement in all circumstances, he allowed the wise man to assent provisionally to any view which seemed probable, while remaining open to contrary argument. The New Academics used several methods to combat rash claims of certainty. They emphasized the variety of possible viewpoints (*diaphonia*); they would argue successively on both sides of a question, or undertake to find arguments against whatever view was offered by the opponent. These methods were to provide Cicero with an excellent vehicle for objective exposition of the doctrines of the various schools.

However, in the *Republic* and *Laws* his position is somewhat different. It is true that in the third book of the *Republic* he presents arguments both for and against justice in the Academic manner, recalling the opposing theses of Carneades (see note on *R*. 3. 8); but it is clear that he has changed the whole drift of Carneades' arguments. There is no sceptical reservation of judgement. The whole debate is explicitly directed towards establishing the case for justice and refuting the opposing view. The speaker Philus, who puts the case against justice, does so unwillingly (3. 8), and the outcome is never left in doubt. Furthermore, in the *Laws*, Cicero explicitly keeps the sceptical Academy at a distance (1. 39) so that it will not disturb his neatly constructed theory of divine providence and natural law; and the views on the *summum bonum* given in *L*. 1. 54 ff. are explicitly in line with those of Antiochus.

It has been thought, therefore, that he had at this time deserted

---

[16] Cicero's 'Academic books' are the main source for the debate between Philo and Antiochus on the possibility of knowledge. Cf. further Glucker (1).

[17] For a convenient list see Powell (3) xiii–xvii.

Introductionxv

scepticism in favour of the views of Antiochus;[18] and a passage in
a later work, the *Academica* (1. 13, cf. 1. 43), has been taken to
indicate that Cicero was at that time converted back from the 'Old
Academy' (as interpreted by Antiochus) to the scepticism of Philo.
But it may be going too far to speak of a change of allegiance.
Rather, it seems that Cicero has here consciously and temporarily
relinquished the stance of a sceptic, to which he would later return
when his context and purposes demanded it. In some of the later
dialogues it suited him to stress the difficulty of coming to a firm
conclusion on the philosophical questions he was discussing, but
this would not have been appropriate in the context of the *Republic* and *Laws* (cf. *L.* 1. 37). In fact, as Görler has pointed out,
there are also signs of the persistence of a sceptical attitude in the
Laws: in *L.* 1. 54 Cicero stops short of confessing total allegiance
to Antiochus, and in *L.* 1. 36 he proclaims his own freedom of
judgement. A certain measure of distancing is effected, too, by the
dialogue form. But we are left in little doubt as to the views of
which Cicero wishes to convince us. Cicero here appears as a
Roman consular speaking on his own authority about matters that
lie well within his experience, and in the *Laws* he assumes the
mantle of a legislator after the Platonic manner. The whole edifice
of the *Laws* depends on certain assumptions about the nature of
law, morality, and the order of the universe. Cicero realizes that
these assumptions are open to sceptical attack. If challenged, he
would be unable to claim certainty for them. But from a legislator's point of view it was important not just that they should be
believed, but also that they should not be called into question.
Hence, for the time being, the sceptical Academy is respectfully
asked to keep its distance.

The *Republic*: Literary Form, Characters, and Setting

In 55 BC, feeling perhaps that his supreme oratorical gifts had not
been given their due or even that they had failed him, Cicero
turned first to an examination of the nature of oratory and its role
in politics (the *De Oratore*). The genre of the Platonic dialogue

[18] See Glucker (2) for the 'conversion' hypothesis, and, for the arguments
against this, Görler.

suggested itself, partly as a means of presenting competing views, but also to draw attention to the reminiscences of Platonic ways of thinking that lay behind Cicero's concept of the ideal orator. It was not unnatural that Cicero should be led on from there to consider more generally the nature of the *res publica*, and to define the nature of the ideal exponent of the political profession, the statesman or 'best citizen' (*optimus civis*).[19]

The obvious literary model was Plato's *Republic*. Cicero's direct homage to the master was expressed in the lost section at the beginning of the work,[20] and is embodied in the concluding vision of the cosmos and the afterlife (the Dream of Scipio) which reflects the Myth of Er at the end of Plato's tenth book. Plato is directly quoted or referred to a number of times, sometimes for purposes of criticism. Cicero's Scipio says (*R.* 2. 3, cf. 2. 51–2) that, rather than invent a city for himself as Plato did, he prefers to examine a real historical instance (the Roman constitution) which comes closest to the ideal; in 2. 21 Laelius criticizes Plato's state as impractical; and the fragments of the fourth and fifth books indicate fairly clearly that Plato's schemes for the abolition of marriage and private property were rejected. But it is a mistake to suppose that, because Cicero departs from Plato in certain specific ways, his *Republic* is in any deep sense anti-Platonic.[21] Plato underlies the *De Republica* in a number of important ways: particularly the treatment of politics as a skill or art that can (theoretically) be an object of knowledge, the search for organic harmony in the state (especially at the end of Book 2), the analogy between state, individual, and cosmos (1. 60; 6. 26), and the ideal of the philosophical statesman which was, it seems, described in the last two books, but which is also actually illustrated in the characters of the main speakers in the dialogue. Cicero's Scipio is enough of a Platonist to regard philosophy and astronomy as the wise man's true occupation, and to declare that one should under-

[19] The subject of the *Republic* is defined more fully in *Q. fr.* 3. 5. 1 as *de optimo statu civitatis et de optimo cive* ('on the best condition of the State and the best citizen').

[20] He apparently called himself a 'companion of Plato', fr. 1b Ziegler, quoted by Pliny the Elder, *Natural History*, pref. 22.

[21] In contrast, Sharples, followed by Zetzel (p. 14), has emphasized the un-Platonic features of the *De Republica*.

take political offices only out of a sense of duty or necessity, as Plato's Guardians do (1. 26–9).[22] In *R. 1. 56–64*, Scipio is made to present quite strongly the case for monarchy, Plato's favoured mode of government, although the other interlocutors withhold their full assent and he himself states quite clearly that he regards the Roman constitution as superior. The Ciceronian ideal states- man bears at least some resemblance to a Platonic Guardian (alias philosopher-king) and also to the ideal statesman in Plato's *Politi- cus*, who has true knowledge of the art of government. Even where Cicero is clearly drawing on later sources, the issues are often the same as those discussed by Plato: the theory of constitutions and the ways in which one type of constitution turns into another, the notion of justice and its defence against cynical pragmatism, and the intense interest in education and morals. Cicero, it can be argued, does not reject Plato, but brings him up to date and down to earth.

Influences from Greek writers after Plato may also be divined. Cicero elsewhere mentions a dialogue by Aristotle also entitled *Politicus* (now lost) which dealt with the character of the ideal citizen or statesman.[23] It is possible that Cicero did not have access to the *Politics* of Aristotle known to us, but some of Aristotle's ideas may have reached him indirectly through Peripatetic philosophers such as Theophrastus and Dicaearchus.[24] The dis- cussion on justice in the third book explicitly owes a great deal to the New Academic philosopher Carneades, though its main lines are already present in Plato's *Republic*. The historian Polybius, a portion of whose remarks on the Roman constitution has sur- vived, was used by Cicero as a source for factual information (*R. 2. 27*) and opinions (4. 3), and there is clearly a great deal in common between Cicero and Polybius as regards the framework of ideas within which they view the constitutional history of Rome, although there are some considerable differences in judge- ment and emphasis.[25] But in general, as with the rest of Cicero's philosophical works, it is probably a mistake to insist too much

[22] Cf. also Plato, *Republic* 347c–d; see Powell (4).
[23] Referred to in Cic. *De Finibus* 5. 11; *Q. fr.* 3. 5. 1.
[24] See Frede.
[25] See notes on 1. 45, and Zetzel 22–4.

on the influence of lost Hellenistic writings. Cicero's pride in his own authority as an experienced Roman statesman and in his own literary abilities was such that, while he might freely plunder Greek writings for facts and ideas, he is not likely to have followed them closely as regards the literary form, the presentation of his argument, or the opinions he expresses (cf. *R.* 2. 21).

We happen to have particularly clear evidence for the progress of Cicero's work on the *Republic* from a letter of November 54 BC.[26] He had at first envisaged a dialogue in nine books, between Scipio and his friends, set during a nine-day holiday in 129 BC. He tried out the first two books on a friend named Sallustius (probably not Sallust the historian), who suggested recasting the work so that Cicero himself spoke in his own person, in order to appear more authoritative than the speakers in a fictional dialogue would, and to enable direct discussion of contemporary events. Cicero eventually followed a plan of this kind in the *Laws*; but for the *Republic* he evidently reverted to something more like the original scheme. The dialogue in its final form comprises six books of conversation between Scipio, Laelius, Philus, Manilius, Sp. Mummius, and four younger men, arranged in pairs of books with a preface to each pair written in Cicero's own person. The work appears to have been dedicated by Cicero to his brother, Quintus.[27]

The choice of characters and setting is of some significance. Scipio Aemilianus, destroyer of Carthage and Numantia, was the most glorious figure of the mid-second century BC and appealed to Cicero's tendency to idealize the great statesmen of the past. Although his rise to power had been an extraordinary one in which popular favour had often overridden the letter of the law, Scipio never appeared to threaten the stability of the Roman state in the way that the later generals, Marius, Sulla, Caesar, and Pompey did. In the last year of his life, the year in which the dialogue is set, he had represented the interests of the Italians and allied communities in their opposition to the agrarian commission

---

[26] *Q. fr.* 3. 5. 1–2; cf. also *Att.* 4. 16.

[27] The allusion in *R.* 1. 13 suits Quintus rather than Atticus, the other main possibility. It may be relevant that Cicero discussed the progress of the work in letters to his brother.

set up by Tiberius Gracchus.[28] Cicero regarded the conflicts over the Gracchan redistribution of land as the beginning of the end for the Roman Republic, and he had himself, as consul in 63, pursued the same kind of policy when he opposed the land bill of the tribune Rullus; it was therefore natural that he should admire Scipio, whose premature death (perhaps murder—at least Cicero thought so) just after his political victory in 129 left behind a hero's memory.

Scipio was also well known for his patronage of writers and intellectuals, and could be presumed to share some of their interests. Polybius the historian says himself that he was among Scipio's closest associates, and it was not in any way unrealistic for Cicero to make Scipio talk about constitutional theory in terms which are clearly very similar to those used by Polybius. Cicero took considerable pains to ensure historical accuracy in the settings of his dialogues. On the other hand, one may expect a certain measure of imaginative idealization in the portrait; the Scipio of the dialogue is designed to be exemplary rather than precisely realistic, and the question of the relationship of the portrait to the historical Scipio is not only difficult to answer in detail but also largely irrelevant to the appreciation of the work.[29]

The characters in the *De Republica* are well-defined individuals; in this respect, at any rate, the dialogue form is more than a mere literary convention. While Scipio is an idealist and a theoretician, his friend Laelius, in real life less distinguished and nicknamed *Sapiens* perhaps more on account of his political caution than because of his philosophical leanings,[30] is more practical and down-to-earth. In the opening conversation (1. 19), Laelius calls the discussion back from astronomical speculation to practical politics in a way strongly reminiscent of Socrates. Manilius is the venerable legal expert (1. 20). Philus is a man of great personal rectitude who nevertheless takes on the defence of injustice for the sake of the argument, as an Academic philosopher might do (3. 8). Mummius is a confirmed conservative and anti-democrat (3. 47). Tubero, Scipio's nephew, is an eager student of

---

[28] Appian, *Bella Civilia* 1. 19; cf. Cic. *Laelius de Amicitia* 12.

[29] On Scipio in general see Astin; for the idealism of Cicero's portrait of him cf. Zetzel 12–13.

[30] Cf. Plutarch, *Tiberius Gracchus* 8; Cic. *De Finibus* 2. 24, etc.

philosophy who is the first to arrive at the house of Scipio, and raises the question of the portent of the double sun (1. 14). The other young interlocutors, Rutilius, Fannius, and Scaevola, are less clearly characterized, at least in the extant portions of the text; but this may well be because of the strong precedence accorded to seniority among the Romans, which is reflected also in Cicero's other dialogues.[31] Another feature of dialogue technique that should not be overlooked is that the characters are able to change their minds: Scipio in 3. 43 signals a change from his position of the previous day.

Finally, although the inspiration of the dialogue is Platonic, the setting is entirely Roman. Socratic dialectic did not come naturally to the hierarchically-minded Romans or to the rhetorically-minded Cicero. Although dialectical argument is occasionally used to good effect, as for example in *R.* 1. 56–64, the exposition more often recalls the connected discourses of Socrates in many parts of Plato's *Republic*. The tone of the conversation is urbane and relaxed; and if the characters compliment each other in a way that may seem laboured to modern taste, that should be seen as reflecting the courtesies of a more formal age than ours.

The Purpose of the *Republic*, and Cicero's Subsequent Career

Cicero's *Republic* is not a political manifesto. The genre of the Platonic dialogue itself suggests an exploration of issues rather than a dogmatic exposition, and the second-century setting precludes direct comment on contemporary events. But certain points are made with unmistakeable conviction. The superiority of the Roman Republican constitution is asserted with great emphasis by Scipio in *R.* 1. 70, and by Cicero as participant in the dialogue in *L.* 2. 23, while Cicero as author insists, in the preface to *R.* 5, on the degenerate state of contemporary Rome. At the same time, alternative viewpoints are given their due. The prominence accorded to the arguments for monarchy in Book 1 has suggested to many interpreters that they represent Cicero's real opinions, but the context shows that they are merely being given an airing. The

[31] Cf. Becker.

same is true of the parallel arguments for aristocracy stated just before, although scholars still sometimes quote them as though they were Cicero's authentic views. In the Philus–Laelius debate it is made quite clear which side we are supposed to approve of, although one cannot help wondering what the consequences would have been for modern views of Cicero if parts of Philus' speech had survived out of context.

Cicero set the dialogue in the past in order to avoid offence (*Q. fr.* 3. 5. 2); the fact that offence would otherwise have been given shows that he intended the work to be relevant to contemporary politics. At the time of writing, traditional modes of government were manifestly not working. The role of the Senate was a subject of controversy, mob violence and gang warfare were increasing, and eventually (in 52) a temporary solution to the disorder was found by granting Pompey extraordinary powers as sole consul.[32] The arguments about monarchy, aristocracy, and democracy, presented with a careful appearance of theoretical objectivity by Cicero, should be seen against this background. His conclusion that the existing Roman constitution is the best is not mere unthinking nostalgia, but is put forward after a full consideration of the alternatives. It amounts to a conclusion that radical constitutional change (as opposed to the relatively minor changes proposed in the *Laws*) was not the answer. Cicero is also criticized for trying to apply the theory of the Greek city-state to an imperial capital, but such criticisms would not have been so readily made if we possessed the whole of Book 3; it is clear from the fragments that one of the central issues in the debate on justice was the relationship between Rome and her empire.

Because so much of what survives of the *Republic* is devoted to constitutional theory and history, it is often assumed that this is what the work was largely about. But the discussion of constitutions occupied somewhat less than a third of the whole dialogue. The third book was about justice, the fourth about education and morals, and the fifth and sixth about the character of the ideal statesman. Cicero himself may have regarded this last part as the most important, as he refers to it several times in subsequent

---

[32] Geiger (to my mind not altogether convincingly) tries to link *R.* with attempts to make Pompey dictator.

letters.[33] There has been considerable controversy as to the exact implications of the phrase *rector rei publicae*,[34] but there is no good evidence that Cicero meant it as anything other than the name of an occupation or profession, i.e. 'politician' or 'statesman' pure and simple. Earlier Latin had no exact word or phrase to express this concept, and Cicero had to coin one (in fact he uses several variants on the phrase). Once this is seen, it becomes clear why the constitutional part of the *Republic* is over so early. What ultimately matters is not the (obviously necessary) constitutional framework within which the politician operates, but the profession of politics itself and the quality of its practitioners. Cicero was concerned not just to encourage political participation, but to present politics as a branch of knowledge which needed to be studied and mastered, and which aimed at the greatest good not of the politicians themselves but of the governed. He used the medium of the literary dialogue to make an appeal to the patriotic sense of the Roman ruling class, and his ideal of the wise and just statesman is by implication an indictment of current politics and politicians. In a letter to Atticus (8. 11) written in February 49, just before the outbreak of civil war, he is still more explicit. Neither Pompey nor Caesar, he says, has given a thought to the proper aims of the statesman as defined in the *Republic*; each only wants power for himself.

The relevance of the *Republic* to the current political situation was quite real, but it was not of the kind that was likely to have an immediate practical effect. Cicero could do nothing to avert the civil war, which broke out barely two years after the *Republic* was put into circulation. The murder of Caesar in 44 BC revived

---

[33] *Att.* 6. 1. 8; 6. 2. 9; 6. 3. 3; 6. 6. 2; 7. 3. 2; 8. 11. 1.

[34] *Rector* literally means 'ruler', 'controller', or 'helmsman'. The phrase has often been taken to imply an office or function within the state: a permanent or temporary position of supreme power, or of supreme informal authority whether or not recognized by law (a conception obviously similar to that of the Augustan principate; cf. n. 8 above). This assumption once made, the question inevitably followed: who was envisaged as a candidate for the job? Some have thought that Cicero had Pompey in mind, others suppose that he was putting himself forward. But the more likely view (argued for more fully by Powell (2)) is that the phrase *rector rei publicae* was intended to mean simply 'statesman', and that the ideal of the *rector* delineated in the lost parts of the fifth and sixth books was one to which all statesmen could aspire. Cf. also How, esp. 41–2, and see Schmidt for a survey of previous views.

Cicero's hopes; it must have appeared to him that all that he had said in the *Republic* about the killing of tyrants had suddenly come true. But the sequel did not meet expectations.[35] Cicero distrusted Caesar's heir; he is on record as judging that Octavian could not be a 'good citizen' (let alone, one supposes, a type of the 'best citizen' described in the *Republic*).[36] Nevertheless, against his own better judgement, he entered into an intrigue with Octavian in the hope that the latter would restore senatorial rule, and courted open hostility to Antony. However, Octavian and Antony at length came to an understanding; proscriptions were instituted; Octavian agreed to Antony's insistence that Cicero should be outlawed; and Cicero, indecisive as always, failed to escape from Italy and was assassinated. A vivid account of his death is given by Plutarch, who tells how he ordered his litter to be put down and stretched out his neck to meet the murderer's stroke.[37]

The *Laws*

The *Laws* was begun in the same period as the *Republic*, at the end of the 50s. Work was suspended when Cicero went out to govern Cilicia in 51, and, whether or not it was resumed in 46 (*Fam.* 9. 2. 5), it may never have been finished. Though Macrobius refers to a fifth book (*Saturnalia* 6. 4. 8), nothing survives beyond Book 3, and even that book is incomplete. Particularly regrettable is the loss of the sections on education and the law-courts.

The setting is Cicero's home town, Arpinum, just over 70 miles (112 km.) south-east of Rome. This choice enabled Cicero to affirm his love of his native district (2. 2–3), to honour his grandfather (2. 3 and 3. 36) as a bastion of local conservatism, to bring in the powerful figure of Marius, on whom he had written a poem (1. 1–2), and to describe the beauty of the countryside (2. 6), which represented a benign nature, corresponding to the nature of God and human reason. The time is a day in late June—an idea derived from Plato (2. 69).

The opening sections on Marius' oak remind us not only that Cicero was a poet but also that the details of literary works do

[35] For the history of this period, see most conveniently Syme.
[36] *Att.* 14. 12. 2.
[37] See Plutarch, *Life of Cicero* 47–8, translated in E. Rawson (3) 293–5; for other sources see E. Rawson (3) 320 and T. N. Mitchell 323–4.

not have to be historically accurate. The same goes (we are invited to infer) for the *Laws*, which, though containing real characters and much historical material, does not represent an actual conversation. The sections on Roman historiography also have a preparatory function, in that they establish Cicero as a man with a firm grasp of Roman traditions and also an extensive experience of politics.

The two participants in the dialogue (apart from Cicero himself) are Titus Pomponius Atticus and Quintus Tullius Cicero. Atticus (110–32 BC)[38] was a knight who inherited 2 million sesterces from his father and another 10 million from his uncle. Cultivated and charming, he contrived to remain on friendly terms with Marius *and* Sulla; Pompey *and* Caesar; Brutus, Antony, *and* Octavian— an extraordinary feat, which suggests not only a benign and generous peacemaker but also a wily opportunist. He spoke excellent Greek, and spent much of his time in Athens; hence the cognomen Atticus. In spite of his wealth, his life-style was in most respects Epicurean. He avoided public office, and his scholarly research (on genealogy and chronology) was of a kind that involved no political judgements. In a period of drastic change Atticus was a symbol of continuity. His conservative temperament anchored him firmly in the past; unlike his boyhood friend, Cicero, he survived the turmoil of the Roman revolution, and 'he lived to see his granddaughter engaged to the future emperor Tiberius'.[39]

Quintus Tullius Cicero (102–43 BC) was Cicero's younger brother. He was aedile in 65 and praetor in 62 (for these offices see Appendix). He was governor of Asia Minor 61–59, legate of Pompey in Sardinia 57–56, and with Caesar in Gaul 54–51, during which time he took part in the invasion of Britain. He joined Pompey in the civil war and was killed in the proscriptions of 43. Quintus was married to Pomponia, Atticus' sister, from 69–44. He had literary interests, and is known to have written four tragedies. To judge from the *Laws*, he held rather narrow oligarchic views (see, for example, his remarks on the tribunate in 3. 19–22). From Cicero's correspondence he emerges as a con-

---

[38] Nepos' informative, if over-laudatory, account of Atticus' life is printed in the Loeb volume along with Florus. The fullest and most sensitive essay on his life and character is in Shackleton Bailey (1) 3–59.

[39] Horsfall 99.

scientious public servant with considerable physical courage but an uncertain temper and unreliable judgement.[40]

The main phases of Cicero's exposition are noted in the headings in the text. Here it is enough to make a few general points about the nature of the work, along with its value and limitations, especially in regard to Books 2 and 3. At one point (2. 23) Quintus remarks that Cicero's proposals about religion 'are not very different from the laws of Numa and the customs of today'. And it is true that not only those sections but the *Laws* as a whole lack the innovative quality of Plato's work, being designed rather to suit a revived version of the Roman constitution described in the *Republic*. For example, the tribunes' powers are retained in spite of Quintus' objections (*L.* 3. 19–22), and the people keep the right to make laws, elect magistrates, and serve as a court of appeal. Yet some proposals are new. Augurs are to have more power; fetials are given wider diplomatic responsibilities (for these offices see Appendix); and other priests are to be available to advise on private ceremonies. The censorship is never to be left vacant; the importance of the quaestorship is reduced; the aedileship becomes the first step in the *cursus honorum* and brings access to the Senate. The Senate itself is given greater powers (e.g. the right to appoint a dictator in emergencies); members are required to attend regularly and to make themselves familiar with current affairs. They will no longer have the privilege of 'free embassies' (3. 18), and when serving as magistrates they are to be more strictly accountable for their actions. The censors are required to implement these reforms.

It is fair to point out that in his religious measures Cicero is outlining an official system for the country, not a personal creed. We cannot be sure about how much he accepted. He was satisfied, however, that no government could ignore the age-old beliefs and rituals of the people, however much they might be despised by thinkers like Lucretius. Moreover, if the system was properly managed it could contribute significantly to the stability of the state. So much is intelligible. It is disappointing, however, to see a man who could write so eloquently about the majesty of the

---

[40] An interesting character-sketch can be compiled from the index of Shackleton Bailey (2).

gods condoning the manipulation of religious laws for immediate political ends (2. 31, 3. 27). In the speeches a certain amount of pious fraud might be expected, but even the letters show some awkward discrepancies. In *Fam.* 1. 1. 3, for instance (on the restoration of Ptolemy) Cicero supports a bogus oracle, conveniently discovered by C. Cato. But then in *Fam.* 1. 7. 4 he suggests ways of circumventing it. His support of divination is based on its political utility.

The political limitations are more serious. Cicero dreams of Rome as she had been a hundred years earlier, before the structure had begun to give way under the strains of empire. Granted, it was too late to save the Republic now; three years later Caesar would cross the Rubicon. But even if, by some stroke of magic, Cicero's dream had come true, disaster would not have been averted. By the 50s huge problems had developed which could not be solved within the framework of what was, essentially, a city-state. First, an empire of such size and complexity could not be run by a small élite of all-round amateurs, in which within a decade the same man might be expected to manage finances, administer city departments, sit as a judge, and lead a military campaign. The voting-system was over-centralized and out-dated; citizens could no longer be expected to travel to the capital for elections and other meetings of the assemblies. Distance also brought problems of control; governors often exploited the provinces in order to meet their election 'expenses'. There were also intractable economic problems resulting partly from the decay of smallholdings owing to the absence of farmers on military service, partly from new farming methods (large ranches worked by slave labour). All this led to the growth of a workless and resentful urban proletariat, which could easily be inflamed by demagogues. That, in turn, contributed to the worst problem of all. Troops were recruited by promises of loot and land. So at the end of a campaign there were thousands of well-trained fighting men in Italy, who depended for their future, not on the Senate, but on the power of an ambitious general. None of these questions is confronted by Cicero. So, whatever his hopes and intentions, there is an air of unreality about the *Laws*.

Nevertheless, the work contains much of interest in social and political history, in matters of religious ritual, and in a conception of law and nature which recurs again and again in the history of jurisprudence. Finally, the *Laws* throws further light on the personality of a brilliant and warm-hearted man who, without high birth or a military command, strove by his gifts of persuasion to make the old republican system work—a system which in three centuries had extended Roman power from Egypt to the Channel. Many years later, the emperor Augustus (who had acquiesced in Cicero's murder) found one of his grandsons with a work of Cicero's in his hand. The youngster tried to hide the book under his cloak, but Augustus took it from him and read through a large part of it where he stood. Then, handing it back, he said 'That was a master of words, my boy. A master of words and a lover of his country.'[41]

Natural Law

Natural law, as expounded by Cicero in *L*. 1, rests on certain fundamental beliefs.

1. *That the universe is a system run by a rational Providence.* In *L*. 1. 21 Atticus obligingly makes this concession to enable the discussion to begin. Little is said in the *Laws* about the rhythms of the natural world, perhaps because the topic has been explored elsewhere.[42] But in *L*. 2. 16 Cicero says we should be grateful for 'the procession of the stars, the alternation of day and night, the regular succession of the seasons, and the fruits which are produced for our enjoyment'.[43]

2. *That Mankind stands between God and the animals.* In virtue of his physical needs, appetites, and mortality, man is part of the animal kingdom. But, unlike other animals, he has been given the power of reason. This enables him to work the land and to use animals for his own purposes (*L*. 1. 25).[44] Moreover, his rational soul, which can survive death (*L*. 1. 24), makes him akin to God. So, in enacting and acknowledging wise laws he is,

[41] See Plutarch, *Life of Cicero* 49.

[42] e.g. *R*. 6. 15 ff.

[43] Cf. Plato, *Laws* 10. 897 ff., Aristotle (Oxford Trans. vol. 12 nos. 12–15), and the Stoic writers employed by Cicero in *De Officiis* 1. 22 and *De Natura Deorum* 2.

[44] Since animals were supposed to be devoid of reason, there could be no justice between them and men; see D.L. 7. 129; Cic. *De Finibus* 3. 67.

however imperfectly, behaving like his creator; for law is 'right reason in commanding and forbidding' (*L.* 1. 33).[45]

'Nature', then, can be used in connection either with lower beings (animals and men) or with higher beings (men and gods). In the former context brutish nature may be contrasted unfavourably with the nature of civilized life;[46] or corrupt society may be contrasted with the natural life of animals.[47] In the second context nature provides a criterion for human laws and customs, which are only good in so far as they coincide with divine reason.[48]

3. *That human potential can only be realized in communities.* Why did people form communities? Did they come to realize that only in ordered groups could they protect themselves and provide for their needs?[49] Or did God take pity on their savagery and bestow the gifts of respect and justice?[50] Or did people form villages, and eventually city-states, because, as Aristotle put it, Man was 'a political animal'—i.e. he possessed an innate impulse to live in a *polis*, or city-state, an organization which fulfilled his nature just as an oak fulfils the nature of an acorn?[51] Cicero acknowledges the 'need' theory, but gives greater emphasis to the view of Aristotle: 'the primary reason for a people's coming together is *not so much* weakness as a sort of innate desire . . . to form communities' (*R.* 1. 39). Such communities, of course, involve government and laws.

4. *That Man is a distinct species.* The similarities of human beings—in physical and mental powers, in feelings, values, and

---

[45] Cf. Cic. *De Natura Deorum* 1. 36 (Zeno), *SVF* 3. 314 (Chrysippus), 1. 537 (Cleanthes), and Cic. *R.* 3. 33.

[46] Cf. Horace, *Satires* 1. 3. 99–111. A famous later example is Hobbes's description of the life of pre-social man (*Leviathan* i. 13).

[47] Diogenes would often use animals to represent the virtues of nature as opposed to custom; D.L. 6. 22; Dio Chrysostom, *Orationes* 6. 21–2, 27, 32–3.

[48] For the Academic Polemo, Zeno's teacher, the chief good was to live according to nature (Cic. *De Finibus* 4. 14). The idea, with various modifications, was shared by the Stoics; see Sandbach, 53–9.

[49] Diodorus Siculus (1st cent. BC) 1. 8. 1–7; Lucretius, *De Rerum Natura* 5. 958 ff., 1145 ff.

[50] As in Protagoras' story (Plato, *Protagoras* 322c).

[51] Aristotle, *Politics* 1. 2. 8–14 (Barker). Thanks to Darwin, we can push the question further back and assume that our distant ancestors lived in groups before the emergence of *homo sapiens*.

aspirations, as well as in defects and vices—far transcend their differences in nationality, custom, religion, and social organization.[52] So, for all his diversity, Man represents a single concept, embraced in a single definition (*L.* 1. 29–32). In virtue of this unity, he is subject everywhere to the same natural law, which stands above all codes of positive law and governs his survival and welfare. This momentous insight was elaborated by the Stoics with their concept of *oikeiosis*, a process whereby a living being becomes attached to everything that shares its nature. This idea of affinity or kinship lies at the heart of humanism. Its implications for colour, sex, and class are still being worked out, slowly and painfully. Even slavery has not yet been abolished, in spite of the fact that in the fourth century BC Alcidamas of Elis in his *Messenian Oration* said, 'God has sent forth all men free; nature has made none a slave.'[53] A thousand years later, Justinian's *Digest*, incorporating the formulations of Ulpian (early third century AD), says 'all men by natural law were born free'[54]—an assertion memorably echoed by Rousseau.

5. *That law is based on nature, not on opinion.* 'Nature' here means the condition of man as it actually is, within the cosmos. So the law based on this objective nature will be a set of general principles, providing a criterion for the laws of diverse communities. Such laws are not necessarily good. Since all men are fallible and many are wicked, 'it is foolish to imagine that everything decreed by the institutions or laws of a particular country is just' (*L.* 1. 42). This recalls a passage of Aristotle where he distinguishes specific law enacted by various communities from general law, which is based on nature (*kata physin*). He goes on to cite the famous clash between Creon and Antigone in Sophocles' play (in particular, lines 456–7). Antigone, he says, appeals to what is just by nature (*physei dikaion*) in burying her brother, even though that has been forbidden by the ruler.[55]

Unless a law is contrary to nature (in which case it is a bad law, or, as some argued, not a law at all), a citizen has a duty to obey

---

[52] Cic. *De Officiis* 1. 50 (based on the Stoic, Panaetius), *De Finibus* 5. 65 f.
[53] Aristotle, *Rhetoric* 1. 13. 2 (the words are supplied by the scholiast).
[54] *Digest* 1. 1. 4; cf. *Institutiones* I. Title 2. 2.
[55] Aristotle, *Rhetoric* 1. 13. 2, cf. *Nicomachean Ethics* 5. 7. 1, Cic. *De Inventione* 2. 161.

it, whether or not it is in his selfish interests to do so, and whether
or not he can get away with ignoring it (*L.* 1. 40–1, 43–5). Here
Cicero is in line with Plato, who goes to much trouble to refute
the idea that the sensible man will aim at a *reputation* for justice
but will behave badly when he can escape detection.[56] Justice,
then, like the other virtues, should be sought for its own sake,
and vices should be shunned because they are bad in themselves
(*L.* 1. 48–52).

   This is not the place to follow the theory of natural law through
the centuries.[57] It is worth pointing out, however, that in the 1940s
the appalling, but legally sanctioned, excesses of Nazism and
Communism led to a revival of interest in natural law: surely there
had to be *some* criteria, however general, by which evil laws could
be judged and condemned. At the end of the war, Jacques Maritain published his essay *The Rights of Man and Natural Law*.
Though Maritain was a Christian, he called his political philosophy 'humanist' (29), and conceded that non-Christians might
share it. The point here was that, from at least as early as Hugo
Grotius in the seventeenth century, it had been recognized that,
even if the whole theological dimension were removed, natural
law could be seen as a set of principles without which civilized
society could not survive. From the other direction the distinguished positivist, H. L. A. Hart, discerned 'a core of good sense'
in the doctrine of natural law[58]—a step welcomed (with qualifications) by A. P. d'Entrèves.[59] This was the sort of thing that
Dennis Lloyd had in mind when he said 'One of the most significant contemporary characteristics of jurisprudence is the coming
together of positivism and natural law'.[60] Nevertheless, many
problems are still the subject of strenuous debate, including the
basic 'Is-Ought question', that is, can 'ought' ever be reduced to,
or derived from 'is'? Is it logically legitimate to say 'She is your
sister, therefore you should treat her kindly'?[61]

[56] This view is expounded by Glaucon in Plato, *Republic* 2. 359 ff.; cf. Cic.
De Officiis 3. 38 ff. The idea is mentioned earlier in Antiphon, *Fragments* 44
(Freeman, 147), on which see Kerferd, 115–17.
[57] See e.g. the survey by John Kelly.
[58] Hart 193–200.
[59] d'Entrèves 185 ff.
[60] Lloyd 119.
[61] See the essays collected by Hudson.

Such problems, of course, are usually discussed in the general context of moral philosophy. But many would think it reasonable to relate them to the idea of natural law. For example, like every law, 'thou shalt not kill' admits of exceptions—as in self-defence, in a just war, and possibly in the case of an intolerable tyrant. In antiquity suicide, too, was permitted in extreme circumstances, not only by Epicureans but also by the Stoics, who believed in natural law. What, then, of voluntary euthanasia for a person suffering from an incurable illness? Though not new, the problem has now become urgent as a result of modern techniques of prolonging life. Again, procreation (within marriage) was approved of for centuries as fulfilling natural law, and contraception was condemned for violating it (as it still is by the Roman Catholic Church). But before Malthus very few foresaw that overpopulation would become a serious threat to human survival. Or again, until very recently, most people agreed with Cicero and the Stoics in assuming that man's dominion over animals (including birds and fish) was in accordance with natural law. But no one envisaged that man would ever be in a position to treat some species as machines and hunt others to extinction. And what of *inanimate* nature? Does natural law have nothing to say about the squandering of resources and the pollution of the planet? If natural law *is* relevant to such matters, does that mean it has to be changed or extended? Or has it always included certain qualifications—qualifications which are now being discovered by the light of experience? For these and similar questions Cicero's observations are still a good starting point.

NOTE ON THE TEXT

Our evidence for the text of the *Republic* is threefold. (1) The incomplete Vatican manuscript, shelfmarked Vat. lat. 5757, was brought to light in 1820 by Cardinal Angelo Mai, Prefect of the Vatican Library. It is an eighth-century copy of St Augustine's commentary on the Psalms, written at the monastery of Bobbio in northern Italy. Mai detected the traces of an earlier text, which proved to be that of the *Republic*. It was common practice in the early Middle Ages to reuse the parchment from old books, after first making an attempt to wash off the original script. Such recycled manuscripts are called 'palimpsests'. Using chemical reagents to enhance the clarity of the older script, Mai recovered about a quarter of the original text, which was evidently a luxury edition of the *Republic* written in uncial script in the fourth or fifth century. The pages were out of order, but the original order could be reconstructed partly from context and partly from the signature numbers which the original scribes had marked at the foot of some of the pages. Subsequent editors have made only minor adjustments. (A photograph of a page of the manuscript may conveniently be found in Reynolds and Wilson, plate 10.) The text in this manuscript contains many errors, but the correct reading is in many cases inserted by an early annotator who appears to have had access to an equally or more reliable text. (2) A number of fragments of the text are preserved as quotations in later writers, particularly Lactantius, Augustine, and the grammarian Nonius Marcellus. The fragments have been fully re-examined by Heck. We have omitted some of the shorter fragments and those whose placing or authenticity is doubtful. (3) The 'Dream of Scipio' survives, often in association with the commentary of Macrobius, in an independent manuscript tradition of which the earliest representative (Paris, nouv. acq. lat. 454) dates from the ninth century.

The *Laws* survives as part of what is called the Leiden corpus, a collection of Cicero's philosophical works preserved principally in three medieval manuscripts held at the Bibliotheek der Rijksuniversiteit, Leiden. The text as we have it breaks off at or before the end of the third book, though there is evidence that it consisted of at least five books (a fragment attributed to Book 5 is preserved by Macrobius). It may well originally have been planned in six books to parallel the *Republic*. It is not clear that Cicero ever published it himself and he may never have revised it fully; it is ironically in this very work that Cicero admits to being bad at resuming work on a project once laid aside. It has been suggested by Zelzer that the text survived at one period only in a cursive copy, which would naturally lead to difficulties of legibility; but whatever the reason, the text as we have it is corrupt in many places and editorial conjecture is often called for.

NOTE ON THE TRANSLATION

The reader of any Latin text is likely to encounter some words which have no exact equivalent in English. In these works the chief examples are *animus*, *magistratus*, *optimates*, *pietas*, *popularis*, *respublica*, and *virtus*. The Latin *animus* is translated by 'mind', 'soul', and even 'heart', depending on the context. *Magistratus* often meant something more like the minister of a government department than our magistrate. Nevertheless, it has been translated as 'magistrate' since that is the traditional practice in all works on classical antiquity. For *optimates* 'the best people' will not do, for that is a colloquial phrase, usually tinged with irony. In *Pro Sestio* 96 Cicero extends the term to 'right-thinking people'; but in the *Republic* and *Laws* he usually restricts it to the socially, economically, and politically dominant group, i.e. the aristocracy. The word *popularis* was used of a politician who was keen to promote the interests of (and thus gain the favour of) the common people. It did not imply a party or even a programme. 'Populist' seems to be the closest approximation. 'Devotion' has been used for *pietas*, since our 'piety' is predominantly a religious concept. 'The Republic' has been kept as the title of Cicero's work because of the Platonic precedent. Elsewhere 'state', 'country', 'form of government', 'constitution', and 'nation' have been used for *respublica*, according to the context. As for *virtus*, which originally denoted 'manliness' in the sense of 'courage', the term 'moral excellence', or, less frequently, 'valour', 'worth', or 'goodness' has been used. Latin was blest with two general words for 'men', namely *homines* ('human beings') and *viri* ('males'). Often the translation simply uses 'men', relying on the context to make the sense clear.

In the dialogues the names of the speakers have been put at the beginning of every speech, and 'Marcus' or 'Quintus' has been substituted for 'brother'. In the direct interchanges the style is that of a rather formal conversation; but when Cicero warms to his theme he tends to rise, quite spontaneously, to a higher, more rhetorical level. Obvious examples occur in 'The Dream of Scipio' and at the end of *Laws* 1. Little attempt has been made to reproduce the archaic elements in the diction of Cicero's proposed legal code. Cicero himself has aimed only at something 'slightly more old-fashioned' than contemporary speech (*L. 2. 18*).

BIBLIOGRAPHY

Works most suitable for general reading are indicated by an asterisk.

Astin, A. E., *Scipio Aemilianus* (Oxford, 1967).

Barker, E. (ed.), *The Politics of Aristotle* (Oxford, 1958).

*Barnes, J., 'Antiochus of Ascalon', in M. Griffin and J. Barnes (eds.), *Philosophia Togata* (Oxford, 1989), 51–96.

Beard, M., and North, J. (eds.), *Pagan Priests* (London, 1990).

Beare, W., *The Roman Stage*, 3rd edn. (London, 1963).

Becker, E., *Technik und Szenerie des ciceronischen Dialogs* (Osnabrück, 1938).

Bickerman, E. J., *Chronology of the Ancient World*, rev. edn. (London, 1980).

Boyancé, P., 'Les Méthodes de l'histoire littéraire; Cicéron et son œuvre philosophique', *REL* 14 (1936), 288–309.

Bréguet, E. (ed.), *Cicéron, La République* (Budé), 2 vols. (Paris, 1980).

Broughton, T. R. S., *The Magistrates of the Roman Republic*, 2 vols. (New York, 1951–2; supplementary vol., Atlanta, 1986).

Bruck, E. F., 'Cicero vs. the Scaevolas: Law of Inheritance and Decay of Roman Religion', *Seminar*, 3 (1945), 1–20.

*Brunt, P. A. (1), 'Laus Imperii', *Roman Imperial Themes* (Oxford, 1990), ch. 14.

——(2), 'Cicero and Historiography', in *Miscellanea di studi classici in onore di Eugenio Manni* (Rome, 1979), i. 311–40.

Büchner, K. (1), 'Die Beste Verfassung. Eine philologische Untersuchung zu den ersten drei Büchern von Ciceros *Staat*', *SIFC* 26 (1952), 37–140.

——(2) *M. Tullius Cicero, De Re Publica* (Heidelberg, 1984).

Campbell, D. A., *Greek Lyric*, iii (Loeb Classical Library, 1991).

Cornell, T. J., *The Beginnings of Rome* (London and New York, 1995).

Crawford, M. H. (ed.), *Roman Statutes*, 2 vols. (London, 1996).

Crook, J. A., *Law and Life of Rome* (London, 1967).

Cumont, F. (1), *Oriental Religions in Roman Paganism* (1911; repr. New York, 1956).

——(2) *After Life in Roman Paganism* (1922; repr. New York, 1959).

Douglas, A. E., 'Cicero the Philosopher', in T. A. Dorey (ed.), *Cicero* (London, 1965), 135–70.

*d'Entrèves, A. P., *Natural Law*, 2nd edn. (London, 1970).

Favonius Eulogius, *Disputatio de Somnio Scipionis*, ed. R. E. van Weddingen, Collection Latomus, 27 (1927).

Ferrary, J.-L. (1), 'Le Discours de Laelius dans le troisième livre du *de re publica* de Cicéron', *Mélanges de l'École Française de Rome: Antiquité*, 86 (1974), 745–71.

——(2), 'Le Discours de Philus (Cicéron, *de re publica* 3. 8–31) et la philosophie de Carnéade', *REL* 55 (1977), 128–56.

——(3), 'L'Archéologie du *de re publica* (2, 2, 4–37, 63): Cicéron entre Polybe et Platon', *JRS* 74 (1984), 87–98.

——(4), 'The Statesman and the Law in the Political Philosophy of Cicero', in A. Laks and M. Schofield (eds.), *Justice and Generosity: Studies in Hellenistic Social and Political Philosophy* (Cambridge, 1995), 48–73.

Forrest, W. G., *A History of Sparta, 950–192 B.C.*, 2nd edn. (London, 1980).

Frazer, J. G., *The Fasti of Ovid*, 5 vols. (London, 1929).

Frede, D., 'Constitution and Citizenship: Peripatetic Influence on Cicero's Political Conceptions in the *De re publica*', in W. W. Fortenbaugh and P. Steinmetz (eds.), *Cicero's Knowledge of the Peripatos* (New Brunswick, NJ, 1989), 77–100.

Freeman, K., *Ancilla to the Pre-Socratic Philosophers* (Oxford, 1956).

Friedländer, L., *Roman Life and Manners under the Early Empire*, 4 vols. (repr. London, 1965).

Frier, B., *Libri annales pontificum maximorum: The Origins of the Annalistic Tradition* (Rome, 1979).

Garton, C., *Personal Aspects of the Roman Theatre* (Toronto, 1972).

Geddes, A. E. M., *Meteorology: An Introductory Treatise*, i (Glasgow, 1921).

Geiger, J., 'Contemporary Politics in Cicero's *De Republica*', *CP* 79 (1984), 38–43.

Glucker, J. (1), *Antiochus and the Late Academy* (Göttingen, 1978).

——(2), 'Cicero's Philosophical Affiliations', in J. Dillon and A. Long (eds.), *The Question of 'Eclecticism'* (Berkeley and Los Angeles, 1988), 34–69.

*Goar, R. J., *Cicero and the State Religion* (Amsterdam, 1972).

Görler, W. (1), see Ziegler, K.

——(2), 'Silencing the Troublemaker: *De Legibus* 1.39 and the Continuity of Cicero's Scepticism', in J. G. F. Powell (3), 85–113.

Greenidge, A. H. J. (1), *Roman Public Life* (London, 1901).

Greenidge, A. H. J. (2), *The Legal Procedure of Cicero's Time* (1901; repr. New York, 1971).

*Griffin, M., 'Cicero and Rome', in *The Oxford History of the Classical World* (Oxford, 1986), 454–78.

Gruen, E. S., *Roman Politics and the Criminal Courts, 149–78 B.C.* (Cambridge, Mass., 1968).

Hardingham, G. G. (ed.), *The Republic of Cicero* (London, 1884).

Hart, H. L. A., *The Concept of Law*, 2nd edn. (London, 1994).

Hathaway, R. F., 'Cicero *De Re Publica* II and his Socratic View of History', *JHI* 29 (1968) 3–12.

Heck, E., *Die Bezeugung von Ciceros Schrift De re publica* (Hildesheim, 1966).

Hopkins, K., *Death and Renewal* (Cambridge, 1983), ch. 4.

Horsfall, N. (ed.), *Cornelius Nepos* (Oxford, 1989).

*How, W. W., 'Cicero's Ideal in his De Republica', *JRS* 20 (1930), 24–42.

Hudson, W. D. (ed.), *The Is–Ought Question* (Oxford, 1969).

Jocelyn, H. D. (ed.), *The Tragedies of Ennius* (Cambridge, 1967).

Jolowicz, H. F., *A Historical Introduction to Roman Law*, 3rd edn. (Cambridge, 1972).

Jones, A. H. M., *The Criminal Courts of the Roman Republic and Principate* (Oxford, 1972).

*Kelly, J. M., *A Short History of Western Legal Theory* (Oxford, 1992).

Kenter, L. P. (ed.), *Cicero, De Legibus Book 1* (Amsterdam, 1972).

Kerferd, G. B., *The Sophistic Movement* (Cambridge, 1981).

Keyes, C. W., *Cicero: De Re Publica, De Legibus* (Loeb Classical Library: Cambridge, Mass., and London, repr. 1988).

Lewis, C. S., *The Discarded Image: An Introduction to Medieval and Renaissance Literature* (Cambridge, 1964).

Liebeschuetz, J. H. W. G., *Continuity and Change in Roman Religion* (Oxford, 1979).

Lintott, A. W. (1), *Violence in Republican Rome* (Oxford, 1968).

——(2), '*Provocatio*: From the Struggle of the Orders to the Principate', *ANRW* 1.2 (1972), 226–67.

Lloyd, D., *Introduction to Jurisprudence*, 6th edn. by M. D. A. Freeman (London, 1994).

Long, A. A., *Hellenistic Philosophy* (London, 1974).

MacKendrick, P., *The Philosophical Books of Cicero* (London, 1989).

Maritain, J., *The Rights of Man and Natural Law* (London, 1945).

Maxfield, V. A., *The Military Decorations of the Roman Army* (London, 1981).

Michels, A. K., *The Calendar of the Roman Republic* (Westport, Conn., 1978).

Mitchell, R. E., 'The Definition of *patres* and *plebs*: An End to the Struggle of the Orders', in Raaflaub, 130–74.

*Mitchell, T. N., *Cicero, the Senior Statesman* (New York and London, 1991).

Nash, E., *Pictorial Dictionary of Ancient Rome*, 2 vols. (New York, 1981).

Nicolet, C., *L'Ordre équestre à l'époque républicaine* (Paris, 1966).

Ogilvie, R. M., *A Commentary on Livy Books 1–5* (Oxford, 1965).

Pallottino, M., *The Etruscans* (London, 1974).

Pease, A. S. (ed.), *M. Tulli Ciceronis De Natura Deorum*, 2 vols. (Cambridge, Mass., 1955 and 1958).

Peterson, I., *Newton's Clock: Chaos in the Solar System* (New York, 1993).

Platner, S. B., and Ashby, T., *A Topographical Dictionary of Ancient Rome* (London, 1929).

Powell, J. G. F. (1) (ed.), *Cicero: On Friendship and The Dream of Scipio* (Warminster, 1990).

——(2), 'The *rector rei publicae* of Cicero's De Republica', *Scripta Classica Israelica*, 13 (1994), 19–29.

——(3) (ed.), *Cicero the Philosopher. Twelve Papers* (Oxford, 1995).

——(4), 'Second Thoughts on the Dream of Scipio', *Proceedings of the Leeds International Latin Seminar*, 9 (1996), 13–27.

Purcell, N., 'On the Sacking of Carthage and Corinth', in D. Innes, H. Hine, and C. Pelling (eds.), *Ethics and Rhetoric* (Oxford, 1995).

Raaflaub, K. A. (ed.), *Social Struggles in Archaic Rome* (Berkeley and London, 1986).

Rawson, B., *The Politics of Friendship: Pompey and Cicero* (Sydney, 1978).

Rawson, E. (1), 'Cicero the Historian and Cicero the Antiquarian', *JRS* 62 (1972), 33–45.

——(2), 'The Interpretation of Cicero's De Legibus', *ANRW* 1.4 (1973), 334–56.

——*(3), *Cicero, A Portrait* (London, 1975; repr. Bristol, 1983).

Reece, R. (ed.), *Burial in the Roman World* (London, 1977).

Reitzenstein, R., 'Die Idee des Prinzipats bei Cicero und Augustus', *Nachrichten der Göttinger Gesellschaft der Wissenschaften* (1917).

Reynolds, L. D., and Wilson, N., *Scribes and Scholars*, 3rd edn. (Oxford, 1991).

Rich, J. W., *Declaring War in the Roman Republic in the Period of Transmarine Expansion* (Brussels, 1976).

Riginos, A. S., _Platonica: The Anecdotes concerning the Life and Writings of Plato_, Columbia Studies in the Classical Tradition, 3 (Leiden, 1976).

Rudd, N., and Wiedemann, T. (eds.), _Cicero, De Legibus_ 1 (Bristol, 1987).

*Sabine, G. H., and Smith, S. B., _Cicero on the Commonwealth_ (Columbus, Oh., 1929).

*Sandbach, F. H., _The Stoics_ (London, 1975).

Schmidt, P. L., 'Cicero, "_De re publica_": Die Forschung der letzten fünf Dezennien', _ANRW_ 1.4 (1973), 262–333.

Schofield, M., 'Cicero for and against Divination', _JRS_ 76 (1986), 47–64.

Scullard, H. H., _From the Gracchi to Nero_, 4th edn. (London, 1976).

Shackleton Bailey, D. R. (1), _Cicero's Letters to Atticus_, i (Cambridge, 1965).

——(2), _Cicero_ (London, 1971).

Sharples, R. W., 'Cicero's _Republic_ and Greek Political Theory', _Polis_, 5.2 (1986), 30–50.

Skutsch, O., _The Annals of Quintus Ennius_ (Oxford, 1985).

Sorabji, R., _Animal Minds and Human Morals_ (London, 1993).

Stahl, W. H. (tr.), _Macrobius, Commentary on the Dream of Scipio_ (New York, 1952).

Staveley, E. S., _Greek and Roman Voting and Elections_ (London, 1972).

Suerbaum, W., 'Studienbibliographie zu Ciceros _De re publica_', _Gymnasium_, 85 (1978), 59–88.

Sumner, G. V., _Orators in Cicero's Brutus_ (Toronto, 1973).

Syme, R., _The Roman Revolution_ (Oxford, 1939).

*Taylor, L. R. (1), _Party Politics in the Age of Caesar_ (Berkeley and Cambridge, 1949).

——(2), _Roman Voting Assemblies from the Hannibalic War to the Dictatorship of Caesar_ (Ann Arbor, 1966).

Toynbee, J. M. C., _Death and Burial in the Roman World_ (London, 1971).

Traglia, A. (ed.), _Marco Tullio Cicerone: I Frammenti Poetici_ (1962).

*Walbank, F. W., _Polybius_ (Berkeley and London, 1972).

Walsh, P. G., 'Making a Drama out of a Crisis: Livy on the Bacchanals', _Greece & Rome_, 43 (1996), 188–203.

Watt, W. S. (1), 'Notes on Cicero, _De Legibus_', _Collection Latomus_ 196 (1986), 265–8.

——(2), 'Tulliana', _Hermes_, 125.2. (1997), 241–3.

Wiedemann, T., see Rudd, N.

Wood, N., *Cicero's Social and Political Thought* (Berkeley and London, 1988).

Zelzer, M., 'Die Umschrift lateinischer Texte am Ende der Antike und ihre Bedeutung für die Textkritik', *Wiener Studien* 94 = NS 15 (1981), 211–31, esp. 227 ff.

Zetzel, J. E. G. (ed.), *Cicero, De Re Publica, Selections* (Cambridge, 1995).

Ziegler, K. (1) (ed.), *M. Tullius Cicero, De Re Publica*, 5th edn. (Leipzig, 1960).

——(2) (ed.), *M. Tullius Cicero, De Legibus*, rev. W. Görler (Freiburg and Würzburg, 1979).

TABLE OF DATES (BC)

THE REPUBLIC

THE REPUBLIC

BOOK 1

1–12. One should engage in politics

[Seventeen leaves are missing at the beginning of our manuscript. Half way through his preface Cicero is criticizing the Epicureans for their lack of patriotism.]

⟨Had it not been for his sense of patriotic duty, X⟩ would not have   1
delivered ⟨our country⟩ from invasion; nor would Gaius Duilius, Aulus Atilius, and Lucius Metellus have rescued it from the Carthaginian menace; the two Scipios* would not have extinguished with their blood the spreading conflagration of the second Punic war; later, when it had broken out with greater fury, Quintus Maximus would not have sapped its strength; Marcus Metellus would not have beaten it down; and Publius Africanus* would not have dragged it back from the gates of this city and penned it up within the enemy's walls.

Or take Marcus Cato,* an obscure man without consular ancestors, a man to whom all of us who follow the same calling look up to as a kind of model, guiding us to perseverance and probity. He might certainly have enjoyed his retirement at Tusculum*— a healthy spot within easy reach of town. But that maniac, as those fellows call him, without being compelled by any necessity, chose to be buffeted by these stormy waves right into extreme old age, instead of enjoying the delightfully tranquil and easy life which they extol. I say nothing of those countless individuals who in peace and war have brought salvation to this country; and I shall not mention the names of those who are close to the memory of this generation, for I do not want anyone to complain that he or one of his family has been left out. I simply state this basic fact: nature has given to mankind such a compulsion to do good, and such a desire to defend the well-being of the community, that this force prevails over all the temptations of pleasure and ease.

2   Yet it is not enough to possess moral excellence* as a kind of
skill, unless you put it into practice. You can have a skill simply
by knowing *how* to practise it, even if you never do; whereas
moral excellence is entirely a matter of practice. Its most important field of practice, moreover, is in the government of a state,*
and in the achievement (in reality, not just in words) of those
things which our friends in their shady nooks make such a noise
about. For nothing is laid down by philosophers—nothing right
and honourable at any rate—which has not been brought into
being and established by those who have drawn up laws for states.
Where does devotion come from? Who gave us our religious
observances? What is the source of law, either the law of nations
or this civil law of ours? From where did justice, good faith, and
fair dealing come? Or decency, restraint, the fear of disgrace, and
the desire of praise and honour? Or fortitude in hardship and
danger? Why, from those men who have taken these values,
already shaped by teaching, and either established them in custom
3 or confirmed them in law. In fact Xenocrates, one of the most
illustrious philosophers, when asked what his pupils got from him,
is said to have answered 'to do of their own free will what they
are compelled to do by law'. So then, the statesman* who, by official authority and legal sanctions obliges everyone to do what
barely a handful can be induced to do by philosophy lectures,
must take precedence over the teachers who theorize about such
matters. For what philosophy lecture is so fine that it deserves to
be set above the public law and customs of a well-ordered state?
For my own part, I consider what Ennius calls 'great and commanding cities' superior to little villages and outposts; similarly,
in my view, those who govern such cities by their counsel and
authority are in wisdom itself* far above those without any experience of public affairs. We are led by a powerful urge to increase
the wealth of the human race; we are keen to make men's lives
safer and richer by our policies and efforts; we are spurred on by
nature herself to fulfil this purpose. Therefore, let us hold that
course which has always been followed by the best men, ignoring
the bugle for retreat, which tries to recall those who have already
advanced.
4   Against these well-known and well-established principles our
opponents set, first, the hardships which have to be endured in

defending the state—surely a flimsy objection in the eyes of anybody alert and diligent, and one to be treated with contempt not only in matters of such moment but even in things of less importance, such as one's pursuits or social duties or even one's everyday occupations. They point, in addition, to the dangers of public life, using the despicable fear of death to deter brave men—men who normally think it more miserable to decay in the natural course of old age than to have the chance of laying down, as a supreme gift to their country, the life which in any case would have to be given back to nature.

On that topic our opponents wax fluent and eloquent (in their own opinion), reeling off the disasters of highly eminent men and the wrongs they have suffered from ungrateful citizens. Here they cite the familiar Greek examples—how Miltiades, the conqueror and tamer of the Persians, before those wounds which he sustained with his face to the foe in that glorious victory were healed, breathed forth the life that had survived the enemy's onslaught in the fetters of his own compatriots; how Themistocles, cast out and warned off with threats from the country he had freed, found refuge not in the havens of Greece which he had saved but in the shelter of that foreign land which he had brought low. Yes indeed, the caprice and cruelty of Athens towards her greatest citizens can be illustrated again and again. But the habit which started and multiplied there has also, we are told, spread to this sober, responsible, country of ours. One hears of Camillus' exile,* the wrong done to Ahala, the resentment directed at Nasica, Laenas' banishment, Opimius' conviction, Metellus' departure into exile, the appallingly cruel overthrow of Gaius Marius and the murder of his chief supporters,* and the widespread slaughter that followed shortly after. Nowadays they regularly mention my name too; and they speak even more feelingly and affectionately about my case, because (I suppose) they think they were spared to continue in their peaceful way of life as a result of my policy and peril.

Yet I would find it hard to say why, when these very men cross the sea to learn and observe . . . [*one leaf is missing; the gist seems to be:* They think *we* should be deterred by similar risks from more important enterprises. Again, if they believe that the dangers of travel are justified by the knowledge acquired, why should *our* dangers not be justified by the reward obtained?] . . . As I was retiring from the consulship, I swore in a public assembly that the state had been saved* by my actions; and the Roman people swore the same oath. ⟨Even if I had never been recalled from exile,⟩ that would have given me ample compensation for the worry and distress caused by all the wrongs I suffered. And yet my misfortunes brought more gain than pain, less vexation than glory; and the joy I derived from being missed by the good was greater that the anguish I suffered from the glee of the wicked. But if, as I say, things had turned out otherwise, what cause would I have for complaint? Nothing surprising, nothing more grievous than expected, happened in return for my great services. I could have reaped richer rewards than anyone else from peace, thanks to the various delights of those studies in which I had engaged since boyhood. Or if some more dreadful calamity had overtaken the people as a whole, I could have suffered, not any special misfortune, but the same misfortune as everyone else. Yet, being the sort of man I was, I did not hesitate to brave the wildest storms and almost the very thunderbolts themselves to protect my countrymen, and, by risking my own life, to win peace and security for

8 the rest. For our country did not give us life and nurture unconditionally, without expecting to receive in return, as it were, some maintenance* from us; nor did it engage simply to serve our convenience, providing a safe haven for our leisure and a quiet place for our relaxation. No, it reserved the right to appropriate for its own purpose the largest and most numerous portions of our loyalty, ability, and sagacity, leaving to us for our private use only what might be surplus to its needs.

9   Furthermore, we should certainly not entertain for one moment the excuses* to which they resort in the hope of enjoying a quiet life with an easier conscience—when, for instance, they say that most politicians are worthless, that it is demeaning to be classified with them, and disagreeable and dangerous to come into conflict with them, especially when they have stirred up the mob. Hence, they argue, it is no business for a wise man to take over the reins, since he cannot check the mad, uncontrollable rush of the crowd; nor does it befit a free man to struggle with corrupt and uncivilized opponents, lashed with foul abuse and submitting to outrages which would be intolerable to a person of good sense—as if good, brave, and high-minded men could have any

stronger reason for entering politics than the determination not to give in to the wicked, and not to allow the state to be torn apart by such people in a situation where they themselves would be powerless to help even if they wished to do so.

Again, when they deny that a wise man will take part in poli- 10 tics, who, I ask you, can be satisfied with their proviso*—'unless some period of crisis compels him'? As if anyone could face a greater crisis than I did. What could I have done at that time had I not been consul? And how could I have been consul if I had not followed from boyhood the career that would bring a man of equestrian birth like me to the highest office? So the opportunity of rescuing the country, whatever the dangers that threaten it, does not come suddenly or when you wish it, but only when you are in a position which allows you to do so. I find this most aston- 11 ishing in the writings of intellectuals: they plead their inability to steer the ship when the sea is calm, because they have never been taught and have never cared to acquire such knowledge; and yet they proclaim that they will take the helm when the waves are at their highest! Those gentlemen openly admit, and indeed take great pride in the fact, that they have never learned and do not teach anything about how to set up or maintain a government; they think that expertise in such matters does not befit learned and philosophical men and should be left to people with practical experience in that sort of thing. So what sense does it make to promise assistance to the government only if driven to do so by a crisis, when they cannot manage a much easier task, namely to take charge of the government when there is *no* compelling crisis? Even if it were true that the sage does not voluntarily deign to descend to the technicalities of statecraft, and yet does not shirk that duty if forced by circumstances, I should still think it quite wrong for him to neglect the art of politics; he ought to have everything at his fingertips, for he never knows when he may have to use it.

I have set out these points at some length, because in the present 12 work I have planned and undertaken a discussion of the state. To prevent the project from seeming futile, I had, at the outset, to get rid of people's scruples about entering public life. Nevertheless, if any readers are swayed by the authority of philosophers, they should pay attention for a moment and listen to men who enjoy a very great authority* and reputation in the highest intellectual circles. Even if they themselves never actually governed, I still think they did the state some service, because they studied and wrote extensively about it. In fact I note that those whom the Greeks called 'The Seven Wise Men'* in almost every case played a central role in political life. Nor, indeed, is there any occupation which brings human excellence closer to divine power than founding new states and preserving* those already founded.

13–32. Preliminaries, leading to astronomy and its relation to politics

13 Since I have had the good fortune* to achieve something of note in government, and also possess a certain ability in expounding political principles not only as a result of experience but also through my enthusiasm for learning and teaching ⟨I am not unqualified* for this task. This is not true of most⟩ authorities; for some of my predecessors have been highly accomplished in theoretical discussion, without any discernible achievement in practice; others, with a creditable practical record, have lacked analytical skill. Not that this account which I am about to give is novel or original. I intend rather to recall a discussion that took place within a group of people who at a particular time were the wisest and most distinguished of our countrymen. This discussion was once reported by Publius Rutilius Rufus to you and me* in our youth, when we were spending several days with him in Smyrna. In it pretty well nothing, I think, was omitted that was of central importance to the analysis of this whole matter.*

14   It was in the consulship of Tuditanus and Aquilius.* Publius Africanus, the son of Paulus, had decided to spend the Latin holidays* on his estate, and his closest friends had promised to visit him several times over that period. Early on the first day his nephew, Quintus Tubero, arrived before the others. Scipio was glad to see him and greeted him warmly. 'Tubero!' he said, 'why are you here so early? Surely the holiday gave you a welcome chance to extend your reading.'

TUBERO: My books are available to me at any time, for they're never busy. But it's a huge stroke of luck to find you relaxing, especially when the country is in such a state of turmoil.

SCIPIO: Ah yes. You've found me relaxing all right, but more in body, I can tell you, than in mind.

TUBERO: Well, you need some mental relaxation too. Several of us are looking forward to making full use of this holiday with you as planned—provided, of course, it's convenient.

SCIPIO: Happy to agree, I'm sure. It will give us a chance at last to remind ourselves of intellectual activities.

TUBERO: Well then, as you in a sense invite me and encourage 15 my approach, may we consider this question first, Africanus, before the others arrive? What's all this about a second sun* that was reported in the Senate? Quite a number of serious people claim they have seen two suns; so we shouldn't refuse to believe them, but rather look for an explanation.

SCIPIO: I do wish we had our friend Panaetius with us. He always goes into these celestial matters very carefully, like everything else. Yet I'll tell you frankly what I think, Tubero. I don't exactly agree with our friend in all that kind of thing. He pronounces with such confidence on phenomena whose nature we can barely guess that you'd fancy he saw them with his own eyes or held them firmly in his grasp. I always think Socrates was wiser. He refused to concern himself with matters of that kind, holding that problems about the physical universe were either too enormous for reason to comprehend or else quite irrelevant to human life.

TUBERO: I don't know why tradition has it, Africanus, that 16 Socrates ruled out all speculation of that kind and confined himself to the study of everyday moral behaviour. We can cite no higher authority about him than Plato, can we? Yet in Plato's books Socrates speaks in many passages in a way which indicates that, even when he is discussing behaviour, moral values, and political topics, he is still keen to include arithmetic, geometry, and musical theory, just as Pythagoras did.

SCIPIO: That's right, Tubero. But I expect you have heard that on Socrates' death Plato travelled first to Egypt on a study tour, and then to Italy and Sicily to gain a thorough mastery of Pythagoras' discoveries. He spent a lot of time in Tarentum with Archytas, and in Locri with Timaeus, and he obtained the use of Philolaus' notes. As Pythagoras' reputation was high at that time in those centres, Plato* devoted himself to his adherents and interests. That's why, as he was fond of Socrates above all others and wished to attribute everything to him, he interwove Socrates' charm and verbal acuteness with the abstruseness of Pythagoras and his weighty contributions to so many areas of knowledge.

17   When Scipio had finished, he saw Lucius Furius Philus appear suddenly in the doorway. After giving him a friendly welcome, he took him by the arm and showed him to a place on his own couch. He also welcomed Publius Rutilius, our source for this conversation, who had come in at the same time, and bade him sit beside Tubero.

PHILUS: So, what's going on? I hope we haven't caused an interruption by arriving in the middle of your conversation.

SCIPIO: Certainly not. The question that Tubero was raising a moment ago is just the sort of thing that you are usually eager to consider. Our friend Rutilius, too, would sometimes discuss such subjects with me even beneath the walls of Numantia.*

PHILUS: And what, may I ask, was the point at issue?

SCIPIO: Those two suns. I'd like to hear what you think about them, Philus.

18   Scipio had just said this when a servant told him that Laelius* had already left home and was on his way. He at once dressed, put on his shoes, and left the bedroom. After walking up and down for a few minutes in the portico, he greeted Laelius on his arrival, along with his companions, namely Spurius Mummius (a close friend), and Laelius' sons-in-law, Gaius Fannius and Quintus Scaevola, well-educated young men who were now old enough to have been quaestors.* After receiving them all, he turned round in the portico, putting Laelius in the middle. For there was a kind of rule between the two friends that on campaigns Laelius should venerate Africanus as a god because of his outstanding military reputation, while in civilian life Scipio should respect Laelius like a father in that he was the older of the two. Then, after exchanging just a few words while they took a turn or two, and Scipio had expressed his great joy at their coming, it was decided that they should sit in the sunniest part of the lawn, because it was wintertime. They were about to do so when Manius Manilius came in, a great authority on law, who was regarded by all as a delightful friend. After being welcomed by Scipio and the rest, he sat down beside Laelius.

PHILUS: Just because these gentlemen have come, I don't think 19 we need look for another topic of conversation; why don't we consider it more precisely and say something good enough for their ears?

LAELIUS: And what, pray, were you talking about? What subject have we interrupted?

PHILUS: Scipio asked me what I thought about the appearance of the two suns being accepted as a fact.

LAELIUS: Really, Philus? And have we, then, concluded our research on everything relevant to our homes and country, since we are now wondering about goings on in the sky?

PHILUS: Don't you think it relevant to our homes to know what is going on and taking place in the house—not the one surrounded by our walls but this whole universe* which the gods have given us to share with them as a dwelling-place and fatherland? After all, we must remain ignorant of many important things if we are ignorant of these. I myself, yes, and even you, Laelius, and indeed all who aspire to wisdom, take pleasure in learning about and pondering upon the physical world.

LAELIUS: I have no objection, particularly as it's holiday time. 20 But can we hear something about it, or have we come too late?

PHILUS: The discussion hasn't started yet. So, as we have a clean sheet, I would gladly hand over to you, Laelius; do tell us your views on the subject.

LAELIUS: No no, let's hear from you, unless perhaps Manilius thinks some decree* should be framed between the two suns whereby they shall possess the sky on the same terms as each possessed it heretofore.

MANILIUS: Laelius, you will persist in making fun of the profession in which you yourself excel, and without which no one can know what is his own and what is another's. But we'll come to that in due course; now let's hear what Philus has to say. I see he's already being consulted about weightier matters than Publius Mucius or I deal with.

PHILUS: I have nothing new to tell you; nothing that I have 21 worked out or discovered by myself. I remember that Gaius Sulpicius Galus* (a very learned man, as you know) happened to be staying with Marcus Marcellus, his one-time colleague in the consulship, when this same visual phenomenon was reported. He

asked for the globe to be brought out—the one which Marcus
Marcellus' grandfather had removed from Syracuse on the capture
of that wealthy and much-adorned city, though he had shipped
nothing else home from such a vast collection of booty. I had often
heard tell of this globe* thanks to the fame of Archimedes; yet I
was not so impressed with it when I saw it. For the other one,
also made by Archimedes, which the same Marcellus had put in
the temple of Valour,* was more beautiful and more widely known
22 to the public. But when Galus began to give a very expert account
of this device, I came to the conclusion that the famous Sicilian
possessed more genius than any human being seemed capable of
containing.

According to Galus, that other globe,* which was solid throughout, was an ancient invention; it had first been turned on the lathe
by Thales of Miletus; then it was marked by Eudoxus of Cnidus,
reputedly a pupil of Plato's, with the constellations and stars
which are fixed in the sky. Many years later, Aratus, taking over
the whole structure and design from Eudoxus, celebrated it in
verse—not with any knowledge of astronomy but with a certain
amount of poetic talent. This newer type of globe, however, dis-
playing the movements of the sun and moon and of the five stars
which are called wanderers or 'planets', could not be fitted on to
the surface of the earlier, solid, globe. Archimedes' invention was
amazing in that he had worked out how a single rotation could
reproduce the diverse paths of the various bodies with their different speeds. When Galus operated this sphere the result was that
the moon was as many revolutions behind the sun on that brass
contraption as it was days behind it in the sky. Hence the very
same eclipse of the sun took place in the sky and on the globe;
and the moon then came round to the cone-shaped shadow* of
the earth cast by the sun from the opposite side . . .

[*Five leaves have been lost. Scipio is now speaking of the Galus
mentioned above.*]

23 . . . for I myself was fond of the man, and I knew that my father
Paulus had particularly liked and approved of him. I remember
when my father was consul in Macedonia and we were in camp
(I was quite young at the time), our army was troubled with super-
stitious fear because on a clear night the bright full moon suddenly failed. Galus was then our staff officer, about a year before

he was elected consul. On the next day, without any hesitation, he made a public statement in the camp to the effect that this was not an omen; it had happened then, and would continue to happen at fixed times in the future, when the sun was in a position from which its light could not reach the moon.

TUBERO: Really? Did he manage to put this across to fellows who were virtually peasants? And did he risk saying such things in front of ignoramuses?

SCIPIO: He did indeed, and with great . . . [*Some lines have been lost, describing the nature of Galus' speech.*] There was no 24 arrogant display, nothing in his manner that was out of keeping with the character of a deeply serious man. He relieved those desperately worried soldiers from groundless superstition and fear. That was a highly important feat.

Something of that kind also happened in the great war which 25 was fought with such ferocity between Athens and Sparta.* When an eclipse of the sun brought sudden darkness, and the Athenians' minds were in the grip of panic, the great Pericles is said to have told his fellow-citizens a fact which he had heard from his former tutor Anaxagoras, namely that this thing invariably happened at fixed intervals when the entire moon passed in front of the sun's orb; and so, while it did not occur at every new moon, it could not occur except in that situation. By pointing out this fact and backing it up with an explanation he released the people from their fear. At that time it was a new and unfamiliar idea that the sun was regularly eclipsed when the moon came between it and the earth—a fact which was reputedly discovered by Thales of Miletus. On a later occasion the point was also noted by our own Ennius. He writes that about three hundred and fifty years after the foundation of Rome

> On June the fifth the moon and night* blocked out
> The sun.

In this area there is so much scientific sophistication that earlier solar eclipses are calculated from this day (recorded by Ennius and the Major Annals*) right back to the one which occurred on July the seventh in the reign of Romulus.* In that darkness nature carried Romulus* off to a normal death; yet we are told that on account of his valour he was raised to heaven.

26   TUBERO: Do you realize, Africanus, that not long ago you thought otherwise . . .

[*One leaf is missing. When the text resumes, the speaker is Scipio.*]

SCIPIO: . . . which the rest may see. Moreover, what can seem impressive in human affairs to one who has contemplated those divine realms, or long lasting to one who has comprehended eternity, or glorious to one who has perceived the smallness of the earth (both as a whole and in the areas inhabited by human beings) and to how tiny a part of it we are confined, and how countless nations have never heard of us, in spite of our hopes

27   that our fame flits and wanders far and wide? As for estates, buildings, herds, and huge amounts of silver and gold—how blessed should we count that man who does not think or speak of such things as 'goods', because he regards their enjoyment as frivolous, their usefulness slight, and their ownership precarious, and observes that the worst kind of person often has them in measureless quantities! He alone can truly claim everything as his in virtue, not of the citizen's, but of the wise man's right,* not by the guarantee of civil law, but by the universal law of nature. (For nature decrees that nothing belongs to anyone except the person who can handle and use it.) Such a man considers that our military commands and consulships belong to the class of necessary rather than desirable things,* that they should be undertaken from a sense of duty, not coveted for the sake of glory or rewards. Such a man, finally, can say of himself what, according to Cato, my grandfather Africanus used to say: that he was never doing more than when he was doing nothing, and was never less alone than when alone.

28   Who can really believe that when Dionysius, by every conceivable exertion, deprived his citizens of their liberty, he did more than his fellow-citizen Archimedes, when the latter, by apparently doing nothing,* constructed the aforementioned globe? Again, who believes that people who can find no one to talk to in the crowded forum are not more alone than those who, with no one present, either converse with themselves or share the company, as it were, of the greatest minds by enjoying their discoveries and writings? Who would think anyone richer than the man who lacks nothing—nothing, at least, that is required by nature, or anyone

more powerful than the man who obtains all he desires, or anyone more blessed than the man who is free from emotional disturbance, or anyone more secure in his prosperity than the man who possesses everything that he could, as they say, take with him from a shipwreck? What power, what office, what kingdom can be more desirable than the ability to look down on all things human, ranking them lower than wisdom, and never turn over in one's mind anything except what is divine and eternal, or the conviction that, while others are *called* men, only those who are skilled in the specifically human arts are worthy of the name? That 29 remark of Plato's (or whoever made it) strikes me as very apt. When he had been driven by a storm at sea to an unknown land and cast up on a lonely shore, and the others were in terror because they knew nothing of the place, he is supposed to have noticed some geometric figures drawn in the sand. On seeing them he cried 'Take heart! I see the traces of men!' He drew this conclusion, evidently, not from any crops which he saw growing in the fields, but from the signs of intellectual activity. That is why, Tubero, I have always valued learning, and educated men, and those interests of yours.

LAELIUS: I hesitate to say, Scipio, that you or Philus or 30 Manilius are so ⟨devoted⟩ to those questions . . . [*One leaf is lost in which Laelius said that while he is not hostile to physics and astronomy he regards them as less important than legal and political matters.*] . . . that friend of ours, who was related to him* on his father's side, is well worth taking as his model; I mean

Aelius
Sextus, a shrewd and very able man,

who was called 'shrewd' and 'very able' by Ennius, not because he sought for things which he could never find, but because he gave answers which relieved his clients' anxiety and worry. When he spoke against the astronomical interests of Galus, he would always quote the famous words of Achilles in *Iphigenia*:*

> Why should diviners seek celestial signs?
> When goat or scorpion or some other beast
> Comes up, then no one sees what lies before
> His feet; they scan the regions of the sky.

Yet this same man would say (for I have often listened to him—
yes, with pleasure) that Pacuvius' Zethus* was too antagonistic to
culture. He approved more of Ennius' Neoptolemus, who said he
wanted to practise philosophy 'fitfully', not 'totally'. But if you
are so keen on the interests of the Greeks, there are other, less limiting and more wide-ranging, subjects, which can be applied to
practical life and even to the conduct of politics. If *your* skills are
good for anything, it is for sharpening up a bit and, as it were,
provoking the minds of youngsters, to help them learn more
important things more easily.

31   TUBERO: I don't disagree with you, Laelius; but I wonder what
more important things you have in mind.

LAELIUS: Well then, I'll tell you, at the risk of incurring your
derision. You asked Scipio about those celestial phenomena,
whereas I should regard what happens before our very eyes as
more worthy of study. Why, I ask you, does the grandson of Lucius
Paulus, and the nephew of our friend here, born into an illustrious family and this far-famed country, enquire how two suns can
have been seen, but does not enquire why in one country there
are now two senates and almost two nations? As you realize, the
death of Tiberius Gracchus and, even before that, the whole policy
of his tribunate, split a single people into two camps. The critics
and opponents of Scipio were initially inspired by Publius Crassus
and Appius Claudius. Now that those two are dead the critics still
ensure that one section of the Senate, led by Quintus Metellus and
Publius Mucius, is opposed to you. They have stirred up the allies
and our Latin comrades; they have broken treaties; every day the
three commissioners* contrive some new act of sedition; and the
one man, here, who is capable of rectifying this dangerous situa-
32   tion is not allowed to do so. Take my advice, then, my young
friends, and don't worry about the second sun. It may not exist
at all; or, as it has been seen, let it exist provided it does no harm.
In any case we can know nothing of such things, and even if
we come to know a great deal, that kind of knowledge will not
make us better or happier people. To have one Senate and
one citizen body is achievable; if it isn't achieved, we are in
serious trouble. The opposite is obviously true at present, and we
can see that if unity is brought about we shall live better and
happier lives.

33–7. Scipio is asked what form of government is best

MUCIUS: So what do you think we should learn, Laelius, in 33 order to achieve what you require?

LAELIUS: Those skills which make us fit to serve the community. That, in my opinion, is the finest duty that wisdom has, and the greatest proof and function of moral excellence. So then, to make sure that we spend this holiday in discussions that are primarily of benefit to the state, why don't we ask Scipio to tell us what form of government he regards as the best? Then we'll go on to other questions. After clarifying them, we will come step by step, I hope, to these very problems, and will get a systematic understanding of the difficulties that now beset us.

After Philus, Manilius, and Mummius had given their whole- 34 hearted approval . . . [*One leaf is missing here. When the text resumes, Laelius is addressing his request to Scipio.*]

. . . I wanted this to happen, not just because it was right that a talk about the state should be given, preferably, by a statesman, but also because I recalled that you used to have frequent conversations with Panaetius in the company of Polybius* (the two Greeks who were possibly most expert in political theory); you would adduce numerous arguments to prove that much the best form of government was the one we had inherited from our ancestors. Since you are more *au fait* with that debate, you would do us all a favour (if I may also speak for the others) by presenting your views about the state.

SCIPIO: Well, I can't pretend that there's any subject to which 35 I give more attention than the one which you are suggesting, Laelius. I am aware that every craftsman in his own work, if he is any good, thinks, ponders, and strives for nothing except to improve in that field. I have inherited this task from my parents and ancestors, that is, the supervision and management of the country. So I suppose I would be admitting that I was lazier than any craftsman* if I devoted less effort to that great art than they do to their little ones. Yet I am not satisfied with what the fore- 36 most and wisest Greeks have left us in their writings about that topic. Nor do I venture to set my own opinions above theirs. So, as you listen, I suggest you think of me as not wholly ignorant of the Greek views, nor as ranking them above our own, especially in this field. Think of me rather as one of the toga-wearing people,* who has been given a liberal education thanks to his father's kindly concern, and has been fired from boyhood with a love of learning, but who has, nevertheless, been trained by experience and family sayings much more than by books.

37   PHILUS: I'm quite sure, Scipio, that you have no superior in ability, and that you far surpass everyone else in your experience of the great affairs of state. We know what studies you have always pursued. So if, as you say, you have also paid some attention to this science (or should I say art?), I am most grateful to Laelius for his suggestion. I expect that what you have to say will be more richly rewarding than anything which the Greeks have written for us.

SCIPIO: Well, you are saddling my talk with great expectations—a heavy burden indeed for anyone about to speak on such an important subject.

PHILUS: However great our expectations, you will still surpass them, as you always do. There's no danger that your rhetorical powers will fail when you are talking about political theory.

38. Scipio clears the ground

38   SCIPIO: I'll do my best to oblige. I begin by observing a rule which all speakers, I fancy, must adhere to if confusion is to be avoided: that is, if the name of the subject under discussion is accepted (whatever it is), the meaning of the name* should be explained. Only when that has been agreed can the discussion begin. For the scope of the subject under investigation will never be understood unless people first understand what it is. Since, then, we are examining the state, let us first ascertain what precisely we are examining.

Laelius nodded assent; so Scipio resumed: As the topic of discussion is so well known and familiar, I shan't go back to the basic elements which professionals usually deal with in such cases. That is, I shan't begin with the initial union* of male and female, and then go on to their offspring and degrees of kinship. Nor shall I offer frequent definitions of what each thing is and the ways in which it is expressed. After all, the audience consists of intelligent men who have served this great country with enormous distinction in war and peace; so I shan't allow my talk to be more obscure than the actual subject I have chosen. In undertaking this task, I don't aspire to give an exhaustive account like a professional teacher; nor do I promise that not one single detail will be overlooked.

LAELIUS: For myself, I'm looking forward to just the kind of talk that you have promised.

39–42. The three simple forms of government

SCIPIO: Well then, a republic is the property of the public.* But a public is not every kind of human gathering,* congregating in any manner, but a numerous gathering brought together by legal consent and community of interest. The primary reason for its coming together is not so much weakness* as a sort of innate desire on the part of human beings to form communities. For our species is not made up of solitary individuals or lonely wanderers. From birth it is of such a kind that, even when it possesses abundant amounts of every commodity . . . [*One leaf is lost in which Scipio presumably speaks of mankind's intrinsic impulse to form societies.*]

. . . ⟨Without⟩ certain seeds, as it were, ⟨of that kind⟩ no means could be discovered of establishing the other virtues or even the community itself. So these groups, formed for the reason just explained, first founded a settlement in a fixed place for the purpose of building houses. When, with the help of the terrain and their own manual labour, they had made it secure, they called such a collection of dwellings a town or, when it had been laid out with shrines and public spaces, a city. So then, every people (which is a numerous gathering of the kind described), every state (which is an organization of the populace), and every republic (which, as I said, is the property of the public) must be governed by some decision-making process* if it is to last. That process must, in the first instance, always come into being for the same reason as that which gave rise to the state. Then this process must be entrusted to one man, or a select group, or else be carried on by the whole populace. When the supreme authority is vested in one man, we call him a king, and the government of that state is a monarchy. When it is vested in a select group, that state is said to be ruled by the power of an aristocracy.* The state in which everything depends on the people is called a democracy. Provided the bond holds firm, which in the first place fastened the people to each other in the fellowship of a community, any of these three types may be, not indeed perfect, nor in my view the best, but at least tolerable, though one may be preferable to another. A just and wise king, or a select group of leading citizens, or the populace itself (though that is the least desirable type) can still, it seems, ensure a reasonably stable government, provided no forms of wickedness or greed find their way into it.

43–5. The defects of each form

43 Nevertheless, in monarchies the rest of the populace plays too small a part in the community's legislation and debate; in aristocracies the masses can have hardly any share in liberty, since they are deprived of any participation in discussion and decision-making; and when the government is carried on entirely by the people (however moderate and orderly) their equality is itself unequal, since it acknowledges no degrees of merit. Hence, although Cyrus of Persia was an exceptionally just and wise monarch, that form of government was not, in my view, the most desirable; for the property of the public (which is, as I said, the definition of a republic) was managed by one man's nod and wish.* Similarly, if it is true, as it is, that our clients, the Massilians, are governed with exemplary justice by a select group of leading citizens, yet even still the people are in a position somewhat akin to slavery. If at one period after the abolition of the Areopagus Athens discharged all its business through the resolutions and decrees of the people, that state failed to maintain its high reputation, for it did not observe different levels of merit.

44 I am speaking here about these three types of government, not when they have become mingled and blended, but when they retain their pure form. These types are each imperfect in the ways described above. They have also other potentially destructive defects. In fact each of these governments follows a kind of steep and slippery path which leads to a depraved version* of itself. Cyrus (to take the most conspicuous example) was a tolerable, even (I grant you) a likeable monarch. Yet below him stands the

cruelly capricious* Phalaris. His is the image into which, by a
smooth and easy process, the rule of one man degenerates. The
government of Massilia, which consists of a few leading citizens,
has as its close counterpart the Thirty—that notorious junta which
at one time ruled Athens. The supreme power exercised by the
Athenian people (to take no other instance) was transformed into
the mad and irresponsible caprice of the mob . . . [*A leaf is gone
and there is something wrong with the opening words of 45; they
have been omitted from the translation. It is clear, however, that
they referred to the process whereby one constitution arose from
another.*]

. . . likewise, one of those types which I have just described usually   45
bursts forth from it. The cycles* and, so to speak, revolutions
through which governments pass in their successive changes are
quite amazing. It is the business of the intelligent man to be aware
of them; but to see them coming, to modify their effects, and to
keep control of their course while governing the state—that calls
for a great citizen and a man of almost superhuman powers. That
is why, in my view, a fourth kind of government is to be judged
the best; that is, a carefully proportioned mixture* of the first three
described above.

46–50. A defence of democracy

LAELIUS: I know that's what you prefer, Africanus; I've often   46
heard you say so. Still, if it's not a nuisance, I'd like to know which
of your three forms you consider the best. For it would help us to
appreciate . . .

[*One leaf is lost. Scipio is presenting the arguments for
democracy.*]

SCIPIO: . . . and the nature of every state depends on the   47
character and will of its ruling body. So liberty has no home in
any state except a democracy. Nothing can be sweeter than liberty.
Yet if it isn't equal throughout, it isn't liberty at all. For how can
liberty be equal throughout, I will not say in a monarchy, where
slavery is evident and unmistakable, but in those states where
everyone is free in name only? They register their votes, they
bestow military commands and political offices, they are can-
vassed, and asked to say yea or nay; but they confer what they

would have to confer even if they didn't want to—things which they themselves don't have, in spite of being asked for them by others. For they have no share in the supreme power, or in national policy-making, or in legal decisions (those are made by specially appointed judges). All such things are apportioned on the basis of one's ancient lineage or wealth. But in a free community of the Rhodian* or Athenian kind there is no citizen who . . . [*A leaf is lost. Scipio is still speaking on the same topic.*]

48 . . . We are told that, when one or more exceptionally rich and prosperous men emerge from the populace, ⟨a despotism or an oligarchy⟩ comes into being as a result of their arrogance and contempt; for the faint-hearted and the weak give way and succumb to the haughtiness of wealth. But if the people would hold fast to their rights, nothing, they say, would be superior in power, liberty, or happiness, inasmuch as they would be in charge of laws, courts, war, peace, treaties, individual lives, and wealth. They maintain that this form of government is the only one that deserves the name of 'republic' (i.e. the property of the public); and that for this reason the republic tends to be restored to freedom from the domination of a king or a senate, whereas kings or rich and powerful aristocrats are not summoned to take over from free peoples.

49 They insist that the whole concept of a free people should not be rejected because of the crimes committed by an undisciplined mob. When the people, in a spirit of unity, judge everything in the light of their own security and freedom, nothing, they say, is less liable to change or collapse. Harmony is readily maintained in a state where everyone has the same interests. It is from incompatible interests, when different policies suit different people, that discord arises. And so, when a senate held power, the stability of the state was never assured. Far less was it assured in the case of monarchy, which, as Ennius* says, possesses 'no holy partnership or trust'. Since, then, law is the bond which holds together a community of citizens, and the justice embodied in the law is the same for everyone, by what right can a community of citizens be held together when their status is unequal? If the equalization of wealth is rejected, and the equalization of everybody's abilities is impossible, legal rights at least must be equal among those who live as fellow-citizens in the same state. For what is a state other than an

equal partnership in justice? . . . [*One leaf is lost. The topic remains the same.*]

. . . The argument runs that the other types of state have no right to the names by which they themselves wish to be called. Take a man who is greedy for domination or absolute power, lording it over an oppressed people. Why should I call him 'king', using the title of Jupiter the Best, instead of 'despot'? Despots can be benevolent, just as kings can be oppressive. So, as far as the people are concerned, the only question is whether they are the slaves of a kind or a harsh master. Either way, they must necessarily be slaves. When Sparta was thought to excel in its political organization, how could it be sure of enjoying good and just kings when it was obliged to accept as a king whoever was born into a royal family?* As for those 'aristocrats' who have not been granted the title by the people's consent but have appropriated it through their own electoral assembly, who could endure them? For on what criteria is a man to be judged 'the best'? Why, on the basis of his learning, his skills, his activities, I hear it said . . . [*Two leaves are lost.*]

51–3. A defence of aristocracy

[*Scipio continues*] . . . If ⟨the state⟩ leaves the process to chance, it will be overturned as quickly as a ship in which a man chosen by lot* from among the passengers has taken over the helm. If, however, a free people chooses the men to whom it will entrust itself, and if, with a genuine desire for security, it chooses only the best men, then without a doubt the security of such states depends on the policies of aristocrats, especially as nature has decreed not only that men of superior character and ability should be in charge of the less endowed, but also that the latter should willingly obey their superiors.

But they maintain that this ideal state has been ruined by people who cannot think straight—people who, knowing nothing about worth (which resides in a few, and is discerned and assessed by a few), imagine that aristocrats are those with large fortunes and possessions or those who belong to famous families. When, as a result of this vulgar misconception, a few with money, not worth, have gained control of the state, those leaders seize the name of 'aristocrats' with their teeth, though lacking any right to it in fact. Money, name, and property, if divorced from good sense and skill in living one's own life and directing the lives of others, lapse into total degradation and supercilious insolence. And indeed there is

52 no more degenerate kind of state than that in which the richest are supposed to be the best. But what can be more splendid than a state governed by worth, where the man who gives orders to others is not the servant of greed, where the leader himself has embraced all the values which he preaches and recommends to his citizens, where he imposes no laws on the people which he does not obey himself, but rather presents his own life to his fellows as a code of conduct?

If one man alone could meet all these requirements there would be no need for more than one. If the whole populace could perceive what was best and reach agreement about it, no one would advocate appointing leaders. It is the difficulty of initiating policies that has transferred authority from kings to larger groups, and the bad judgement and recklessness of popular bodies that has transferred it from the masses to the few. Hence the aristocrats have taken over the middle ground between the inadequate autocrat and the reckless mob. Nothing could be more moderate than that. With such men protecting the state the people must be very fortunate; they are freed from all trouble and anxiety, having made others responsible for their carefree life. Those others must protect it and not give the people cause to

53 complain that their interests are being ignored by the leaders. That is always a risk, for equality before the law, which free people so cherish, cannot be maintained indefinitely; for the people themselves, even when free from all restraint, give many special privileges to many persons, and even among the people there is much favouritism in regard to men and their status. So-called equality is most inequitable; for when the same respect is accorded to the highest and the lowest (who must be present in every nation), equity itself is most unequal. That cannot happen in states ruled by the best. Those, more or less, are the arguments, along with others of a similar kind, that are advanced by those who maintain that this is the most desirable form of government.

54–64. Pressed to choose one of the simple forms, Scipio prefers monarchy but acknowledges its precarious nature

LAELIUS: But what about yourself, Scipio?* Which of those 54 three do *you* most approve of?

SCIPIO: You are right to ask which of the three I *most* approve of, for I do not consider any one of them ideal by itself. Rather than any one of the separate types, I prefer a mixture of all three. But if one has to be preferred in its pure form, I would prefer monarchy . . . [*In the last few lines of this section the text is defective.*] The name of king is like that of father, in that a king takes thought for his subjects as if they were his children, and looks after them more conscientiously than . . . that they are supported by the dedication of one man, the best and most highly esteemed.

Here now are the aristocrats, who claim to perform this func- 55 tion more effectively, claiming that there is more good sense in a group than in an individual, and yet also the same degree of fairness and reliability. But here come the people, shouting at the top of their voices that they will obey neither an autocrat nor an oligarchy; that nothing is sweeter than liberty, even to wild animals; and that this blessing is denied to anyone who serves a king or an aristocracy. Accordingly, kings attract us by affection, aristocracies by good sense, and democracies by freedom. So in comparing them it is hard to choose which one likes best.

LAELIUS: I'm sure you're right; but the problems ahead can hardly be cleared up if you leave this one unresolved.

SCIPIO: Well then, let's follow the example of Aratus,* who at 56 the opening of his great exposition thinks it right to begin with Jove.

LAELIUS: Why with Jove? And what has your talk in common with his poem?

SCIPIO: It just seems right that we should begin our discussion with that being who is acknowledged by everyone, learned and unlearned alike, to be the sole king of all gods and men.

LAELIUS: Why?

SCIPIO: Why do you think? The reason's obvious. One answer is that rulers of states have, for reasons of practical expediency, promoted the belief that there is one king in heaven who, in Homer's words,* 'shakes the whole of Olympus with his nod'; and that he should be regarded as king and father of all. In that case there is weighty authority and many witnesses (if universal testimony may be so described) that, in obedience to their rulers' decrees, countries have agreed that there is nothing superior to a king, in the belief that all the gods are ruled by one divine power. If, however, we have been brought up to think that this belief is a kind of fable, founded on the misconceptions of the ignorant, let us listen to people who may be described as the common teachers of educated men—those who have, as it were, seen with their eyes things which we barely take in through our ears.

LAELIUS: And who, may I ask, are they?

SCIPIO: Those who have studied the nature of reality as a whole, and have realized that this entire world ⟨is controlled⟩ by ⟨one⟩ mind ... [57 *Two leaves are missing. Scipio continues to* 58 *argue in favour of monarchy*.] ... But if you like, Laelius, I will present witnesses who are not excessively ancient nor in any sense barbarous.

LAELIUS: I'd like to hear them.

SCIPIO: Well, do you realize that this city has been without a king for less than four hundred years?

LAELIUS: Of course.

SCIPIO: Well then, this period of four hundred years is not particularly long, is it, for a city or a state?

LAELIUS: No. The place has barely grown up.

SCIPIO: So four hundred years ago there was a king in Rome.

LAELIUS: Yes, and a proud one* too.

SCIPIO: And before that?

LAELIUS: A very just one;* and from him they reach right back to Romulus, who lived six hundred years before our time.

SCIPIO: So even he didn't live all that long ago, did he?

LAELIUS: By no means. Greece was already growing old.*

SCIPIO: Tell me, then: were Romulus' subjects barbarians?

LAELIUS: If, as the Greeks say, all people other than Greeks are barbarians, I'm afraid his subjects *were* barbarians. But if the name should be applied to character rather than language, then the Romans, in my view, were no more barbarous than the Greeks.

SCIPIO: Yet in this discussion of ours we are not concerned with nationality but with nature. If sensible men, not very long ago, wanted to have kings, then my witnesses are not so very ancient; nor are they wild and uncivilized.

LAELIUS: I grant, Scipio, that you have an ample supply of witnesses! But with me, as with any good judge, arguments have greater force than witnesses. 59

SCIPIO: Very well, Laelius; you can employ an argument based on your own self-awareness.

LAELIUS: What awareness?

SCIPIO: Whenever—or *if* ever—you are aware of being angry with someone.

LAELIUS: I have had that experience more often that I could wish!

SCIPIO: Ah. So, when you are angry, do you allow anger to take control of your mind?

LAELIUS: Certainly not. I take my cue from Archytas of Tarentum. Once, on arriving at his country house, he found that all his instructions had been ignored. 'Why, you worthless wretch!' he said to his agent, 'if I weren't angry I would have beaten you to death on the spot!'

SCIPIO: Very good! So evidently Archytas rightly looked on 60 anger (that is, when it was at variance with his judgement) as a kind of revolt within the mind, and he was anxious to quell it by rational reflection. Bring in greed, bring in lust, bring in the desire for power and glory; then you realize that if there is to be a ruling power in the human mind, it will be the sovereignty of a single element, namely reason (for that is the best part of the mind). As long as reason is supreme there is no room for lust, anger, or irresponsible behaviour.

LAELIUS: That's right.

SCIPIO: So you approve of a mind which is ordered in that way?

LAELIUS: Certainly; there's nothing better.

SCIPIO: So you would not approve of one where reason had been ousted, and where lust in its countless forms and anger held total sway?

LAELIUS: In my opinion that sort of mind, and the person who possessed it, would be the vilest thing in creation.

SCIPIO: So you agree, then, that every activity of the mind

should be under the rule of one element, that element being reason?

LAELIUS: I do.

SCIPIO: Why, then, do you have any doubt regarding your opinion of the body politic? There, if the thing is put in the hands of more than one person, clearly there will be no power in charge; for if power is not a unity it may well be nothing at all.

61   LAELIUS: What, pray, is the difference between one and more than one being in charge, if the latter are inspired by justice?

SCIPIO: I notice, Laelius, that you are not much impressed by my witnesses! But I shan't give up. I shall continue to use *you* as a witness to confirm what I'm saying.

LAELIUS: Me? And how do you propose to do that?

SCIPIO: Recently, when we were at your villa in Formiae, I observed that you gave the staff strict instructions to take orders from one person only.

LAELIUS: Quite; my agent.

SCIPIO: What about your house in town? Do several people run your affairs?

LAELIUS: No indeed; just one.

SCIPIO: What of the whole establishment? Is anyone else in charge of it apart from you?

LAELIUS: Certainly not.

SCIPIO: So why don't you admit that in a state, too, the rule of one man is best, provided he is just?

LAELIUS: I'm almost persuaded to agree with you.

62   SCIPIO: You'll agree more readily, Laelius, if I leave aside the analogies of the ship's captain and the doctor* (which show that, provided they are qualified in their respective professions, a ship should be entrusted to the former alone and an invalid to the latter alone) and move on to more striking instances.

LAELIUS: What have you in mind?

SCIPIO: Well, I take it you're aware that it was because of the overbearing and arrogant nature of Tarquin alone that the name of king has become anathema to our people.

LAELIUS: I am, indeed.

SCIPIO: In that case you are also aware of another fact, on which I shall probably enlarge in the course of my talk, namely that after Tarquin's expulsion the populace revelled in an extraordinary excess of liberty. That was when innocent people were driven into exile, when many had their property seized as plunder, when two consuls were elected each year, when the rods of authority were lowered in the presence of the people, when appeals of all kinds became possible, when secessions of the common people took place, when, in fact, most of the measures enacted ensured that everything should be in the hands of the people.

LAELIUS: Yes; that's what happened.

63

SCIPIO: And that's what tends to happen in periods of peace and security. For you can act irresponsibly when you have nothing to be afraid of. The same is true on board ship, and often in the case of a mild illness. But as the seafarer and the invalid beg the help of one individual when the sea suddenly grows rough and the illness more serious, so our people, which at home in peacetime gives orders, threatens the actual magistrates, refuses to obey them, appeals against them, and challenges their decisions, in wartime defers to each magistrate as though he were king; for then safety takes precedence over personal desires. In times of more serious conflict, our countrymen have decreed that the supreme power should not be shared, even with one colleague, but should rest in the hands of an individual whose very name reflects the nature of his power. For a dictator* is so called in virtue of the fact that his appointment is dictated (though in our augurs' books,* Laelius, you will remember that he is called 'master of the people').

LAELIUS: Yes, I do.

SCIPIO: And so those men of old wisely . . . [*One leaf is lost.*] . . . When the people are deprived of a just king, they are like   64 orphans. A sense of loss lingers within their hearts. As Ennius says* in the lines following the death of that excellent king:

> And all the time they say among themselves
> 'O Romulus, O Romulus divine,
> Sent down from heaven as guardian of our land,
> O sire, O father, offspring of the gods!'

They did not give the name 'lords' or 'masters' or even 'kings' to those whose just rule they obeyed, but 'guardians of our land', 'fathers' and 'gods'—with good reason; for what do they say next?

> You brought us forth into the realms of light.

Life, honour, glory—these were the blessings they thought they had received from their just king. The same goodwill would have continued in later generations if the character of the king had remained the same. But, as you know, owing to the wickedness of one individual that whole form of government collapsed.

LAELIUS: Yes indeed. And I'm interested to hear how those changes have taken place, not just in our country but in countries in general.

65–8. The instability of simple forms

65   SCIPIO: When I've told you my opinion about what I regard as the best type of constitution, I shall have to talk in greater detail about how constitutions in general pass into one another, even though the best one, I think, will not readily undergo such changes. But the first and most inevitable of all changes is that which overtakes a monarchy. As soon as a king begins to rule unjustly, that kind of government vanishes on the spot, for that same man has become a tyrant. That is the worst kind of government, and at the same time the closest neighbour to the best. If a tyranny is overthrown by an aristocracy, as usually happens, the country then moves into the second of these constitutions. It is somewhat like monarchy in being a paternal council of leading men who have the best interests of the people at heart. If the tyrant has been killed or expelled by the people acting directly, the latter behave with reasonable restraint as long as they remain wise and sensible. They take pleasure in what they have done, and are keen to preserve the constitution which they themselves have set up. But if, violently or otherwise, the populace deposes a *just* king, or if, as more frequently happens, it tastes the blood of the aristocracy and subjects the entire state to its wild caprice (and make no mistake about it, no tempest or conflagration, however great, is harder to quell than a mob carried away by the novelty of power), then the result is what Plato* so brilliantly described, if I can

66   express it in Latin. (It's not easy, but I'll try.) 'When', he says, 'the insatiable throat of the mob is parched with thirst for freedom, and when, thanks to the wicked servants it employs, it thirstily quaffs a freedom which instead of being sensibly diluted is all too potent, then, unless its magistrates and leaders are extremely soft

and indulgent, and administer that freedom generously in its favour, it denounces them, arraigns them, and condemns them, calling them despots, kings, and tyrants.' I expect you know the passage.

LAELIUS: Very well.

SCIPIO: Well, this is the next bit: 'Those who take orders from 67 the leading men are harassed by the populace and called willing puppets. Public officials who try to behave like private citizens, and private citizens who manage to abolish the distinction between ordinary people and officials, are overwhelmed with praise and showered with honours. In a state of that kind total freedom must prevail. Every private household is devoid of authority—a disease which infects even domestic animals. Father fears son, son ignores father, respect is completely absent. In the interests of universal freedom there is no distinction between citizen and foreigner; a teacher is afraid of his pupils and truckles to them; they treat their teachers with contempt. Youngsters assume the authority of older men; the latter lower themselves to take part in youngsters' amusements for fear of becoming unpopular and disliked. As a result even slaves behave with excessive freedom, wives enjoy the same rights as their husbands, and in this all-pervading freedom dogs and horses and even asses charge around so freely that one has to stand aside for them in the street. As this unlimited licence comes to a head,' he says, 'citizens become so tender and hypersensitive that at the slightest hint of authority they are enraged and cannot bear it. In consequence they begin to ignore the laws too; and the final outcome is total anarchy.'

LAELIUS: Yes, that's a pretty accurate account of what he says. 68

SCIPIO: To revert, then, to my own conversational style, he goes on to say that this excessive licence, which the anarchists think is the only true freedom, provides the stock, as it were, from which a tyrant grows. As the death of an aristocracy comes from its own excessive power, so freedom itself plunges an over-free populace into slavery. All excess, whether the over-luxuriance has occurred in the weather or on the land or in people's bodies, turns as a rule into its opposite. The process is especially common in states. In communities and individuals alike, excessive freedom topples over into excessive slavery. Extreme freedom produces a tyrant, along with the extremely harsh and evil slavery that goes with him. For from that wild, and indeed savage, populace a chief is usually chosen to oppose the leaders who have now been persecuted and ousted from their position—a brazen dirty fellow, who has the impudence to harass people who in many cases have served their country well, a fellow who presents the people with other folks' property as well as their own.

If he remains a private citizen, such a man faces many threats. So he is given powers, which are then extended. Like Peisistratus at Athens, he is surrounded by a bodyguard. He ends up by tyrannizing over the very people from whom he emerged. If that man is overthrown, as often happens, by decent citizens, constitutional government is restored. But if he is supplanted by unscrupulous thugs, then a junta is created which is just another form of tyranny. The same kind of group can also arise from an often excellent aristocratic government when some crookedness diverts the leaders from their course. And so political power passes like a ball from one group to another. Tyrants snatch it from kings; aristocrats or the people wrest it from them; and from them it moves to oligarchic cliques or back to tyrants. The same type of constitution never retains power for long.

69. A mixed constitution is the best

69 That is why, though monarchy is, in my view, much the most desirable of the three primary forms, monarchy is itself surpassed by an even and judicious blend of the three simple forms at their best. A state should possess an element of regal supremacy; something else* should be assigned and allotted to the authority of aristocrats; and certain affairs should be reserved for the judgement and desires of the masses. Such a constitution has, in the first place, a widespread element of equality which free men cannot long do without. Secondly, it has stability; for although those three original forms easily degenerate into their corrupt versions (producing a despot instead of a king, an oligarchy instead of an aristocracy, and a disorganized rabble instead of a democracy), and although those simple forms often change into others, such things rarely happen in a political structure which represents a combination and a judicious mixture—unless, that is, the politicians are deeply

corrupt. For there is no reason for change in a country where everyone is firmly established in his own place, and which has beneath it no corresponding version into which it may suddenly sink and decline.

70–1. The example of the Roman constitution

However, I'm afraid that you, Laelius, and you, my kind and 70 learned friends, may get the impression that in talking like this I am setting myself up as a preacher or a teacher instead of collaborating with you in a joint inquiry. So I shall move on to matters which are familiar to everyone, and which indeed we have long been working towards. I hold, maintain, and declare that no form of government is comparable in its structure, its assignment of functions, or its discipline, to the one which our fathers received from their forebears and have handed down to us. So, if you approve (because you wanted me to talk on a subject which you yourselves knew well), I shall describe its nature and at the same time demonstrate its superiority. Then, after setting up our constitution as a model, I shall use it as a point of reference, as best I can, in all I have to say about the best possible state. If I can keep this aim in view and bring it to a conclusion, I shall have amply fulfilled, I think, the task which Laelius assigned me.

LAELIUS: Well it's certainly your task, Scipio, and yours alone. 71 For who is better placed than you to talk about our forefathers' institutions, since your forefathers were themselves especially distinguished? Or about the best possible state? If we were to have such a state (which we don't have even now), who could play a more active role than you? Or who could better formulate our future policies? For by repelling the two dangers* that threatened our city you yourself* have made provision for all the years that lie ahead.

FRAGMENTS OF BOOK I

1. [Loeb, 34] So do, please, bring your talk down from the sky to these more immediate problems (Nonius 1. 121 and 2. 446).

2. [Loeb, frag. 2] Therefore, since our fatherland brings more blessings, and is a more long-standing parent than the one who

begot us, it must surely claim a greater debt of gratitude than a father (Nonius 3. 688). [*This seems to belong to the prologue.*]

3. [Loeb, frag. 3] Nor would Carthage have enjoyed such prosperity for some six hundred years without sound policies and a sound system of training (Nonius 3. 845).

BOOK 2

1–11. The foundation of Rome

As everyone was consumed with eagerness to hear what he had ¹ to say, Scipio began as follows:

My first point is taken from old Cato. As you know, I was especially fond of him and admired him greatly. On the recommendation of my two fathers* and, even more so, because of my own interest, I devoted myself to him, heart and soul, from my early days. I could never hear enough of his talk—so rich was the man's political experience, which he had acquired during his long and distinguished career in peace and war. Equally impressive were his temperate way of speaking, his combination of seriousness and humour, his tremendous zest for obtaining and providing information, and the close correspondence between his preaching and his practice.

Cato used to say that our constitution was superior to others, ² because in their case there had usually been one individual who had equipped his state with laws and institutions, for example, Minos of Crete, Lycurgus of Sparta, and the men who had brought about a succession of changes at Athens (Theseus, Draco, Solon, Cleisthenes, and many others) until finally, when it lay fainting and prostrate, it was revived by that learned man, Demetrius of Phalerum. Our own constitution, on the other hand, had been established not by one man's ability but by that of many, not in the course of one man's life but over several ages and generations. He used to say that no genius of such magnitude* had ever existed that he could be sure of overlooking nothing; and that no collection of able people at a single point of time could have sufficient foresight to take account of everything; there had to be practical experience over a long period of history.

Accordingly in my discourse I shall go back, as Cato used to ³ do, to the 'origin'* of the Roman people (I gladly borrow his actual word). Moreover, it will be easier to carry out my plan if I describe for you the birth, growth, and maturity of our state, which eventually became so firm and strong, than if I deal with some imaginary community, as Socrates does in Plato.

4   Everyone agreed to this; so he continued: Have we ever heard of any state with so splendid and famous a beginning as this city founded by Romulus?* He was the son of Mars—let's not argue with a popular tradition which is not only ancient but also wisely transmitted by our forefathers, namely, that great public servants should be deemed divine by birth as well as in ability. Romulus, then, is said to have been exposed at birth on the banks of the Tiber, along with his brother Remus, on the orders of Amulius, King of Alba, who feared the overthrow of his kingdom. There he was suckled by an animal from the forest before being rescued by herdsmen, who brought him up as an agricultural labourer. They say that when he grew up he was so far ahead of the others in physical strength and force of character that all the people who lived in that part of the countryside where the capital stands today willingly and cheerfully accepted his leadership. Putting himself at the head of their forces (to move, now, from legend to history) he is supposed to have crushed Alba Longa, a strong and formidable city at that time, and to have put King Amulius to death.

5   After this splendid achievement, Romulus' first thought, we are told, was to found a city by means of augury* and to establish a political community. He chose an incredibly advantageous site for the city—a thing which has to be planned with careful foresight by anyone trying to create a permanent community. He did not move it to the coast, though with troops and resources of that size he could easily have marched into the territory of the Rutulians and Aborigines; or he could have started a new city at the mouth of the Tiber, where King Ancus founded a colony* many years later. With his exceptional imagination the great man realized clearly that coastal sites were not particularly suitable* for cities founded in the hope of permanence and power, first because coastal sites were exposed to numerous, and also unforeseeable,

6   dangers. For, in the case of an inland settlement, advance warning is given of an enemy's approach, not only when it's expected but also when it isn't, by many indications, including a certain amount of unavoidable noise and din. No enemy can come across country, at whatever speed, without our knowing that he's there, and also who he is and where he comes from. But a maritime, naval enemy

can be upon us before anyone knows he is on the way; and when he comes he doesn't advertise his identity or his nationality or even his intentions. There is no means of discerning or inferring even whether he is friend or foe.

Furthermore, the moral character of coastal cities is prone to corruption and decay. For they are exposed to a mixture of strange talk and strange modes of behaviour. Foreign customs are imported along with foreign merchandise; and so none of their ancestral institutions can remain unaffected. The inhabitants of those cities do not stay at home. They are always dashing off to foreign parts, full of airy hopes and designs. And even when, physically, they stay put, they wander abroad in their imagination. No factor was more responsible for the ultimate overthrow of Carthage and Corinth* (which had already been long undermined) than the restlessness and dispersal of their citizens; for in their craving for mercantile voyages and commercial profit they failed to attend to their land and their army. The sea also brings enticements to luxury in the form of booty or imports, which cause serious damage to states. Apart from anything else, the attractiveness of their site represents many temptations to sensual indulgence, whether through extravagance or idleness. What I have just said about Corinth could be said with equal justice, I suspect, of Greece as a whole. For the Peloponnese is pretty well surrounded by the sea, and apart from Phlius* there are no communities whose territory does not touch the sea. Outside the Peloponnese, only the Aenianes, the Dorians,* and the Dolopes are far from the sea. I need hardly mention the Greek islands, which are surrounded by the waves and almost float on their surface along with the customs and institutions of their cities. These places, as I said earlier, belong to the Greek motherland. But think of all the colonies she has sent out to Asia, Thrace, Italy, Sicily, and Africa. Except for Magnesia, every one of them is washed by the waves. As a result, a Greek coast seems to have been tacked on, as it were, to the lands of barbarians. Of the barbarians themselves none originally sailed the seas, except the Etruscans, who did so as pirates, and the Phoenicians, who did so for trade. Seafaring was clearly the cause of Greece's misfortunes, including her political instability, since it gave rise to the characteristic vices of coastal cities which I touched on briefly a little while ago. But along with those endemic faults there is one enormous advantage. The products of every land can come by sea to the city where you live; conversely your people can export and deliver the produce of their fields to whatever country they wish.

10   How then could Romulus have achieved with more inspired success the advantages of a coastal city, while avoiding its faults, than by founding Rome on the bank of a river which flowed with its broad stream, smooth and unfailing, into the sea? Thus the city could import by sea whatever it needed, and export its surplus; and thanks to the same river it could not only draw in by sea the commodities most necessary for its life and culture, it could also bring them down from the hinterland. And so Romulus, in my view, already foresaw that this city would eventually form the site and centre of a world empire. A city founded in some other part of Italy could hardly have held so easily such vast political power.

11   As for the city's own natural defences, can anyone be so unobservant as not to have them etched, clear and familiar, on his mind? Thanks to the wisdom of Romulus and the other kings, the line and course of its wall were designed to run in every direction through steep precipitous mountains. The only access, between the Esquiline and Quirinal hills, was covered by a high rampart and a huge ditch; and the citadel, thus protected, was built all round on steep crags which looked as if they had been cut away on every side, so that even in the dreadful period of the Gallic invasion it remained impregnable and inviolate. The chosen site also enjoyed an abundance of spring water and a healthy atmosphere in spite of the region's plague-ridden character; for breezes blow through the hills, and they in their turn provide shade for the valleys.

12–44. The period of the kings

12 Romulus achieved all this in a very short time. He founded the city, which he decreed should be named Rome after him; then, to strengthen the new community, he followed a novel and somewhat crude plan* which nevertheless bore the stamp of a great and far-seeing man, in that it consolidated the resources of his kingdom and people. Well-born Sabine girls had come to Rome

on the festival of Consus to attend the yearly games which Romulus had inaugurated. On his orders they were seized and assigned in marriage to young men of the foremost families. The 13 Sabines, consequently, attacked the Romans, and the outcome of the battle was confused and uncertain. Romulus, therefore, made a treaty with Titus Tatius in response to the appeals of the very wives who had been abducted. By the terms of this treaty he admitted the Sabines to Roman citizenship with shared religious observances, and he accepted their king as a partner in his kingship.

After Tatius' death the entire sovereignty reverted to Romulus. 14 Previous to that, he, together with Tatius, had chosen a royal council made up of leading citizens, who were called 'Fathers'* on account of the affection in which they were held. He had also divided the populace into three tribes,* named after himself, Tatius, and Lucumo (a supporter of Romulus who had been killed in the struggle with the Sabines), and into thirty voting-districts which he named after the Sabine girls who, from among those abducted, had appealed for a peace treaty. But although these administrative divisions had been set up in Tatius' lifetime, after his death Romulus relied still more on the authority and advice of the Fathers in discharging his royal duties.

In doing so he was the first to realize and accept something 15 which Lycurgus had realized a little earlier in Sparta,* namely that states are better governed and controlled by the king's sole power and authority when the influence of all the best men is allowed to act upon the absolute monarch. So, protected and supported by this council, which was a kind of senate, Romulus waged many highly successful wars against his neighbours; and, though he brought no plunder to his own house, he continually increased the 16 wealth of the citizens. Moreover, Romulus was most scrupulous in observing the auspices, a habit which we still retain, much to the benefit of the state. He himself took the auspices when founding the city—an act which marked the beginning of our state; and at the beginning of every public event he appointed augurs, one from each tribe, to assist him in taking the auspices. He also arranged for the common people to be assigned to the leading citizens as clients (the great advantages of this scheme will be explained later*); and instead of controlling them by violent

punishments he imposed fines of sheep and cattle; for wealth at
that time consisted of livestock* (*pecus*) and land (*loci*), hence
people were called 'rich in livestock' (*pecuniosi*) and 'wealthy in
land' (*locupletes*).

17   Romulus reigned for thirty-seven years and laid those two
admirable foundation-stones of the state, namely the auspices
and the Senate. So great were his achievements that when, after a
sudden eclipse of the sun,* he failed to reappear, it was assumed
that he had been admitted to the company of the gods, an idea
which could never have gained currency for any human being
18 who had not possessed an outstanding reputation for valour and
integrity. This was the more astonishing in the case of Romulus,
in that the other men who are supposed to have attained apotheosis lived in less educated periods of history, when the mind was
prone to fabricate myths, and simple people were easily induced
to believe them; whereas we know that the age of Romulus existed
less than six hundred years ago, at a time when writing and learning had long been familiar, and when all those primitive supersti-
tions that belong to an ignorant society had been swept away. If,
as Greek chronology informs us, Rome was founded in the second
year of the seventh Olympiad,* the age of Romulus came at a
period when Greece was already full of poets and musicians, and
less credence was given to fables, except in the case of remote
events. The first Olympiad is dated a hundred and eight years after
Lycurgus began to codify the law, though some people think it
was inaugurated by that same Lycurgus, owing to a confusion
over the name.* Now Homer, at a conservative estimate, lived
19 about thirty years before the age of Lycurgus. Hence it may be
inferred that Homer lived many years before Romulus. So by then,
when men were educated and the times themselves were enlight-
ened, there was hardly any scope for myth-making. Antiquity
accepted fabulous stories even though they were sometimes clumsily conceived;* but that later age, which was by now sophisticated, made a point of deriding sheer impossibilities and rejecting
them with scorn.

[*There is a gap at this point, and the next lines are based on a
fragmentary text. Scipio seems to have mentioned some Greek
poets who lived at the time when Romulus' apotheosis was
accepted.*]

... his daughter's son, as some people said. In the fifty-sixth 20
Olympiad, the very year when ⟨Stesichorus⟩ died, Simonides was
born. This helps us to appreciate that Romulus' immortality was
believed at a time when the nature of human life had long been a
familiar subject, discussed and understood. There is no doubt that
it was due to Romulus' exceptional intelligence and force of character that people believed what the peasant Proculus Julius said
about him—a thing which had not been believed about any other
mortal for many generations. At the behest of the Senate, which
was keen to dispel the ill-feeling and suspicion following Romulus'
death, Proculus is supposed to have declared at a public meeting
that he had seen Romulus on the hill now called the Quirinal;
Romulus had instructed him to ask the people to build him a
shrine on that hill; he himself, he said, was a god and bore the
name of Quirinus.

You appreciate, then, don't you, that it was thanks to the good 21
sense of one man not only that a new people came into being but
that, when he departed, it was not a baby crying in its cradle, but
rather a youth on the verge of manhood.

LAELIUS: Yes, we are aware of that, and also of the fact that at
the outset you are using a novel method of exposition which is
not to be found in any Greek treatise. The doyen of writers* on
this theme chose a stretch of virgin territory where he could build
a state according to his own specifications. It was a remarkable
state no doubt, but quite out of touch with men's lives and habits. 22
His successors have presented their opinions about types and
systems of political organization without reference to any definite
model or form of constitution. It looks to me as if you intend to
do both. For in your opening remarks you prefer to attribute your
discoveries to others rather than, like Plato's Socrates, to claim
them for yourself; in talking about the site of the city you discuss
in theoretical terms what Romulus did by chance or necessity; and
instead of wandering from one state to another you confine your
discussion to a single example. So carry on as you have begun. As
you work your way through the other kings I fancy I can foresee
the emergence of a fully-fledged state.

SCIPIO: So then, after Romulus' death, his Senate, which com- 23
prised the best men*—men whom the king held in such high
regard that he wished them to be called 'Fathers' and their

children 'Patricians'*—tried to rule the state by itself, without a
king. But the people would not have it, and in their grief at the
loss of Romulus they persisted in calling for a king. Therefore the
leading citizens astutely devised a new procedure unknown to any
other nation, namely the introduction of an interregnum.* This
practice ensured that, pending the appointment of a permanent
monarch, the state should not be without a king, nor yet have a
long-reigning substitute. It thus guarded against a situation in
24 which a person, having grown used to power, should be too slow
in laying down the sovereignty or too well placed for usurping it.
Even at that stage, you see, that newly established people perceived something that escaped the Spartan Lycurgus. He thought
that a king should not be chosen (if indeed that lay within Lycurgus' power), but should be accepted, whatever he was like, provided he was a descendant of Hercules. But our peasant ancestors
perceived even then that one should look for valour and good
sense in a king rather than noble lineage.

25 As Numa Pompilius was reputedly outstanding in these
respects, the people passed over its own citizens, and on the
Senate's recommendation brought in a king from outside, inviting
a Sabine from Cures to reign at Rome. When he arrived here,
although the people had already held an Assembly of Voting
Districts* to appoint him king, he still had a law passed by that
same body to confirm his regal powers. Then, as he saw that the
Romans, following the precedent set by Romulus, were intensely
keen on military pursuits, he thought they should be diverted a
little from that way of life.

26 First, he divided among the citizens, man by man, the territory*
which Romulus had conquered, pointing out that if they gave up
pillage and plunder they could obtain all the commodities they
needed by working the land. At the same time he instilled a love
of peace and relaxation, which provide the most favourable
conditions for the growth of justice and good faith, and the best
kind of security for cultivating the fields and enjoying their
produce.

Pompilius also extended the scope of the auspices, adding two
augurs to the original number; and he appointed five priests* from
among the leading citizens to take charge of the various religious
rituals. He introduced the laws* which we still have in our records,

and by turning their attention to religious ceremonies he tempered those ardent spirits which were accustomed to, and eager for, continual warfare. In addition, he created flamens, Salii,* and vestal virgins, and organized most scrupulously every aspect of religious 27 life. It was Numa's wish that, while religious observances themselves should be minute and complicated, the equipment should be very simple. He devised many rituals* which had to be learned by heart and adhered to, but they did not involve any expense. In this way he directed more attention to religious duties but removed the cost.

Numa also instituted fairs and games and all kinds of other occasions for crowded gatherings. By organizing these activities he won over to mild and civilized behaviour characters who were fierce and brutalized by their enthusiasm for warfare. After reigning in unbroken peace and harmony for thirty-nine years (and here let us take as our principal guide our friend Polybius, a man of unrivalled accuracy in problems of chronology), Numa died. By then he had established on a firm basis those two factors which, above all others, ensure that states will last, namely religion and humane behaviour.

When Scipio had reached this point, Manilius asked: Is it an 28 authentic tradition, Africanus, that King Numa, whom you have just been talking about, was a pupil of Pythagoras, or at least a Pythagorean? This assertion has often been made by our elders, and one gathers that the opinion is widely held. Yet an inspection of the public records shows that it is not properly documented.

SCIPIO: No, Manilius. The whole thing is quite wrong. It is not only a fabrication, but a clumsy and absurd fabrication too (it is particularly hard to tolerate the kind of falsehood which is not just untrue but patently impossible). Research has established that it was only when Lucius Tarquinius Superbus had been on the throne for over three years that Pythagoras came to Sybaris, Croton, and that part of Italy. The sixty-second Olympiad witnessed both the beginning of Superbus' reign and the arrival of 29 Pythagoras. So when the years of the kings have been added up it follows that Pythagoras first reached Italy about a hundred and forty years after Numa's death. No doubt has ever been cast on this conclusion by the experts in chronological research.

MANILIUS: Good Lord! What a gigantic howler! And to think that people have accepted it for so long! Still, I'm happy to learn that we got our culture, not by importing foreign expertise but through our own native qualities.

30   SCIPIO: Indeed. But you'll appreciate the point more easily if you think of our country developing and moving by a kind of natural process along the road to the best constitution. And you will judge that our ancestors' wisdom was the more praiseworthy in that, as you will find, even the features borrowed from elsewhere have been made much better here than they were in the places where they originated and from which we derived them. You will also find that the Roman people became strong, not by chance, but through their own good sense and their firm system of values—though, granted, fortune has not been against them.

31   On the death of King Pompilius the people made Tullus Hostilius king at a meeting of the Assembly of Voting Districts chaired by the interrex. And Tullus, following Pompilius' example, had his position officially ratified by each district in turn. He was a man with a brilliant military reputation, earned by his great feats on the battlefield. From the sale of his plunder he built and enclosed a senate house* and a place for the people's assembly.* He also drew up a legal procedure for declaring war. To be more precise, he formulated the procedure himself in very fair terms, and then, by incorporating it in the fetials'* ceremonies, he enacted that every war which had not been declared and proclaimed should be deemed unjust and unholy. Note how firmly our kings already grasped the point that certain rights should be granted to the people (I shall have a lot to say on this matter later on). Tullus did not even venture to assume the symbols of kingship without the people's permission. To make it lawful for twelve lictors* with their rods to walk in front of him . . .

[*A leaf has been lost here. According to St Augustine (De Civitate Dei 3. 15), Scipio says that, unlike Romulus, Tullus Hostilius was not alleged to have been deified.*]

33   LAELIUS (?): . . . for since you have begun your account the state is not creeping, but flying, towards the best constitution.

SCIPIO: After him Ancus Marcius, the son of Numa Pompilius' daughter, was appointed king by the people, and he, too, had a law passed in the Assembly to ratify his position. Ancus defeated the Latins in war and then admitted them to citizenship. He also extended the city to include the Aventine and Caelian hills. He shared out the land he had taken, handed over to the public all the forests he had taken on the coast, founded a city at the mouth of the Tiber and settled colonists there. After a reign of twenty-three years he died.

LAELIUS: Yes, he too was an admirable king. But Roman history is indeed obscure if we have a record of that king's mother but know nothing of his father.

SCIPIO: That's true; but, except in the case of kings, names at that period tended to be shrouded in darkness.

Nevertheless, now for the first time our state seems to have 34 taken a step forward in culture by having, as it were, a foreign system of education grafted on to it. For it was no tiny stream that flowed into this city from Greece, but rather a rich flood of moral and artistic teaching. There was a Corinthian, we are told, called Demaratus who was easily the foremost citizen in prestige, influence, and wealth. Finding the tyranny of Cypselus at Corinth intolerable, he is supposed to have escaped with a large sum of money and made his way to Tarquinii, the most flourishing city in Etruria. Hearing that Cypselus' dictatorship was taking root, this brave, freedom-loving man turned his back on his country for good. He was enrolled as a citizen of Tarquinii, and set up his hearth and home in that community. When his Tarquinian wife had borne him two sons, he trained them in all subjects in accordance with Greek practice . . . [*A leaf has been lost at this point. Scipio is now talking of Demaratus' son, Lucumo*] . . . ⟨Lucumo⟩ 35 easily obtained ⟨Roman⟩ citizenship. Owing to his agreeable personality and his intellectual stature he became a friend of King Ancus—so much so that he was regarded as a participant in all his decisions and almost a partner in the kingship. He possessed, moreover, the greatest charm and kindness, giving help, assistance, protection, and financial aid to every citizen who needed it. As a result, when Marcius died, the monarchy passed, by the unanimous vote of the people, to Lucius Tarquinius. (He had chosen this form as an adaptation of the Greek name, to show that he was conforming in every way to the customs of this country.) After having his position ratified by law, he first doubled the original number of the Senate, calling the older members 'Fathers of the

greater families' and those whom he had enrolled 'Fathers of the
lesser families'.* He would always invite the former to speak first.

36   Then he organized the knights* in the system which has survived to our own day. He could not change the names of the Tities,
Ramnes, and Luceres, though he wanted to do so, because Attus
Navius, a most venerable augur, refused to sanction it. (I notice,
incidentally, that the Corinthians, too, at one time carefully distributed horses at public expense and charged childless men and
unmarried women the cost of maintaining them.)* Anyhow,
Lucius added new detachments of cavalry to the older ones,
making twelve hundred* cavalrymen in all, and thus doubling
their number. Subsequently he defeated the Aequi in battle, a large
fierce tribe which represented a threat to Roman interests. He also
drove off the Sabines from the city walls, scattered them with his
cavalry, and gained a decisive victory. We are told in addition that
Lucius was the first to hold the great games which are called 'The
Roman Games';* that in the Sabine War, in the very heat of battle,
he vowed a temple to Jupiter Optimus Maximus* on the Capitol;
and that he died after reigning for thirty-eight years.

37   LAELIUS: This provides further confirmation of Cato's saying
that our country's constitution is not the work of one man or one
period; for it is clear that as one king succeeds another more and
more benefits and advantages are accruing. But of all the kings it
was the next in line who, in my view, had the deepest understanding of constitutional matters.

SCIPIO: That's right. Tradition has it that Servius Tullius, who
succeeded Tarquin, was the first to rule without being formally
chosen by the people. His mother is supposed to have been a slave*
from Tarquinii, his father one of the king's clients. He was brought
up among the servants and waited at the king's table; but the
brightness of the lad's intelligence was already too clear to remain
unnoticed—he was so capable in all his duties and in everything
he said. And so Tarquin, whose children were then quite small,
became so fond of Servius that the latter was commonly treated
as his son. The king had him educated with the greatest care in
all the accomplishments which he himself had learnt, to meet the
most exacting standards of Greece.

38   When Tarquin was killed as the result of a conspiracy hatched
by the sons of Ancus, Servius began to rule, as I said above,

without being duly elected by the people, but not without their consent and goodwill. This happened because of an official fabrication* to the effect that Tarquin, though suffering from a wound, was still alive. Servius, wearing the king's regalia, made legal decisions, rescued debtors at his own expense, and by exercising considerable charm satisfied the people that he was administering the law on Tarquin's instructions. He did not submit himself to the Senate, but after Tarquin's burial he asked the people to endorse his position. He was pronounced king by acclamation, and had the decision legally ratified by the Assembly of Voting Districts. He began his reign with a war of revenge against Etruria; as a result . . . [*A leaf is missing. Scipio is now describing the constitutional reforms of King Servius, especially with regard to the Assembly of Centuries.*]

. . . the eighteen richest ⟨centuries of knights⟩. Then, after marking 39 off a large number of knights from the whole body of the people, he distributed the rest of the populace into five classes, distinguishing the older from the younger members in each. By distributing them in this way he contrived that the preponderance of the votes should be in the hands, not of the masses, but of the wealthy. He thus safeguarded a principle which should always be observed in politics, namely that the greatest power should not rest with the greatest number. If you weren't familiar with that system of divisions I would explain it. As it is, you can see that it now works out as follows: if you take the equestrian centuries (including the original six*) together with the first class, and add in the century which is allocated to the carpenters* because of their usefulness to the city, the total is eighty-nine.* That leaves a hundred and four. And so, if only eight more centuries vote the same way, the influence of the people as a whole is done for, and the much greater numbers in the ninety-six remaining centuries ⟨*have no say in the result. Thus Servius' system ensured that the mass of the people**⟩ was neither excluded from the right to vote (for that would have been high-handed), nor given too much power, which would have been dangerous. In carrying out these measures 40 Servius was careful even in the matter of names and titles. He called the rich *assidui** from *as* [a coin] and *do* [I give]. As for those who had no more than fifteen hundred sestertii or nothing at all to count towards their assessment except their heads, he

called them *proletarii*,* conveying the idea that they were expected
to contribute children [*proles*], that is to say, the country's
next generation. At that time any one of those ninety-six
42 centuries contained almost more members than there were in the
whole of the first class. Thus, while no one was deprived of the
right to vote, the greatest voting power lay in the hands of those
who were most concerned that the state should be in the best possible order. Moreover, when the reservists, trumpeters, buglers,
and 'child-givers' had been added in . . . [*Two leaves have been
lost.*]

. . . ⟨A similar situation existed in Carthage, which is⟩ sixty-five
years older ⟨than Rome⟩; for it was founded in the thirty-ninth
year before the first Olympiad. The famous Lycurgus, too, saw
much the same point. Hence this fairness, this triple form of constitution, seems to me to have been shared by us with those countries. But I shall trace out in finer detail, if I can, the peculiar
feature of our state. It is one of surpassing excellence, and it will
prove to be of a kind which cannot be found in any other country.
Those elements which I mentioned before were combined in early
43 Rome, Sparta, and Carthage,* but quite without balance.* In
whatever country a single man holds permanent authority, especially that of a king—even though there may also be a senate, as
there was in Rome in the days of the kings, and in Sparta under
Lycurgus' system, and though there may also be a degree of
popular power, as there was in the period of our kings—still, that
royal title outweighs everything else, and a country of that kind
is inevitably a monarchy in fact as well as in name. Now that form
of constitution is most liable to change; for when it is upset by
the incompetence of one man, there is nothing to stop it from
falling headlong into utter ruin. Monarchy in itself is not only free
from blame; it is, I am inclined to think, far preferable to the other
two simple types of constitution (if I could bring myself to approve
of any simple type), but only as long as it retains its proper form.
The proper form requires that the security, the equal rights, and
the peace of the community should be controlled by the permanent power, and the comprehensive justice and wisdom of a single
man.

At the same time, a community that lives under a king is totally
deprived of many advantages, in particular, freedom, which is not

a matter of having a just master, but of having none at all . . . [*A leaf has been lost here. Scipio is now speaking of Tarquinius Superbus, who represented the degeneration of monarchy.*]

. . . For some years ⟨the people⟩ put up with him, because, harsh 44 and unjust as he was, that master enjoyed success in his undertakings. He conquered the whole of Latium and occupied Suessa Pometia, a prosperous and well-stocked town. After enriching himself with huge quantities of plunder in the form of gold and silver, he fulfilled his father's vow by building on the Capitol. He founded colonies, and following the custom of his forefathers he sent splendid gifts to Apollo at Delphi, offering him, as it were, the first-fruits of his booty.

45–51. Tarquinius Superbus turns into a tyrant and is expelled

Soon now the cycle* will begin to turn. You should become famil- 45 iar from the start with its natural movement and circuit; for it is the crowning achievement of political wisdom (and that is what my talk is all about) to divine the course of public affairs, with all its twists and turns. Then, when you know what direction things are taking, you can hold them back or else be ready to meet them.

Now this king I'm speaking of had, right from the start, an uneasy conscience; for he was stained with the blood of an excellent king. Terrified, as he was, of paying the ultimate penalty for his crime, he was determined to terrify others. Later on, buoyed up by his conquests and wealth, he allowed his insolence to run riot, being quite unable to control his own behaviour or the lusts 46 of his family. Finally his elder son violated Lucretia (Tricipitinus' daughter and wife of Collatinus); and that modest and noble woman punished herself for the outrage by taking her own life. Whereupon Lucius Brutus, a man of exceptional courage and ability, struck the cruel yoke of harsh servitude from the necks of his fellow-Romans. Though just a private citizen, Brutus took the whole country on his shoulders, and he became the first in this state to show that, when it comes to preserving the people's freedom, no one is just a private citizen. Following his example and leadership, the country was roused by this new complaint on the part of Lucretia's father and relatives, as well as by the memory of Tarquin's arrogance and the many injuries done by him and his sons in the past. As a result, the king himself, along with his sons and the entire Tarquin family, was sent into exile.

47   You see, then, don't you, how a king turned into a despot, and how, by the wickedness of one man, that type of government swung from good to the worst possible. This latter type is represented by the kind of political master which the Greeks call a 'tyrant'. By 'king' they mean one who, like a father, takes thought for his people and maintains his subjects in the best possible sort of life. That, as I said, is a good form of government, but one

48   which is precarious and prone, as it were, to topple over into the most pernicious form. As soon as a king takes the first step towards a more unjust regime, he at once becomes a tyrant. And that is the foulest and most repellent creature imaginable, and the most abhorrent to god and man alike. Although he has the outward appearance of a man, he outdoes the wildest beasts in the utter savagery of his behaviour. How can anyone be properly called a man who renounces every legal tie, every civilized partnership with his own citizens and indeed with the entire human species? However, there will be another, more suitable, place to speak about such people when the theme itself obliges me to deal with men who have tried to seize despotic power* even when their country has already been liberated.

49   So there you have the initial emergence of a tyrant; for that is the Greek name for a wicked king. Our own countrymen have applied the word 'king' to all who have held absolute power over their people on a permanent basis. Hence Spurius Cassius, Marcus Manlius, and Spurius Maelius are said to have attempted to seize the kingship, and recently . . . [*One leaf has been lost, which doubtless contained a reference to Tiberius Gracchus. Scipio is now talking of the body of elders in Sparta.*]

50   . . . ⟨Lycurgus⟩ called them 'Elders' in Sparta. That body was remarkably small in number—twenty-eight, in fact; yet he wanted them to hold the top advisory power while the king retained the top executive power. Our countrymen followed his example, taking over the same idea. What he called 'the Elders' they called 'the body of elders' [*senatus*]. (I mentioned that Romulus had already taken this step after choosing the Fathers.) Nevertheless,

the power, influence, and title of the king always remain pre-eminent. Suppose you grant a certain amount of power to the people, too, as Lycurgus and Romulus did; you will find that by giving them permission just to taste freedom you have not satisfied their hunger for it but only whetted their appetite. And, hanging over them all the time like a cloud will be the fear that, as usually happens, the king will turn out to be unjust. The fate of the people, then, is precarious when, as I said before, it depends on the goodwill and good character of a single man.

So the earliest example of the form, type, and emergence of tyranny is to be found, not in the state which Socrates described from his own imagination in Plato's well-known dialogue, but here, in the state founded with heaven's blessing by Romulus—I mean how Tarquin, without assuming any new powers but by abusing those which he had, completely wrecked a government of this monarchical kind. Let us contrast with him the other figure*— that of the good wise man who thoroughly understands what enhances the interests and prestige of the state, who is, as it were, a guardian and overseer of his country; for those titles are due to whoever directs and steers the community. Make sure you can recognize such a man, for he is the one who, by his good sense and devoted efforts, can preserve the country. As this concept has not been commonly used in our language up to now, and as that type of man will figure quite often in the remainder of my talk . . . [*Six leaves have gone.*]

52–6. Publicola maintains the Senate's authority by making concessions to the people

. . . ⟨Plato⟩ constructed a state which was desirable rather than feasible. It was the smallest he could contrive, and, though not actually possible, it enabled the reader to see how politics worked. I, however, if I can manage it, while using the same principles as he deduced, will try to show them operating, not in a shadowy country of the mind, but in a very great nation. In doing so I shall touch, as though with a pointer, on the cause of every good and every evil in public life.

When the two hundred years of monarchy were over (or perhaps a little more, if one takes account of the interregna), and

when Tarquin had been expelled, the Romans were gripped with
a hatred of the name of king, just as strong as the sense of longing
which had gripped them after the death, or rather the departure,
of Romulus. Then they could not do without a king; now, after
getting rid of Tarquin, they could not bear the word . . . [*Eight
leaves are lost.*]

53 . . . that law* was totally abolished. This was the mood which
induced our ancestors to expel the innocent Collatinus, whom
they regarded with suspicion because of his family connection
⟨with Tarquin the Proud⟩, and to banish the other Tarquins on
account of the odium attached to the name. In view of this same
mood, Publius Valerius for the first time ordered the rods to be
lowered when he began to speak at a meeting of the people. Then
he moved house to the bottom of the Velian Hill when he realized that he was arousing the people's resentment by starting to
build near the top of the hill, on the very site where King Tullus
had lived. He also showed himself 'the people's friend'* *par excellence* by proposing to the people a law, which was in fact the first
law passed by the Assembly of Centuries, to the effect that no
magistrate should have a Roman citizen flogged or put to death
54 without permitting an appeal.* (The pontiffs' records, however,
state that even the king's verdicts were subject to appeal, and this
is confirmed by our augurs' books. The Twelve Tables likewise
indicate in several of their laws that it was legitimate to lodge an
appeal against every verdict and sentence. Moreover, the tradition
that there was no right of appeal against the decisions of the Ten
Men who drafted the laws is sufficient proof that there *was* such
a right in the case of the other magistrates. The consular law introduced by Lucius Valerius Potitus and Marcus Horatius Barbatus,
men who wisely courted the populace in the interests of peace,
laid it down that no magistrate should be appointed unless his
rulings were subject to appeal. Finally, the Porcian Laws, which,
as you know, were three laws, proposed by three different Porcii,
did not introduce anything new, except a clause prescribing a
penalty for violation.)

55   So then, after carrying that law about appeal, Publicola at once
gave orders for the axes to be removed* from the bundles. On the
next day he had Spurius Lucretius elected as his colleague; and he
ordered his own lictors to attend Spurius instead, because he was

the older. He also initiated the custom whereby lictors should walk before each consul in alternate months.* This was to prevent the symbols of power being more numerous in the free republic than they had been under the kings. It was no ordinary man, in my view, who by granting the people a modest amount of freedom preserved more easily the authority of the leading citizens. You see I do have a reason for warbling on to you about these old out-dated things. In those famous figures and times I am noting examples of men and events for use as reference-points in the remainder of my talk.

In those times, then, the Senate maintained the state in the fol- 56 lowing condition: though the people were free, not much was done through them; most things were done on the authority of the Senate according to custom and precedent. The consuls had a power which, though limited in length to one year, was in its nature and legitimacy equivalent to that of a king. And (a factor that was perhaps the most vital in maintaining the power of the aristocracy) the rule was staunchly retained whereby the people's corporate decisions were not valid unless endorsed by the Senate's authority. At this same period, about ten years after the first consuls, Titus Larcius was appointed dictator. That was regarded as a new kind of power, very similar to the regal model. Yet, with the people's consent, all the power was firmly held in the hands of the leading citizens; and in those times great military feats were accomplished by valiant men who wielded supreme power, whether as dictators or as consuls.

57–60. More substantial concessions are exacted by the people

A little later, however, about fifteen years after the Republic's 57 inception, in the consulship of Postumus Cominius and Spurius Cassius, the people, now rid of the kings, arrogated to itself a somewhat larger amount of legal authority—a development which, in the nature of things, was bound to take place. There was, perhaps, a lack of calculation in the matter; but then the very nature of politics often prevails over calculation. One must bear in mind what I said at the outset, namely that unless a state maintains a fair balance of rights, duties, and functions (the magistrates

having adequate power, the aristocratic council adequate influence, and the people adequate freedom) its constitutional organi-
58 zation cannot be preserved from change. Anyhow, at a time when
the community was in a state of turmoil over debt, the common
people occupied first the Sacred Mount and then the Aventine.
Remember that not even the system of Lycurgus kept the Greek
population under so tight a rein. For in Sparta too, in the regime
of Theopompus, five officials called ephors (and in Crete ten,
called cosmoi) were appointed to offset the power of the king, just
as here the tribunes of the plebs were elected to limit the authority of the consuls.*

59   In the case of that widespread debt our ancestors, perhaps, did
have available a method of relief which had been perceived by
Solon at Athens not long before and which our Senate took note
of some time later. (Then, as a result of one man's sadistic lust,*
all the citizens' bonds were undone and were never fastened again.
Ever since, on occasions when the common people have wilted
and fainted under their financial burden,* some relief or remedy
has always been devised in order to ensure the community's stability.) But at that time the Senate failed to take such a step, and
so the people were given an excuse for creating two tribunes of
the plebs through seditious action, in order to reduce the power
and authority of the Senate. This authority, however, remained
weighty and far-ranging, because the wisest and most valiant men
protected the state by a combination of good sense and military
force. Their authority was widely respected, because, while they
far exceeded others in prestige, they enjoyed fewer pleasures and
were not, as a rule, any richer. Each man's worth was the more
esteemed in public life in that, when it came to private matters,
they helped individual citizens most conscientiously by their
actions, advice, and financial support.

60   That was the state of affairs when Spurius Cassius, a man who
enjoyed enormous popularity with the masses, was accused by the
quaestor of plotting to seize the throne. As you know, when his
father testified that he had found Spurius to be guilty, he was put
to death with the people's consent. Roughly fifty-three years after
the first consuls another welcome law was introduced by the
consuls Spurius Tarpeius and Aulus Aternius about fines and forfeits,* and was passed by the Assembly of Centuries. Twenty years

after that, because large numbers of cattle had been transferred from private to public ownership as a result of fines imposed by the censors Lucius Papirius and Publius Pinarius, lighter assessments were fixed in penalties involving cattle by a law proposed by the consuls Gaius Julius and Publius Papirius.

61–3. The Board of Ten draft a code of law. Their successors prove inferior

Some years earlier, when the supreme authority resided in the 61 Senate and the people were docile and obedient, an idea was adopted whereby both the consuls and the tribunes of the plebs should resign from office and ten men* should be appointed. This board was to have very great authority, not subject to appeal. In addition to their supreme power, these men were to have the task of drafting laws. When they had drawn up with great wisdom and fairness a code of Ten Tables, they nominated ten other men to serve for the following year.

The second group has not enjoyed a similar reputation for integrity and fairmindedness. Nevertheless, one member, Gaius Julius,* has won great approval. He stated that he had been present when a corpse was exhumed in the bedroom of Lucius Sestius, a nobleman. Yet although as one of the Ten he held absolute power which was not subject to appeal, he simply ruled that Lucius should give bail. He would not, he said, contravene that excellent law which laid it down that no sentence could be passed on the life of a Roman citizen except in the Assembly of Centuries.

A third year of the decemvirate followed. The personnel 62 remained the same, because they had refused to appoint successors. With the government in this situation (which, as I have said several times before, could not last long, because it was not equally just to all ranks of society) the whole country was in the hands of the leading citizens. Ten men of the highest birth were in control, unopposed by any tribunes of the plebs; no other magistrates had been added; and no appeal to the people had been left 63 open against flogging and execution. Therefore, as a result of the board's injustice, a massive and sudden upheaval took place, followed by a total change of government. The ten men added two

tables of unjust laws, enacting that there could be no intermarriage between plebeians and patricians—a most outrageous
measure, since that privilege is normally allowed even between citizens of different states. (The prohibition was later rescinded by
Canuleius' plebeian decree.) In all their official acts they behaved
irresponsibly, and they were cruel and greedy in their domination
over the people. The episode of Decimus Verginius is, of course,
well known, and is related in countless works of literature. He
killed his virgin daughter in the forum with his own hand to save
her from the lust of one of the Ten. When, in his grief, he fled to
the army, which was then on Mount Algidus, the soldiers called
off the war on which they were engaged, and, with weapons in
hand, occupied first the Sacred Mount, as they had done earlier
for a similar reason, and then the Aventine . . . [*Four leaves
are lost.*]

⟨We have now arrived at the form of government which⟩ I
believe our ancestors most approved of and were very wise to
retain.

64–6. Scipio recapitulates

64 After these words from Scipio, when everyone was waiting in
silence for the rest of his talk, Tubero said: Since these senior gentlemen have nothing to ask you, Africanus, perhaps you would let
me say what I find missing in your talk.

SCIPIO: Certainly; I'd be happy to hear it.

TUBERO: You seem to me to have praised our form of government, though Laelius asked you to discuss, not ours in particular,
but forms of government in general. Even so, I did not learn from
your talk what moral system, what customs and laws, we should
employ in founding and preserving the kind of government which
you advocate.

65 SCIPIO: I think, Tubero, we shall shortly have a more suitable
place for discussing the foundation and preservation of states. As
for the best constitution, I thought I had given an adequate reply
to Laelius' question. For I distinguished, first, three acceptable
forms of government along with their three objectionable coun-
terparts. I then showed that no one of these simple forms was
66 ideal, but that each of them was surpassed by a moderate blend

of the three acceptable types. As for my using our own state as a model, that had value, not for defining the best constitution (for that could have been done without a model), but for illustrating, from the actual experience of the greatest state, what was being described in my theoretical exposition. But if you ask about the nature of the best state in itself, we shall have to draw on the model presented by nature,* since you ⟨are not satisfied with⟩ the model of a city and its people which we have been using . . . [*At least two leaves have disappeared.*]

67–70. The ideal statesman

SCIPIO: . . . I have long been looking for him, and I am keen to 67 meet him.

LAELIUS: Perhaps you are looking for the man of good sense?

SCIPIO: The very man.

LAELIUS: Well, you can find plenty of specimens in our present company. What about yourself, for a start?

SCIPIO: Yes. If only one could find the same percentage in the Senate as a whole! Still, take the man who, as we often saw in Africa, sits on an enormous wild beast,* controlling it and directing it wherever he wishes and turning the great brute this way and that by a gentle touch or word of command—now *he* is a man of good sense.

LAELIUS: I know the sort you mean; I often saw them when I was on your staff.

SCIPIO: Well, that Indian or Carthaginian controls one animal, which is docile and familiar with human ways. But the faculty which lies within the human mind, forming part of it, and is called the reason, tames and controls not just one animal, and one, at that, which is easily broken in—if, indeed, it succeeds in doing so, which it rarely does. For that fierce creature calls for firm handling . . .

[*Two leaves have fallen out, in which Scipio talks about the difficulties of a statesman. See the fragments at the end of the book.*]

LAELIUS: I now see the duty and function which you assign to 69 the man for whom I was waiting.

SCIPIO: Why, he should have virtually no duty apart from this, for it embraces all the rest—namely that he should never cease inspecting and examining himself, challenging others to imitate him, and by the splendour of his mind and conduct offering himself as a mirror to his fellow-citizens. Just as with string instruments* or pipes or in singers' voices a certain harmony of different sounds must be maintained (and trained ears cannot bear the effect if that harmony is thrown out or becomes discordant), and as that harmony, though arising from the management of very different notes, produces a pleasing and agreeable sound, so a state, by adjusting the proportions between the highest, lowest, and intermediate classes, as if they were musical notes, achieves harmony. What, in the case of singing, musicians call harmony is, in the state, concord; it constitutes the tightest and most effective bond of security; and such concord cannot exist at all without justice.

[*About a dozen leaves are missing. Augustine (*De Civitate Dei 2. 21) *says that Philus asked for a fuller discussion of justice in view of the common opinion that no state could be governed without injustice.*]

70   SCIPIO: I do agree, and I would stress that what we think has been established so far about the government of the state amounts to nothing, and that we have no basis for further progress, unless we refute the contention that government cannot be carried on without injustice, and, more than that, prove conclusively that it cannot be carried on without the highest degree of *justice*. But, if you don't mind, we will let that do for today and postpone the rest until tomorrow, for there is still quite a lot to say.

This was agreed, and so discussion ended for that day.

FRAGMENTS OF BOOK 2

1. [Loeb, 41] ⟨I hold⟩ that the best possible political constitution represents a judicious blend of these three types: monarchy, aristocracy, and democracy. It does not inflame by punishments a mind which is rough and uncultivated ... (Nonius 2. 542).

2. [Loeb, 53] And so, after Romulus' splendid constitution had remained unshaken for about two hundred and twenty years ... (Nonius 3. 845) *Also relevant may be Augustine's statement that, finding the king's domination intolerable, the Romans appointed*

two chief magistrates annually; they were called consuls from the verb meaning to consult (De Civitate Dei, 5. 12).

3. [Loeb, 68] . . . which thrives on blood, which so revels in every kind of cruelty that it is barely satisfied with the pitiless slaughter of men (Nonius 2. 466).

. . . greedy, covetous, lascivious, and wallowing in carnal pleasures (Nonius 3. 788)

. . . fourthly, anxiety, given to lamentation, grieving, and always distressing itself (Nonius 1. 102).

. . . to be affected with pain and misery or to be grovelling in fear and cowardice (Nonius 1. 338–9).

. . . as an incompetent driver is dragged out of his chariot, trampled on, lacerated, and crushed to death (Nonius 2. 453).

4. . . . ⟨I must ask you⟩ to address your replies to Carneades, who with his intellectual dishonesty often makes very sound cases appear absurd (Nonius 2. 402).

BOOK 3

1–7. The abilities and achievements of man

[*Cicero is speaking in his own person. Four leaves are missing, but according to Augustine,* Contra Iulianum 4. 12. 60, *Cicero affirms that in spite of man's physical weakness, his fears and moral failings, he, unlike other animals, has deep within him the divine fire of rational intelligence.*]

3 . . . and ⟨intelligence enabled him to compensate⟩ for his slowness by means of vehicles. Also, on hearing the confused and jumbled noise which men were making with their inarticulate sounds, ⟨intelligence⟩ split those sounds up and divided them into units, imprinting words, like signs, on things, and bringing together people who previously dwelt apart through the delightful bond of a common speech. Thanks to that same intelligence, vocal sounds, which seemed to be numberless, were all set down and represented by the invention of a few marks. Those marks allowed conversations to be carried on with people who were far away, wishes to be indicated, and records of things past to be preserved. Then came number, a thing which is necessary for life and is also, uniquely, changeless and eternal.* That was what first induced us to look up to the sky, and enabled us to gaze with understanding at the movements of the stars, and by marking off nights and days ⟨to calculate the year⟩.

[*Four leaves are missing. Cicero is speaking of the different activities of moral philosophy and statesmanship, and the possibility of combining the two.*]

4 . . . their minds rose higher and succeeded in achieving, in thought or action, something worthy of what I have previously called the gift of the gods. So let us regard those who theorize about ethical principles as great men, which indeed they are; let us grant that they are scholars and teachers of truth and moral excellence, provided we acknowledge the fact that this other branch of study is by no means contemptible, whether it was invented by men engaged in the ever-changing world of politics or was practised by those philosophers in the course of their peaceful

studies—I am speaking of the art of governing and training peoples, an art which in the case of good and able men still produces, as it has so often in the past, an almost incredible and superhuman kind of excellence. If, then, someone thinks, like the men who are taking part in the discussion recorded in these books, that he should add scholarship and a deeper understanding of the world to the mental equipment which he possesses by nature and through the institutions of the state, no one can fail to acknowledge his superiority over everybody else. For what can be more impressive than the combination of experience in the management of great affairs with the study and mastery of those other arts? Who can be regarded as more completely qualified than Publius Scipio, Gaius Laelius, and Lucius Philus—a trio who, to make sure of including everything that brought the highest distinction to eminent men, added this foreign learning derived from Socrates to the native traditions of their forefathers? Hence my opinion that anyone who achieves both objectives, familiarizing himself with our native institutions *and* with theoretical knowledge, has acquired everything necessary for distinction. If, however, one has to choose between these paths to wisdom, then, even though some people think that a life passed quietly in the study of the highest arts is happier, there can be no doubt that the statesman's life is more admirable and more illustrious. That is the kind of life which makes the greatest men famous—like, for instance, Manius Curius,

> Whom none could overcome with steel or gold,

or . . . [*Three leaves are missing at this point.*]
. . . ⟨though one grants that both approaches⟩ have led to wisdom, the methods of the two groups have differed in this respect: one has nourished people's natural potential by verbal skills, the other through laws and institutions. Now this country on its own has produced more men who, if not 'philosophers' (for the former group clings so tenaciously to that name), certainly deserve the highest praise, since they have promoted the precepts and discoveries of the philosophers. Think, moreover, of all the states that have been and still are admirable, given that in the nature of things it requires practical wisdom of the very highest order to devise a form of government that will last. If we assigned just one such

man to each of those states, what a huge number of outstanding individuals we would have before us! If, within Italy, we were prepared to survey Latium or the Sabine or Volscian peoples, going on to Samnium, Etruria, and Magna Graecia; and if then ⟨we took account of⟩ the Assyrians, the Persians, the Phoenician peoples . . . [*Six leaves have been lost.*]

8–28. Philus argues that injustice is necessary and advantageous

8   PHILUS: What a splendid case you are putting in my hands when you ask me to undertake the defence of wickedness!

LAELIUS: Still, if you make the points which are usually made against justice, you needn't worry* about giving the impression that you actually believe what you say. After all, you yourself are an absolute model of old-fashioned honesty and good faith; and everyone knows your habit of arguing both sides of a case,* because that, in your view, is the simplest way of getting at the truth.

PHILUS: Well, all right then. I'll play the game your way and deliberately cover myself with mud. That's something that gold prospectors don't shirk; so I suppose that in digging for the truth, a thing far more precious than all the gold in the world, we shouldn't try to avoid the consequences, however nasty. I only wish that, as I am going to use someone else's argument, I could also use someone else's mouth. As it is, Lucius Furius Philus will have to say the things that Carneades* ⟨used to assert⟩, a Greek fellow who used to devise verbal arguments for whatever was expedient . . . [*Two leaves have fallen out.*]

12   . . . ⟨Plato⟩ strove to discover and defend ⟨justice⟩, the other ⟨Aristotle⟩ filled four pretty hefty books on that very subject. I never expected anything important or impressive from Chrysippus, who argues in his usual style, investigating every problem through the function of words rather than the weight of things. It was the aim of those heroic souls to raise up that virtue from the ground—that virtue which, when it occurs, is the most generous and open-handed of all, which loves everyone better than itself, and whose *raison d'être* is to secure other people's welfare rather than its own—and to set it close to wisdom on that heavenly throne.

Certainly they did not lack such good intentions; what other 13
motive or what possible purpose did they have for writing? Nor
did they lack intellectual ability (in that respect they were
supreme). But the weakness of their case was too much for their
good intentions and their powers of expression. For the justice
which we are considering is a political phenomenon, not an
element in nature. If it *were* part of nature, like hot and cold
or bitter and sweet, then just and unjust would be the same for
everyone.

As it is, if someone riding in Pacuvius' famous chariot of winged 14
snakes* could look down and survey many different cities and
countries, he would see first of all in Egypt, a land which has
escaped change more successfully than any other, and which preserves in written records the events of countless centuries, a bull
called Apis by the inhabitants being treated as a god, and many
other extraordinary things too, including beasts of every kind
being worshipped among the gods. Then in Greece, as with us, he
would see splendid temples consecrated to statues in human form,
which the Persians regarded as sacrilegious. Xerxes,* in fact, is
supposed to have ordered the temples of Athens to be burnt,
simply because he believed it was impious to confine within walls
gods whose abode was the whole universe. Later Philip, who
planned to make war on Persia, and Alexander, who actually did 15
so, claimed in their defence that they wanted to take vengeance
on behalf of the Greek temples. The Greeks themselves thought
the temples should be left unrestored, so that later generations
might have before their eyes an ageless monument of Persian
profanity.

Think of all those nations, like the Taurians on the Black Sea
coast, Busiris, King of Egypt, the Gauls and the Carthaginians,
who have regarded human sacrifice as a holy act, most welcome
in the sight of the immortal gods. Peoples' customs, in fact, are
vastly different. The Cretans and Aetolians think that armed
robbery is an honourable occupation. The Spartans maintain that
every piece of land that they can reach with a javelin belongs to
them. The Athenians used to swear a public oath to the effect that
every land producing olive oil and corn was their property. The
Gauls consider it disgraceful to obtain corn by sowing seed; so 16
they send in troops to gather someone else's harvest. We Romans,

paragons of justice as we are, forbid the tribes beyond the Alps to plant olive-trees and vines, in order to enhance the value of our own products. In doing so we are said to be acting wisely, but not justly. So you can see that wisdom is something different from fairness. Lycurgus, who devised such unrivalled laws and such an equitable code, gave the land of the rich to the common people—for the latter to work as slaves.

17   If I wanted to describe the varieties of laws, institutions, customs, and habits, I could show not just that different kinds have existed among so many nations but that a thousand changes have taken place within a single city—even in this one. Our friend Manilius here, who is a learned lawyer, would now give a different opinion about the rights of women in regard to bequests and legacies from that which he used to give in his youth before the *Lex Voconia** came into force. That law, I may point out, which was passed in the interests of men, involves a serious injustice to women. For why shouldn't a woman possess money of her own?* Why should a vestal virgin* be allowed to make a will, but not her mother? Why, if the amount of a woman's assets had to be limited, should Publius Crassus' daughter, provided she were his only child, have been legally entitled to a hundred million sesterces, whereas mine was not allowed three million? [*One leaf has dropped out. Philus is still speaking.*]

18   . . . ⟨If nature⟩ had laid down our system of justice, every country would have the same laws, and one country would not have different laws at different times. If it is the duty of a just man and a good citizen to obey the laws, would someone tell me which laws are intended? Is it every law in existence? But moral excellence does not accept contradictions; nature forbids variations; and anyhow laws are enforced by penalties, not by our sense of justice. So there is nothing natural about justice. It follows that not even just individuals are just by nature. Or do they mean that, as there are various laws, naturally good men abide by *real*, not merely putative, justice? We are told that the duty of a good and just man

19   is to give everyone his due. So what, for a start, shall we give to dumb animals? Pythagoras and Empedocles* (no average men, but thinkers of the greatest eminence) proclaim that all living creatures have the same standing in law, and they loudly assert that anyone who injures an animal faces inescapable punishment. So

it's a crime to harm a beast, and whoever is prepared ⟨to commit⟩ this crime . . . [*of the next 80 leaves only 4 survive. Some of what is missing can be supplied from certain passages of Lactantius and Tertullian which are paraphrased below.*]

Why are national codes dissimilar? Is it not because each community enacts what seems to suit its own conditions? The Romans themselves illustrate the difference between justice and expediency. By declaring war through the fetial priests they have given a specious legality to lawless behaviour; and by seizing other people's land they have acquired a world empire (Lactantius, Divinae Institutiones 6. 9. 2–4).

Every empire is gained by war, which always involves harm for the gods of the conquered as well as for the conquered themselves (Tertullian, Apologeticus 25. 14–15).

Carneades argued that there was no natural law. All living creatures, he said, including human beings, seek what is in their own interests. If there is such a thing as justice, it is the height of folly; for by acting in the interests of others a person does injury to himself. If the Romans decided to be just and return other people's property, they would at once revert to poverty and live in huts (Lactantius, Div. Inst. 5. 16. 2–4).

Your advantages are the disadvantages of others. Hence building an empire involves expropriating other people's territory and enriching yourself at their expense. Aggressive generals are held to be the embodiment of valour and excellence. Teachers of philosophy give the cloak of tradition and authority to folly and crime (Lactantius, Div. Inst. 6. 6. 19 and 23).

PHILUS: . . . for all who have the power of life and death over   23 a community are tyrants, but they prefer to be called kings—the name borne by Jupiter the Best. When certain men control a state thanks to wealth or birth or some other advantage, that is an oligarchy, but the members are called aristocrats. If the people hold the supreme power and everything is done according to their decisions, that is called liberty, though in fact it is licence. But when there is mutual fear between one individual and another, and between one class and another, then, because no one can rely on his own strength, a kind of pact is made between the people and the powerful few. From that emerges the compromise recommended by Scipio, i.e. the mixed form of government. You see, the mother of justice is not nature, nor good intentions, but weakness. For when one is faced with a threefold choice: (*a*) to do injury without experiencing it, (*b*) to do it and to experience it, (*c*) neither to do it nor to experience it, the best choice is to do it, preferably with impunity. The next best is to avoid doing it or undergoing it; the worst is to be constantly at daggers drawn, inflicting and suffering injury in turn. [*Four leaves have disappeared. Philus is still speaking.*]

24   Wisdom encourages us to make money, increase our possessions, and extend our boundaries (for what sense would there be in the tribute inscribed on the monuments of our greatest generals, 'He advanced the bounds of empire', if nothing had been gained from anyone else?); also to rule over as many subjects as possible, enjoy pleasures, and revel in power, supremacy, and dominion. Justice, on the other hand, teaches us to spare all men, take thought for the interests of mankind, give everyone his due, and not lay hands on the things belonging to the gods, the state, or somebody else. What, then, is gained by obeying wisdom? Wealth, positions of power, possessions, offices, military commands, and dominion over individuals or nations. But as we are talking of the state, and national activities are more conspicuous, and since justice is essentially the same in both cases, I think we should confine our discussion to wisdom in its public context. Leaving others aside for the moment, consider this nation of ours, whose history Africanus, in yesterday's conversation, traced from its roots, and whose empire now controls the world. Was it through justice or wisdom that it rose from the smallest to the greatest thing in existence? [*Probably two leaves are missing.*]

25   ... except Arcadia and Athens, who, I fancy, were afraid that this decree from the hand of justice* might at some time come into effect, and so invented the claim that they had sprung from the ground like these little field-mice.

26   Against these points the following arguments are usually advanced in the first place by a group of thinkers* who are by no means dishonest in debate, and who have the more weight in this case because, when discussing the good man (whom we all wish to be open and straightforward) they do not argue like cunning old hands full of evil intent. These people maintain that a wise man is not good because he takes pleasure in goodness and justice

in themselves for their own sake, but because good men live a life which is free from fear, worry, anxiety, and danger, whereas the wicked always have some qualms which they can't get out of their minds, continual visions of trials and punishments; that no profit or reward, if dishonestly obtained, is enough to make up for the constant dread, the conviction that some punishment is constantly at hand or constantly impending . . . [*Four leaves are lost, but half of section 27 (in which Philus is still speaking) is supplied from Lactantius,* Divinae Institutiones *5. 12. 5–6.*]

Now consider this possibility. Let us imagine two people—one 27 a man of the highest character, wholly fair-minded and just and exceptionally reliable, the other a man of remarkable wickedness and effrontery. And let us assume that a country is so mistaken as to think that the good man is wicked, villainous, and evil, while believing that the vicious man is entirely blameless and honest. Let us then suppose that, in keeping with this misconception which is shared by all the citizens, the good man is harassed, seized, has his hands cut off and his eyes gouged out; he is then condemned, clapped in irons, branded, expelled, suffers destitution, and finally, for the best of reasons, is regarded by all as utterly wretched. The villain, on the other hand, is praised, made much of, universally adored; offices, military commands, wealth, and riches of every kind are heaped upon him; in a word, he is judged by everyone to be supremely good and eminently worthy of all the gifts of fortune. Now tell me, who would be mad enough to doubt which of the two he would prefer to be?

What is true of individuals is also true of nations. No state is 28 so stupid as not to prefer wicked dominion to virtuous subjection. I need not go far to find an instance. While I was consul and you were my advisory committee, I consulted you about the treaty of Numantia. As everybody knew, Quintus Pompeius had made a treaty, and Mancinus was in the same position. The latter, admirable man that he was, actually supported the bill which I introduced in accordance with a senatorial recommendation; the former vehemently defended his action. If self-respect, integrity, and honour are what we are looking for, Mancinus brought all these virtues to the debate; but if we want clear-headedness, practical common sense, and an awareness of our real interests, Pompeius comes out on top.

29–31. Philus concludes his defence of injustice

[Some leaves have been lost here, but Carneades' remarks on wisdom as opposed to justice, reported by Philus, can be recovered in part from Lactantius, Divinae Institutiones 5. 16. 5–13, of which the following is a paraphrase.]

If a man has faulty goods for sale, should he declare their defects? If he does, he will act justly but will foolishly lose money. If he doesn't, he will act unjustly but to his own advantage. More seriously, suppose in a shipwreck a strong man sees a weaker man on a plank, will he not push him off to save himself, especially if there are no witnesses? If he doesn't, he will act justly but will foolishly throw away his own life. So, said Carneades, political justice is really not justice but prudence; natural justice is indeed justice, but it is at the same time folly. These are subtle and seductive arguments, and Cicero could not refute them. When Laelius is brought on to reply to Philus, he carefully avoids them. As a result he apparently fails to defend natural justice against the charge of folly; instead he defends political justice against the charge of being merely prudent.

32–41. Laelius maintains that justice is necessary for a state's stability

32   SCIPIO (?): . . . I wouldn't mind, Laelius, ⟨taking up the defence of justice⟩, but I believe our friends here want what I want too, namely that you also should make some contribution to our discussion, especially as you yourself promised yesterday that we'd hear more than enough from you. But that just can't happen. So, if I may speak for the rest, please don't let us down (Gellius 1. 22. 8).

LAELIUS: ⟨No doubt Carneades is a very clever man⟩ but he certainly ought not to be allowed to address our young people; for if he believes what he says, he is a filthy scoundrel; if he doesn't, as I hope is the case, his remarks are still outrageous (Nonius, 2. 507 and 2. 508).

33   . . . law in the proper sense is right reason in harmony with nature. It is spread through the whole human community, unchanging and eternal, calling people to their duty by its commands and deterring them from wrong-doing by its prohibitions. When it

addresses a good man, its commands and prohibitions are never in vain; but those same commands and prohibitions have no effect on the wicked. This law cannot be countermanded, nor can it be in any way amended, nor can it be totally rescinded. We cannot be exempted from this law by any decree of the Senate or the people; nor do we need anyone else to expound or explain it. There will not be one such law in Rome and another in Athens, one now and another in the future, but all peoples at all times will be embraced by a single and eternal and unchangeable law; and there will be, as it were, one lord and master of us all—the god who is the author, proposer, and interpreter of that law. Whoever refuses to obey it will be turning his back on himself. Because he has denied his nature as a human being he will face the gravest penalties for this alone, even if he succeeds in avoiding all the other things that are regarded as punishments . . . (Quoted by Lactantius, *Divinae Institutiones* 6. 8. 6–9.)

[*According to Augustine,* De Civitate Dei *22. 6, this book contained a discussion of the view that the best kind of state never resorts to war except in defence of its honour or its security. The same passage has the following words which editors attribute to Laelius.*]

. . . As for the punishments which even the stupidest can feel— 34 destitution, exile, jail, flogging—individuals often escape them by choosing the option of a quick death; but in the case of states, death, which seems to rescue individuals from punishment, is itself a punishment. For a state should be organized in such a way as to last for ever. And so the death of a state is never natural, as it is with a person, for whom death is not only inevitable but also frequently desirable. Again, when a state is destroyed, eliminated, and blotted out, it is rather as if (to compare small with great) this whole world were to collapse and pass away.

[*The following quotation from Cicero's* Republic *is contained in Isidore,* Etymologiae *18. 1. 2*]

. . . wars are unjust when they are undertaken without proper 35 cause. No just war can be waged except for the sake of punishing or repelling an enemy . . . no war is deemed to be just if it has not been declared and proclaimed, and if redress has not previously been sought . . .

[*Laelius is now arguing that it is just for superior to rule over inferior. The following fragment comes from Augustine.*]

36   Do we not perceive that whatever is best has been granted domination by nature herself, to the great advantage of the weak? Why else does God rule over man, mind over body, reason over desire, anger, and the other wicked elements in the same soul? (*Contra Iulianum* 4. 12. 61).

37   . . . But one has to recognize that there are different kinds of ruling and serving. The mind is said to rule over the body and also over desire; but in the former case its rule is like that of a king over his subjects, or a father over his children; in the latter case its rule resembles that of a master over his slaves, in that it subdues and crushes desire. The rule of kings, magistrates, senates, and people's assemblies over citizens and allies is like that of mind over body; but masters break the spirit of their slaves, just as the best element in the soul, namely wisdom, breaks the hold of the unruly and wicked elements in the same soul, such as desire, anger, and the other disruptive forces . . . (Ibid.)

. . . that control over the body's limbs resembles control over one's own sons, because of their ready obedience, whereas the bad elements of the soul are kept in subjection, like slaves, by a harsher discipline (Augustine, *De Civitate Dei* 14. 23).

[*Laelius is now talking about the rewards which goodness (virtus) may expect. The passage survives in Lactantius, whose comments are paraphrased in the parentheses.*]

40   Goodness clearly likes to be honoured, and it has no other reward. (*But the Bible, which you knew nothing about, shows that there is another reward.*) Yet, while it readily accepts the reward of honour, it does not stridently demand it. (*You are seriously mistaken if you think that goodness can ever receive its reward from men. Why, you yourself in another passage rightly said*) What riches will you offer as an incentive to such a man? What kinds of power? What kingdoms? Such things in his view are human possessions; he regards his own goods as divine. (*Inconsistencies of this kind arise from your ignorance of the truth. You then go on to say*) But if everyone is ungrateful, or many are resentful, or the powerful few are hostile, and so deprive goodness of its rewards (*Only a feeble and vacuous goodness can be deprived of its rewards. If, as you said before, its rewards are divine, how can such malicious people withhold them? It is true, however, that as Laelius says*) it consoles itself with many com-

forts, and sustains itself above all with its own beauty *(Divinae Institutiones* 5. 18. 4–8).

[*Laelius now refers to great men who rose above worldly rewards.*]

... their bodies ⟨i.e. the bodies of Hercules and Romulus⟩ were not raised to heaven; for nature would not allow that something with an earthly origin should exist anywhere except on earth (Augustine, *De Civitate Dei* 22. 4.)

... the most valiant men never ⟨fail to receive the rewards⟩ of valour, energy, and endurance (Nonius, 1. 181).

... I suppose Fabricius felt deprived of the riches offered by Pyrrhus, or Curius of the Samnites' costly presents! (Nonius, 1. 192).

... When he was staying at his Sabine villa, our great friend, Cato, as he told us himself, used to visit this man's hearth. That was where ⟨Curius⟩ had sat when he refused the gifts of the Samnites, once his enemies but now his clients (Nonius, 1. 95 and 3. 840).

[*Laelius now refers to Tiberius Gracchus, perhaps as one who failed to eschew worldly rewards.*]

... Tiberius Gracchus continued ⟨to act properly⟩ in the case of 41 Roman citizens, but he ignored the rights which had been guaranteed by treaty to the allies and to those with Latin status. If that kind of lawless behaviour becomes more widespread and drags our empire away from justice into violence, so that people who up to now have willingly accepted our authority are kept loyal by terror, then, even if we in our generation have been reasonably alert to this danger, I am still worried about our descendants, and about the survival of our empire—an empire which could remain permanent if people continued to live by our forefathers' principles and values.

42–8. Scipio reverts to his original definition of a republic as the property of the public. Tyranny, oligarchy, and mob rule fail to meet this definition, since they lack justice. The book breaks off as the speakers begin to discuss the uncorrupted versions of the three simple forms of government

When Laelius had finished speaking, all present indicated 42 their great pleasure at what he had said. But Scipio, carried away with something approaching fervour, went beyond the others.

SCIPIO: Well, Laelius, you have defended many a case so ably that I would put you not only above my colleague Servius Galba, whom you used to judge supreme in his lifetime, but even above any of the Attic orators* in charm . . .

[*Six leaves are missing.*]

43   SCIPIO: . . . So who would call that a republic, i.e. the property of the public, when everyone was oppressed by the cruelty of a single man, and there was not one bond of justice nor any of that social agreement and partnership which constitute a community? The same was true of Syracuse. That was an outstanding city. Timaeus calls it the largest in Greece and the finest in the world. Yet its striking citadel, its harbour, which extended right into the heart of the town and lapped against the foundations of its buildings, the broad streets, the porticoes, temples, and walls still did not succeed in making it a republic as long as Dionysius was in power. For nothing belonged to the public, and the public itself belonged to one man. Therefore, wherever there is a tyrant, one cannot say, as I maintained yesterday, that there is a *defective* republic; logic now forces us to conclude that there is no republic at all.

44   LAELIUS: You've put it admirably. I now see where the argument is moving.

SCIPIO: And do you see, then, that a place totally controlled by a clique cannot truly be called a republic either?

LAELIUS: Yes, I'm quite clear about that.

SCIPIO: And you're absolutely right. For what became of 'the property of the Athenian public' when, after the great Peloponnesian war, the notorious Thirty exercised their power without a semblance of justice? Did the country's ancient glory, or the celebrated beauty of the city with its theatre, gymnasia, porticoes, its famous Propylaea, its citadel and the marvellous works of Phidias, or the magnificent Piraeus make it a republic?

LAELIUS: Certainly not, because it was not the property of the public.

SCIPIO: Well then, what about the time when the Board of Ten ruled in Rome without permitting appeals, in that third year when freedom itself had lost all its rightful possessions?

LAELIUS: The property of the public did not exist. Or rather, the public had to take action to *recover* its property.

SCIPIO: I come now to the third type of government [*i.e.* 45 *democracy*]. Here there may seem, perhaps, to be some difficulty. When everything is supposed to be done through the people and to be in the people's control, when the masses punish whoever they please, when they seize, carry off, hold on to, or squander whatever they like, can you deny then, Laelius, that a republic exists, when everything belongs to the public? After all, our definition of a republic is 'the property of the people'.

LAELIUS: Actually there is no state to which I should be quicker to refuse the name of republic than the one which is totally in the power of the masses. If we decided that there was no republic in Syracuse or Agrigentum or Athens when tyrants held sway, or here in the regime of the Ten, I don't see how there is any stronger case for applying the name of republic to a state enslaved by the mob. In the first place, for me there is no public except when it is held together by a legal agreement, as you rightly laid down, Scipio. That rabble is just as tyrannical as one man, and all the more repellent in that there is nothing more monstrous than a creature which masquerades as a public and usurps its name. It is quite inconsistent that, when the property of the insane is placed by law in the hands of male relatives because the former ⟨are no longer capable of managing it themselves, the property of the public should be left in the hands of an insane mob⟩ . . . [*Four leaves are missing, in which Scipio argued that monarchy, in its uncorrupted form, could be regarded as a republic.*]

. . . The points which I have just adduced in connection with 46 monarchy could also be used to show why ⟨an aristocracy, too,⟩ is a republic and the property of the people.

MUMMIUS: Yes, and with much greater force; for a king, being a single individual, is more accurately compared to a master. On the other hand, nothing could be more fortunate than a state in which *several* good men are in charge of affairs. Yet I still prefer even a monarchy to an unfettered democracy. That third type of government, which you have still to discuss, is the most defective of all.

SCIPIO: That shows, Spurius, your well-known anti- 47 democratic attitude! Still, though such a system can be more easily put up with than you admit, I agree that of the three types it is the least desirable. But I don't agree with you that aristocracy is superior to monarchy. If it is good sense that governs a state, what does it matter whether that quality is exercised by one or by a group? But in arguing like this we are misled by a confusion of terms. When a group is called an aristocracy, nothing, it seems, could be more impressive (for what is conceivably better than 'the best'?). But when mention is made of a king, we think at once of a *bad* king.* Here, however, we are not talking about a bad king; we are concerned with the concept of a state ruled by a monarch. So imagine that your king is a Romulus or a Pompilius or a Tullius. Perhaps you will not be so critical of a state like that.

48   MUMMIUS: So what remains to be said in favour of democracy?

SCIPIO: Well, tell me, Spurius, do you not think that Rhodes, which we visited together not so long ago, has some kind of republic?

MUMMIUS: I think it does—and by no means a contemptible one at that.

SCIPIO: Quite right. But, if you recall, all the citizens were both common people and senators. A rota system decided which months they should serve as commoners and which as senators. They received payment in both capacities for attending meetings. The same men heard all cases, including those of a capital nature, in the theatre and in the senate house. The senate had as much power, and as much prestige, as the masses . . .

FRAGMENTS OF BOOK 3

1. [Loeb, 24] . . . for when he was asked what criminal urge impelled him to plague the sea with his solitary sloop, he answered 'the same urge that makes you plague the world' (Nonius 1. 181; 2. 498; 3. 856–7).

2. [Loeb, 35] . . . Our nation has now attained world power by defending its allies (Nonius, 3. 800).

3. [Loeb, 38] . . . for there is a type of unjust slavery when people who *could* be their own masters are subject to somebody else; but in the case of those who are ⟨fit only to be⟩ slaves ⟨no injustice is done⟩ (Nonius, 1. 155).

4. [Loeb, 42, about Isocrates?] . . . that he was lacking in two things which prevented him from addressing the public or speaking in the law-courts, namely confidence and vocal power (Nonius, 2. 401).

5. [Loeb frag. 3] It was the Phoenicians who, with their trade and merchandise, first brought greed, luxury, and an insatiable desire for things of all kinds to Greece (Nonius, 3. 695).

BOOK 4

Education

[*According to Lactantius (*De Opificio Dei *1. 11–13) Cicero touched on the relation of mind (or soul) to body in Book 4. Fragments which seem to belong to that topic are usually placed at the beginning to serve as an introduction to the theme of education. The book is in a pitiful state; the Vatican manuscript contains just parts of sections 2–4.*]

1   ... and the very mind that envisages the future recalls the past ... (Nonius, 3. 803).

    ... If it is true that everybody would sooner die than be turned into some form of animal (even though he retained a human mind), how much more awful it would be to have a human body and the mind of a wild beast! In my view the latter fate would be worse to the degree that the mind is nobler than the body ... (Lactantius, *Divinae Institutiones* 5. 11. 2).

    ... He did not think, he said, that what was good for a ram was also good for Publius Africanus ... (Augustine, *Contra Iulianum* 4. 12. 59).

2   SCIPIO: ... How efficiently the orders are arranged on the basis of age and property! For voting purposes the senate is counted along with the knights. Too many people now, in their folly, want to get rid of this admirable system; they advocate a new distribution of wealth through some resolution of the plebs whereby senators would have to resign their equestrian status.

3–8. A critique of Greek customs

3   Consider now how wisely provision has been made for that partnership of citizens in a happy and honourable life. For that is the primary purpose of forming a community, and that must be achieved for human beings by the state, partly through its institutions and partly through its laws. First, with regard to the training of free-born boys—an area in which the Greeks have worked hard to no avail and in which alone, according to our guest

Polybius,* our institutions have been neglectful—⟨the Romans⟩ have never wished any system to be laid down by law, or officially spelt out, or universally imposed ... [*At least two leaves have dropped out, which may have included the next three fragments.*]

... ⟨In Athens⟩ when ⟨youngsters⟩ enter military service they regularly have guardians assigned to them, whose business it is to supervise them in their first year ... (Servius on Virgil, *Aeneid* 5. 546).

... not only as in Sparta, where boys are taught to filch and steal ... (Nonius 1. 30).

... they thought it reflected badly on the young lads if they did not have lovers ... (Servius on Virgil, *Aeneid* 10. 325).

SCIPIO: ⟨The ancient Romans thought it wrong⟩ that an 4 adolescent should appear naked. So the foundations, as it were, of our modesty go far back in history. How absurd it is for naked young men to exercise in gymnasiums! How frivolous is the kind of training given to ⟨Greek⟩ cadets!* How free and easy are their caresses and liaisons! I say nothing of the Eleans and Thebans.* (With them, in love-affairs among free-born men, lust enjoys a licence which is actually sanctioned and unrestrained.) Even the Spartans, who permit everything short of the act of intercourse in young men's amours, mark off their exception with a pretty flimsy barrier; for they allow partners to lie beside one another and embrace with just a blanket in between.

LAELIUS: You make it very clear, Scipio, that in criticizing those Greek systems you prefer to grapple with the most famous states rather than with your friend Plato. You don't lay as much as a finger on him, even though ...

... and our revered Plato even more than Lycurgus; for he 5 absolutely insists that everything should be held in common,* to prevent anyone from claiming anything as his own private property ... (Nonius 2. 574).

... I, however, ⟨would send him⟩ to the place where he sends Homer from his imaginary city, festooned with garlands* and anointed with perfume ... (Nonius 2. 481).

... The censor's stigma involves nothing for the guilty man 6 apart from a red face. And so, as the verdict centres solely on the man's good name, that kind of censure is called 'de-naming' [*ignominia*] (Nonius 1. 35).

. . . Initially the state is supposed to have shuddered at ⟨the censors'⟩ severity . . . (Nonius 3. 683).

. . . No overseer should be put in charge of women, of the type that is appointed in Greece, but there should be a censor to teach men how to control their wives . . . (Nonius 3. 801).

. . . So the inculcation of modesty has an enormous effect; all the women do without liquor . . . (Nonius 1. 8).

. . . Yes, and if any woman was notorious her relatives would refuse to kiss her . . . (Nonius 2. 476).

7   . . . I disapprove of a nation being at once the world's ruler and its tax-collector. I consider thrift is the best source of revenue in family and state alike . . . (Nonius 1. 35–6).

8   . . . I admire fastidiousness, not only in conduct but also in the choice of words. 'If they disagree,' is what the provision says. A dispute between friends, as distinct from a quarrel between enemies, is called a disagreement . . . hence in the eyes of the law neighbours disagree; they do not quarrel . . . (Nonius 3. 695).

. . . ⟨They did not believe⟩ that men's concerns ended with their life. Hence the sacredness of burial is part of pontifical law . . . (Nonius 1. 255).

. . . ⟨The Athenian commanders⟩ failed to bury the dead because they were unable to recover them from the sea owing to the force of the storm. For this reason, in spite of their innocence, they were put to death (Nonius 2. 455).

. . . and in this dispute I sided not with the people but with the aristocracy . . . (Nonius 3. 836).

. . . for it is not easy to oppose the power of the people if you give them little or nothing in the way of legal rights . . . (Priscian 15. 4. 20).

9–12. The damage done by dramatists

9   . . . When ⟨the playwrights⟩ hear the shouts and cheers of the people, as if the people were a great and wise master, then what darkness they bring on, what fears they arouse, what desires they inflame! (Augustine, *De Civitate Dei* 2. 14).

10   . . . Since ⟨the ancient Romans⟩ regarded the theatre and show

business in general as disgraceful, they thought that such people should not only be deprived of the public offices enjoyed by other citizens but should also be removed from their tribe by the censor's stigma . . . (Augustine, *De Civitate Dei* 2. 13).

. . . ⟨The Greek Old⟩ Comedy would never have succeeded in 11 gaining the audience's approval for its vices if those vices had not been condoned in everyday life . . . Who was not mentioned, or rather attacked, by it? Who was spared? Granted, it injured Cleon, Cleophon, and Hyperbolus—wicked demagogues who stirred up sedition in the country's political life. We might tolerate this, even though it is preferable that such citizens should be pilloried by a censor rather than a playwright. But it was no more seemly that Pericles, after presiding over his country in peace and war with the greatest authority for so many years, should be insulted in verses and guyed upon the stage than if our Plautus or Naevius* had dared to traduce Publius and Gnaeus Scipio, or Caecilius had derided Marcus Cato . . . Contrast our Twelve Tables. Though 12 they treated very few crimes as capital offences, they did include the case where a person chanted or composed a song which brought infamy or disgrace to another. And quite right too; for our life-style should be open to the magistrates' verdicts and the judgements of the law, not to the cleverness of poets; nor should we have to listen to insults unless we are entitled to reply and to defend ourselves in court.

[*According to Augustine,* De Civitate Dei 2. 9, *Cicero's passage concluded with a demonstration that the early Romans thought it wrong that any living person should be praised or blamed on the stage.*]

. . . The Athenian Aeschines, a very accomplished orator, 13 although he had acted in tragedies in his youth, entered public life; and Aristodemus, another tragic actor, was often sent by Athens as an envoy to Philip about the most highly important questions of peace and war . . . (Augustine, *De Civitate Dei* 2. 11).

FRAGMENTS OF BOOK 4

1. [Loeb, section 1] . . . and the same body [i.e. the earth], by interposing itself, causes the shades of night, which are useful both

for counting days and for bringing rest after toil . . . (Nonius 2. 349).

2. [Loeb, section 1] . . . and when in autumn the earth opens up to take in the seed, in winter ⟨closes to protect it, in spring⟩ relaxes to let it come to birth, and in the fullness of summer ripens some crops and parches others . . . (Nonius 2. 543).

BOOK 5

The ideal statesman

[*The Vatican manuscript contains only sections 3, 5, 6, and 7. Augustine says that the quotation in sections 1–2 comes from Cicero's introduction. The position of the other fragments is conjectural.*]

> On ancient customs and old-fashioned men
> the state of Rome stands firm.

The compactness and truth of that line are such that the poet* who uttered it must, I think, have been prompted by an oracle. For neither the men on their own (in a state which lacked such a moral tradition) nor the state on its own (without such men in charge) could have founded or long maintained so great and wide-ranging an empire. Long before living memory our ancestral way of life produced outstanding men, and those excellent men preserved the old way of life and the institutions of their forefathers. Our generation, however, after inheriting our political organiza- 2 tion like a magnificent picture now fading with age, not only neglected to restore its original colours but did not even bother to ensure that it retained its basic form and, as it were, its faintest outlines. What remains of those ancient customs on which he said the state of Rome stood firm? We see them so ruined by neglect that not only do they go unobserved, they are no longer known. And what shall I say of the men? It is the lack of such men that has led to the disappearance of those customs. Of this great tragedy we are not only bound to give a description; we must somehow defend ourselves as if we were arraigned on a capital charge. For it is not by some accident—no, it is because of our own moral failings—that we are left with the name of the Repub- lic, having long since lost its substance . . . (Augustine, *De Civi- tate Dei* 2. 21).

MANILIUS:* . . . ⟨that there was no function so⟩ proper for a 3 king as the administration of justice. That embraced the interpre- tation of law, because private citizens used to ask the kings to rule

on legal questions. To make that possible, rich and extensive
lands, whether for crops, plantations, or herds, were marked out.
These were to be the property of the kings, and were to be
managed without any work or labour on their part so that they
would not be distracted from public concerns by any worries over
their private business. No private citizen acted as a judge or arbitrator in any lawsuit; everything was decided by the king's judgement. In my view Numa, among the Romans, adhered most
closely to this ancient system, which was that of the kings of
Greece. The others, though they did perform this function too,
nevertheless spent a large part of their time waging war and
dealing with the legal problems involved; whereas the long peace
which this city enjoyed under Numa gave birth to its laws and
religion. For he drafted the laws which, as you know, are still in
force. That, indeed, is the proper concern of the citizen whom we
are discussing . . .

[*At least two leaves are missing. Scipio is now drawing an
analogy between the statesman and the farm-manager. Though
both need some theoretical knowledge, that is not their primary
concern.*]

5   SCIPIO: . . . I take it you won't object to finding out about the
nature of roots and seeds, will you?

MANILIUS: No, not if the need arises.

SCIPIO: You don't think that all that sort of thing should be left
to your farm-manager, do you?

MANILIUS: Certainly not; for then the cultivation of the land
would very often lack proper attention.

SCIPIO: So a farm-manager knows about the nature of the land,
and a steward knows how to read and write; but each of them
concentrates on practical efficiency rather than enjoying that kind
of knowledge for its own sake. Similarly our statesman will indeed
have taken trouble to find out about justice and laws and will certainly have studied their foundations. But he should not become
involved in answering queries, reading up cases, and writing decisions. He must be free, as it were, to manage and keep account
of the state. He will be well versed in the fundamental principles
of law (without that, no one can be just); he will have some grasp,
too, of civil law, but only in the sense that a ship's captain will

have a grasp of astronomy and a doctor of natural science. Each of those men draws on those areas of knowledge in practising his skill, without being diverted from his special business. The statesman, moreover, will make sure that . . .

[*An indeterminate number of leaves have been lost.*]

SCIPIO: . . . states in which the best men strive for praise and honour, shunning disgrace and dishonour. They are not deterred so much by fear of the penalty prescribed by law as by a sense of shame—that dread, as it were, of justified rebuke which nature has imparted to man. The statesman develops this sense by making use of public opinion, and completes it with the aid of education and social training. So in the end citizens are deterred from crime by moral scruples as much as by fear. That will do for the question of prestige, which could be discussed at greater length and in greater detail.

For the purposes of life and its practical conduct a system has been devised, consisting of legal marriages, legitimate children, and sacred shrines belonging to the domestic gods of Roman families, so that everyone may enjoy both public and private benefits. The good life is impossible without a good state; and there is no greater blessing than a well-ordered state. In consequence, it always amazes me . . .

[*The palimpsest breaks off here.*]

SCIPIO: . . . The aim* of a ship's captain is a successful voyage; a doctor's, health; a general's, victory. So the aim of our ideal statesman is the citizens' happy life—that is, a life secure in wealth, rich in resources, abundant in renown, and honourable in its moral character. That is the task which I wish him to accomplish—the greatest and best that any man can have (Cicero, *Ad Atticum* 8. 11. 1).

SCIPIO(?): Nothing in a state* should be so free from corruption as a vote and a verdict. So I fail to understand why a man who corrupts them by money should deserve punishment whereas one who does so by eloquence should actually win applause. For my own part, I think that a man who corrupts a judge by his speech causes more harm than one who does it by a bribe; for no honest man can be corrupted by a bribe, but he *can* be by eloquence (Ammianus Marcellinus 30. 4. 10).

... On hearing these remarks of Scipio's, Mummius strongly agreed, for he thoroughly disliked the modern type of rhetorician (Nonius 3. 838).

FRAGMENTS OF BOOK 5

1. [Loeb, section 4] Nevertheless, as a good landowner needs some experience in farming, building, and book-keeping ... (Nonius 3. 798).

2. [Loeb, section 9] That virtue is called bravery which contains greatheartedness and a lofty contempt of pain and death (Nonius 1. 297).

BOOK 6

1–2. The problem of political control

So you are waiting to hear about the ruler's prudence in all its 1
facets—a quality that takes its very name from 'pro-vision' [*seeing
ahead*] (Nonius 1. 60).

Accordingly this citizen must make sure that he is always fore-
armed against the things that upset the stability of the state
(Nonius 2. 389).

. . . and such dissension among citizens is called 'sedition',
because people 'go apart' [*se* + *itio*] to different factions (Nonius
1. 36 and Servius on Virgil, *Aeneid* 1. 149).

. . . and in times of civil conflict, when soundness is more important than numbers, I think citizens should be assessed rather than
counted (Nonius 3. 836).

For our lusts are set over our thoughts like cruel mistresses,
ordering and compelling us to do outlandish things. As there is
no way in which they may be appeased or satisfied, once they have
inflamed a person with their seductive charms they drive him to
every sort of crime (Nonius 3. 686).

. . . whoever crushes its [*i.e. the seditious mob's*] force and its
rampant ferocity . . . (Nonius 3. 789).

This act was the more remarkable in that, although the two col- 2
leagues were in the same position, they were not equally disliked;
more than that, the affection felt for Gracchus* actually mitigated
Claudius' unpopularity (Gellius 7. 16. 11, Nonius 2. 448).

The result was that, as this writer* points out, a thousand
men went down to the forum every day wearing purple-dyed
cloaks . . . (Nonius 3. 805).

In their case, as you recall, a crowd of the least substantial citizens got together, and thanks to the coins which they contributed
a funeral was, quite unexpectedly, provided (Nonius 3. 833).

. . . for our ancestors were keen that marriages should be built
on solid foundations (Nonius 3. 824, Priscian, *Gramm. Lat. K.* 3.
70. 11).

Laelius' speech,* with which we are all familiar, ⟨points out⟩

how welcome the priests' crocks and, as he says, 'the Samian pots' are to the immortal gods (Nonius 2. 640).

[*Laelius complained that no statues had been erected to Nasica for killing Tiberius Gracchus. Part of Scipio's reply has been preserved in the following section, which leads up to the Dream of Scipio.*]

8   SCIPIO: For men of good sense the consciousness of their outstanding deeds is in itself the richest reward for their moral excellence. Nevertheless, that superhuman excellence longs, not for statues held in place by lead nor for triumphs and their withering laurels, but for fresher and more lasting kinds of reward.

LAELIUS: And what, may I ask, are they?

SCIPIO: As this is the third day of our holiday, allow me . . . (Macrobius, *On the Dream of Scipio* 1. 4. 2 ff.).

[*Cicero began by referring to Plato's myth of Er.*]

3   . . . who, after being laid on the funeral pyre, came back to life and revealed many secrets about the world below (Favonius Eulogius* on *The Dream of Scipio* 1, p. 13).

[*Augustine says that, according to Cicero, Plato was presenting an entertaining story rather than the truth*, De Civitate Dei 22. 28.]

9–29 The Dream of Scipio*

9   SCIPIO: As you know, I served in Africa* as military tribune of the fourth legion when Manilius here was consul. On arrival, my first priority was to meet King Masinissa, who for good reasons was a very close friend of our family. When I came to see him, the old man put his arms around me and wept. Then, after a minute or two, he looked up at the sky and said 'I give thanks to you, O Sun most high, and to you other heavenly beings, that before departing this life I see Publius Cornelius Scipio in my kingdom, here in my palace. Simply by hearing his name I feel refreshed; for the memory of that excellent and invincible man [*his grandfather*] remains constantly in my heart.' Then I asked him about his kingdom, and he asked me about our republic. And as our leisurely conversation moved this way and that, the day came to an end.

Later, after he had entertained me in royal style, we continued 10
our talk far into the night. The old man spoke all the time about
Africanus, recalling not only his acts but also his sayings. Then,
after going to bed, I sank into a deeper sleep than usual, for I was
tired after my journey and had stayed up late. Now it happens
from time to time that our thoughts and conversations give rise
to something in our sleep, like what Ennius* writes about in the
case of Homer, whom he obviously thought and spoke about a
good deal in his waking hours. So, I suppose as a result of our
talk, Africanus* now appeared, in a form more familiar to me
from his portrait than from what he was like in life. When I
recognized him I began to tremble, but he said 'Don't be afraid,
Scipio. Listen to me and remember what I say.

'Do you see that city which, through my efforts, was forced to 11
bend the knee to the Roman people—the city which is now reviving the wars of the past and cannot remain at peace?'* (At this he
showed me Carthage from a high place which was clear and
shining in the radiance of starlight.) 'At the present moment, as
you come to attack it, you are little more than a common soldier.
In less than two years you will overthrow it as a consul, and you
will obtain in your own right the name which you have already
inherited from me. When you have destroyed Carthage, you will
celebrate a triumph, become censor, and go as an envoy to Egypt,
Syria, Asia, and Greece. In your absence you will be elected consul
a second time; you will bring a very great war* to an end; you
will sack Numantia. But after riding in a chariot to the Capitol,
you will find the country in turmoil as a result of my grandson's*
policies.

'Then, Africanus, you will have to show our fatherland the light 12
of your spirit, ability, and good sense. But at that point I see a
fork, as it were, in the pathway of destiny. For when your life has
completed eight times seven revolutions* of the sun in its wheel-
ing course, and when those two numbers which are considered
perfect (each for a different reason) have, in the natural cycle,
reached the sum of years allotted to you by fate, then the entire
country will turn to you alone because of your prestige. The
Senate, all good citizens, the allies, the Latins—all will look to
you; you will be the one man on whom the country's safety
depends. In short, you will have to assume the dictatorship* and

restore order in the state, if you manage to elude the unholy hands
of your relatives.'*

At this point Laelius cried out in horror, and the others groaned
heavily. But Scipio with a gentle smile said: Sh! Please don't wake
me from my sleep. Listen for a few minutes to the rest of what
happened.

13   'Yet, to make you all the keener to defend the state, Africanus,
I want you to know this: for everyone who has saved and served
his country and helped it to grow, a sure place is set aside in
heaven where he may enjoy a life of eternal bliss. To that supreme
god who rules the universe nothing (or at least nothing that
happens on earth) is more welcome than those companies and
communities of people linked together by justice that are called
states. Their rulers and saviours set out from this place,* and to
this they return.'

14   At this point I was extremely apprehensive, fearing not so much
death as treachery on the part of my relatives. Nevertheless, I
asked whether he himself and my father Paulus were still alive,
and the others whom I imagined to be dead.

'Why indeed they are,' he said, 'and so are all who have escaped
from the fetters of the body as though from prison. For that life
of yours (as it is called) is really death. But look, here is your father
Paulus coming to meet you.' When I saw him, I burst into tears.
But he put his arms around me, kissed me, and told me to stop
crying.

15   As soon as I had dried my tears and was able to speak, I said
'Best and most revered of fathers, please tell me—since this is life
(as Africanus has just said), why do I linger on earth? Why do I
not hurry here to join you?' 'Things are not like that,' he said.
'There is no possible way for you to come here, unless the god
whose temple is this whole visible universe releases you from the
bonds of the body. Human beings were born on condition that
they should look after that sphere called earth which you see in
the middle of this celestial space. A soul was given to them out of
those eternal fires which you call stars and planets. Those bodies
are round and spherical, animated by divine minds, and they complete their circuits and orbits with amazing speed. That is why
you, Publius, and all loyal men must keep the soul in the custody*
of the body. You must not depart from human life until you

receive the command from him who has given you that soul; otherwise you will be judged to have deserted the earthly post assigned to you by God. Instead, Scipio, be like your grandfather here, and me, your father. Respect justice and do your duty. That is important in the case of parents and relatives, and paramount in the case of one's country. That is the way of life which leads to heaven and to the company, here, of those who have already completed their lives. Released from their bodies, they dwell in that place which you see—a place which you have learnt from the Greeks to call the Milky Way.' (And in fact there was this circle shining with dazzling radiance among the fiery bodies.)

When I beheld the whole universe from that point, everything seemed glorious and wonderful. There were stars which we have never seen from this earth of ours, each of a size which we have never imagined to exist. The smallest star,* which was furthest from heaven and nearest to earth, was shining with a light not its own. The spheres of the stars easily exceeded the earth in size. Now the earth itself seemed so small to me that I felt ashamed of our empire, whose extent was no more than a dot on its surface.

As I gazed more intently upon it, Africanus said 'Well now, how long will your thoughts remain fixed on the earth? Do you not notice what lofty regions you have entered? Everything is joined together by nine circles* or rather spheres. One of them (the outermost) is that of heaven, which surrounds all the others. It is itself the supreme divinity, holding apart and keeping in all the rest. In that sphere are fixed those stars which revolve eternally in their courses. Below it are seven spheres which revolve backwards in a contrary motion* to that of heaven. One of them (that nearest to heaven) belongs to the star which on earth is called Saturn's; then comes that light, called Jupiter's, which brings prosperity and good health to mankind; then comes the red star dreaded by all on earth, which you say belongs to Mars; below that, the band more or less in the middle is occupied by the sun, which is the leader, chief, and ruler of the other lights; it is also the mind and regulator of the universe, so huge that it suffuses and fills everything with its light; the sun is followed by two attendants—Venus in her course and Mercury in his. The lowest sphere is that in which the moon revolves, lit by the rays of the sun. Below that

everything is subject to death and decay, except the souls which
the gods, in their generosity, have granted to the race of men.
Above the moon all is eternal. The earth, the innermost and last
of the nine spheres, does not move; it is the lowest sphere, and all
heavy things fall onto it by virtue of their own weight.'

18   I gazed at all these things in amazement. Then, pulling myself
together, I said 'What is this sound,* so loud and yet so sweet,
that fills my ears?'

'That,' he said, 'is the sound produced by the impetus and
momentum of the spheres themselves. It is made up of intervals
which, though unequal, are determined systematically by fixed
proportions. The blend of high and low notes produces an even
flow of various harmonies. Such vast motions cannot sweep on in
silence, and nature ordains that low notes should be emitted by
one of the boundaries and high notes by the other. From the
uppermost of the heavenly orbits (that which carries the stars)
comes a high note with frequent vibrations, in that its cycle is
more rapid. The deepest note emanates from the lowest orbit, that
of the moon. The earth, which is the ninth sphere, remains fixed
and immobile in one place, filling the central position of the universe. Those eight rotating spheres (of which two [*being an octave
apart*] produce the same effect) give out seven distinctive sounds
according to their intervals. That number is more or less the linch-
pin of everything. By imitating this system with strings and voices
experts have succeeded in opening up a way back to this place, as
have others who, in their life on earth, have applied their out-
19 standing intellect to heavenly subjects. Filled with this sound,
people's ears have become deaf to it. Hearing, in fact, is the most
easily impaired of all your senses. For instance, where the Nile
comes hurtling down from the mountain peaks at a place called
Catadoupa,* the local inhabitants have lost their sense of hearing
because of the loudness of the roar. The noise of the whole universe, then, revolving as it does at an enormous speed, is so loud
that human ears cannot take it in, just as you cannot look straight
at the sun because your sight and vision become overwhelmed by
its rays.'

Though listening to all this with astonishment, I kept turning
20 my eyes repeatedly back to earth. Thereupon Africanus said 'I
notice you are still gazing at the home and habitation of men. If

it seems small to you (as indeed it is) make sure to keep your mind on these higher regions and to think little of the human scene down there. For what fame can you achieve, what glory worth pursuing, that consists merely of people's talk? Look. The earth is inhabited in just a few confined areas. In between those inhabited places, which resemble blots, there are huge expanses of empty territory. Those who live on earth are separated in such a way that nothing can readily pass between them from one populated region to another. More than that, in relation to your position, some people stand at a different angle,* some at right angles, and some directly opposite. You certainly cannot expect any praise from them.

'You notice, too, that the earth is also encircled and surrounded 21 by things like belts.* The two farthest apart from each other, which lie in each direction right beneath the poles of the sky, are, as you see, frozen solid. The belt in the middle (the largest one) is burnt by the heat of the sun. Two belts are habitable; the one to the south, where from your point of view people walk upside down, is in no way related to your race; as for the one which lies open to the north wind—the one where you live—notice how tiny a part of it concerns you. That entire land mass which you occupy has been made narrow from north to south* and broader from east to west. It is like a small island surrounded by the sea which you on earth call the Atlantic, the Great Sea, or the Ocean. Yet observe how small it is in spite of its imposing name. Has your 22 fame, or that of any of us, been able to find its way from these civilized and familiar lands to the far side of the Caucasus, which you see here, or to swim across the Ganges, there? In the remaining areas of the east or west, or in those far to the north and south, who will ever hear your name? When all those regions have been cut out, you can surely see how small is the area over which your glory is so eager to extend. And even those who talk about us now—how long will they continue to do so?

'Even if the children of future generations should want to hand 23 on in their turn the praises of each one of us which they have heard from their fathers, nevertheless, owing to the floods and fires which at certain times will inevitably afflict the earth, we cannot achieve, I will not say eternal, but even long-lasting glory. And what difference does it make that you should be talked of

among people still unborn when you were never mentioned by
those who lived before your time—men who were not inferior in
numbers and were certainly superior in character?

24   'Anyhow, of those who may come to hear our name none will
manage to remember it for more than a year. Granted, men commonly measure the year simply by the return of one heavenly
body, namely the sun. But when all the heavenly bodies return to
the position from which they started, and after a long interval
restore the configuration of the entire firmament, then that can
truly be called the cycle of a year.* I hardly venture to guess how
many generations of men that year contains. In the past, when
Romulus'* soul found its way to this region, people saw the sun
grow dim and go out. When, in the same position and at the same
time, the sun goes out again, then you may take it that all the
planets and stars have returned to their original places, and that
the year has been completed. I can tell you that not one twentieth part of that year has yet rolled by.

25   'If, then, you abandon hope of returning to this place where
great and eminent men have their full reward, of what value, pray,
is your human glory which can barely last for a tiny part of a
single year? If, therefore, you wish to look higher and to gaze upon
this eternal home and habitation, you will not put yourself at the
mercy of the masses' gossip nor measure your long-term destiny
by the rewards you get from men. Goodness herself must draw
you on by her own enticements* to true glory. As for what others
say about you, that's their concern. They'll say it anyhow. All that
is said is confined within those small areas that you see. In no case
does a person's reputation last for ever; it fades with the death of
the speakers, and vanishes as posterity forgets.'

26   When he had finished, I said 'From boyhood, Africanus, I have
followed in your footsteps and those of my father,* and have not
let your reputation down. But if, as you say, there is a kind of
path for noble patriots leading to the gate of heaven, then, in view
of the great reward you have set before me, I shall now press on
with a much keener awareness.'

'By all means press on,' he replied, 'and bear in mind that *you*
are not mortal, but only that body of yours. *You* are not the person
presented by your physical appearance. A man's true self is his
mind,* not that form which can be pointed out by a finger.

Remember you are a god, if a god is one who possesses life, sensation, memory, and foresight, and who controls, regulates, and moves the body over which he is set, as truly as the supreme god rules the universe. And just as the god who moves the universe, which is to some extent mortal, is eternal, so the soul which moves the frail body is eternal too.

'Whatever is in constant motion* is eternal. What imparts motion to something else, but is itself moved by another force, must come to the end of its life when its motion ceases. Therefore only that which moves itself never ceases to be moved, because it never loses contact with itself. Moreover, in the case of everything that moves, this is the source and primary cause of motion. But the primary cause has no beginning; for while everything arises from that primary cause, it itself cannot arise from anything else, for if it *were* produced by something else, it would not be the primary cause. But if it never comes into being neither does it ever die. For once the primary cause is dead it will not be restored to life by anything else; nor will it create anything else from itself, in as much as everything must arise from the primary cause. Hence the origin of motion comes from that which is moved by itself. That, moreover, cannot be born or die, or else the whole firmament must necessarily collapse and the whole of nature come to a standstill; nor could it obtain any force which would deliver that initial push to set it in motion.

'Since, then, it is clear that what moves by itself is eternal, who could deny that this property is possessed by minds? Everything that is propelled by an external force is inanimate; but an animate being is moved by its own internal power, for that is the peculiar property and function of the mind. If the mind is the one and only entity that moves itself, surely it has never been born and will never die.

'Be sure to employ it in the best kinds of activity. Now the best concerns are for the safety of one's country. When the mind has been engaged in and exercised by those concerns it will fly more quickly to this, its dwelling-place and home. And it will do so the more readily if, when still enclosed in the body, it already ventures abroad and, by contemplating what lies beyond, detaches itself as much as possible from the body. As for the souls of those who devote themselves to bodily pleasures and become, so to speak, their willing slaves, and are impelled by the lusts that serve pleasure to violate the laws of gods and men—those souls, on escaping from their bodies, swirl around, close to the earth itself, and they do not return to this place until they have been buffeted about for many ages.'

He departed, and I awoke from sleep.*

UNPLACED FRAGMENTS OF THE *REPUBLIC*

1. [Loeb, frag. 2] It is a difficult matter to praise a boy, Fannius; for then one has to praise promise, not achievement (Servius on Virgil, *Aeneid* 6. 877).

2. [Loeb, frag. 3] 'If it be granted to any man to mount to the regions of the gods, for me alone the huge gate of heaven stands open' . . . That is true, Africanus, for that same gate opened for Hercules also (Lactantius, *Divinae Institutiones* 1. 18).

THE LAWS

THE LAWS

BOOK 1

1–15. Poetic and historical truth. The dearth of Latin historians. The scene is set

ATTICUS: I recognize that clump of trees and also this oak* which belongs to the people of Arpinum; I have often read about it in *Marius*. If that oak still survives, this must be it; and indeed it's a very old tree.

QUINTUS: It does survive, my dear Atticus, and it always will; for it was sown by the imagination. No stem tended by a farmer can last as long as one planted by a poet's verses.

ATTICUS: And how, may I ask, is that, Quintus? What kind of a thing is it that poets plant? I suspect you are flattering your brother to solicit support for yourself!*

QUINTUS: No doubt you're right. But as long as Latin literature has a voice, this place will have an oak-tree called after Marius; and, as Scaevola* says about my brother's poem, 'it will grow grey o'er countless centuries'. Or perhaps the Athens you love has managed to keep the olive-tree* on the Acropolis alive for ever? Or the tall young palm which they point out today on Delos is the very one that Homer's Ulysses* said he had seen there? Many other things in many places have survived longer by virtue of tradition than they could possibly have lasted in the course of nature. So let this now be that 'acorn-laden oak'* from which 'the tawny messenger of Jove in wondrous form' once flew. But when weather or old age has destroyed it, there will still be a tree in this place which they can call Marius' oak.

ATTICUS: I've no doubt about that. But here's a question I want to put—not to you, Quintus, but to the poet himself. Was it your verses that planted this oak, or were you told that this episode was witnessed by Marius as you describe it?

MARCUS: I'll answer that, Atticus; but first you must answer this for *me*: is it a fact that after his death Romulus walked up and down not far from your house* and informed Julius Proculus that he himself was a god, Quirinus by name, and ordered a temple to be dedicated to him in that place? And is it true that in Athens (again not far from your old house) Aquilo carried off Orithyia?* For that's what they say.

4   ATTICUS: What on earth is the point of that question, and why do you ask it?

MARCUS: For no reason at all, except to warn you against inquiring too closely into things that are handed down in that way.

ATTICUS: Still, there are many points in *Marius* which raise the question whether they are fact or fiction; and some people expect you to tell the truth, because you are dealing with the recent past and with a local personality.

MARCUS: I certainly don't wish to be thought a liar. But, my dear Titus, the people you mention are being naïve; they are demanding in this case the kind of truth expected of a witness rather than a poet. I suppose the same folk believe that Numa conversed with Egeria and that an eagle placed a crown on Tarquin's head.

5   QUINTUS: I take it, Marcus, that in your view one set of rules must be followed in a work of history, another in a poem.

MARCUS: Yes, because in the former everything is measured by the standard of truth,* Quintus, whereas in the latter the main purpose is to entertain. And yet there are countless yarns in Herodotus, the father of history, and in Theopompus.

ATTICUS: This gives me an opportunity which I've been waiting for, and I shan't let it slip.

MARCUS: And what's that, Titus?

ATTICUS: You have often been asked, indeed pressed, to write a work of history. People think that if you took it on we would succeed in rivalling the Greeks in that genre too. And if you want my own opinion, I think you owe this as a duty not only to the enthusiastic people who enjoy your writings but also to your country, which you once saved and now have the chance to glorify. For, as I myself recognize and have often heard you say, our literature is lacking in the field of history. You above all people could supply this need, since, as you often maintain, this kind of writing is so closely akin to oratory.*

6   So do, please, take on this work, and devote some time to an

activity which is still unknown or ignored by our own writers. For
after the Annals of the Pontifex Maximus* (the most meagre
source imaginable), if one comes to Fabius or Cato, whom you
are always quoting, or to Piso or Fannius or Vennonius, then,
although one of these has more vitality than another, what could
be more insipid than the entire group? Coelius Antipater, who
was close in time to Fannius, had a bit more spirit in his writing.
Though his power was uncouth and primitive, without any
polish or finesse, he could have stimulated his successors to write
with greater care. But in fact he was succeeded by Gellius,*
Clodius, and Asellio, who cannot stand comparison with him but
hark back, rather, to the older writers with their slackness and
incompetence.

I doubt if Macer is worth counting. His verbosity has a certain 7
shrewdness, but it does not come from the learned storehouse of
Greek rhetoric but from Latin hacks;* his speeches, moreover,
contain a good deal of ill-judged elevation and show a total lack
of propriety.* His friend Sisenna easily surpasses all our writers to
date, except, perhaps, those who have not yet published their
work,* in which case we can have no opinion about them. But he
has never been put in your class as an orator; in his history he has
a childish ambition: he wants to give the impression that he has
read Cleitarchus alone among Greek writers and that he merely
aspires to imitate him. If he had managed to equal him he would
still have been some way from the best. So this is your task,
and yours alone, and people expect it of you—unless Quintus
disagrees.

QUINTUS: Not at all; in fact we have often talked about that. 8
But there is a minor difference of opinion between us.

ATTICUS: And what is that?

QUINTUS: From what period should he begin his narrative? I
think he should start from the earliest times, since those events
are recorded in such a style that they are not even read about. But
he himself claims the right to handle the history of his own period
in order to include the events in which he himself took part.

ATTICUS: I'm inclined to agree with him. For things of enormous moment have happened in the memory of our generation.
In addition, he will glorify the achievements of his great friend,
Gnaeus Pompeius, and will also reach the glorious and
unforgettable year* of his own consulship. I would sooner he

recounted these events than, as they say, 'the story of Romulus and Remus'.

MARCUS: I am aware, Atticus, that this work has long been expected of me. I would not shirk it if I had any free time available. But one cannot embark on a thing of such importance when one's programme of work is full and one's mind is already occupied. Two things are needed: freedom from work and freedom from worry.

9   ATTICUS: What about the other things you have written— works more voluminous than any of our countrymen have produced? What time, pray, did you have available for *them*?

MARCUS: Oh, bits of spare time crop up which I don't allow to go to waste. When I am given a short break in the country, my writing has to be fitted into that number of days. But you cannot start a history without setting free time aside; and it cannot be finished in a short period. Moreover, I tend to become confused if, after starting a project, I have to turn to something else. And it's not so easy to pick up the threads again after breaking off as to take a thing through from start to finish.

10   ATTICUS: What you have just described evidently calls for a diplomatic mission* or a leisurely carefree holiday of that sort!

MARCUS: I was counting rather on the holiday that comes with old age. I would be quite willing to sit on a chair in the good old style advising clients on points of law and carrying out the pleasant and respected function of a reasonably active old age. In that way I would be able to give as much attention as I wished to the project which you desire and to many larger and more rewarding matters.

11   ATTICUS: Ah, but I'm afraid no one will accept that excuse. You will always have to plead in court, especially now that you have changed and adopted a new style of speaking. Just as your friend Roscius in his old age employed a more relaxed delivery in the sung passages* and had the pipes play more slowly, you are gradually modifying those strenuous efforts which you used to make. As a result your delivery is now more akin to a calm philosophical discourse.* Since this style can apparently be maintained even in advanced old age, I don't see you getting any respite from court work.

12   QUINTUS: I was rather thinking that our people might well

approve of it if you spent your time giving advice on points of law. So when you feel inclined I think you should try it.

MARCUS: That would be fine, Quintus, if there were no risk in trying it. But I suspect that in attempting to cut down my work I would actually increase it, and that on top of the court work (which I never undertake without preparation and rehearsal) I would be faced with this business of interpreting the law. That would be a problem, not so much because of the effort involved as because it would prevent me from giving thought to my speeches. Without that, I have never dared to undertake any major case.

ATTICUS: Why don't you explain these matters to us in those 13 'bits of spare time', as you call them, and put together a more thorough account of civil law than others have done? You have always been interested in law from those far-off years when we attended Scaevola's consultations* together, and you have never seemed to be so totally committed to speaking as to neglect the study of civil law.

MARCUS: You are luring me into a lengthy disquisition, Atticus! Still I will undertake it, unless Quintus would sooner we did something else. Since our time is our own, I'm happy to state my views.

QUINTUS: And I'm happy to hear them. There's nothing I'd sooner do; and how could I better spend the day?

MARCUS: Why don't we follow our usual path, where the seats 14 are? When we've had enough walking we can take a rest; and we'll certainly not be short of entertainment as we discuss the various questions.

ATTICUS: Count me in. If you like we can go down here by the Liris—along the bank where there's shade. So now—make a start, please, and tell us your opinions about civil law.

MARCUS: Shall I? Well, there have been able men, I think, in our country who have regularly expounded civil law and answered people's questions about it. But although they have promised great things they have dealt with small details. What is so majestic as the law of the land? Yet what is more petty than the function of those who answer queries? It is, of course, necessary for the public, and I don't mean that the men who performed that task were ignorant of law in general; but they practised what is called civil law only with the intention of making it available to the people. That, though practically necessary, is intellectually undemanding. So what do you want me to do? What are your instructions? That I should write little handbooks about the regulations for party-walls* and gutters?* Or list the rules for contracts or court procedure? Such things have been diligently compiled by many writers, and they are less significant, I fancy, than what you expect from me.

15   ATTICUS: If you want to know what *I* expect, it seems logical that since you have written about the best constitution you should also write about its laws. For that, I notice, is what Plato did— your idol and favourite, whom you revere above all others.

MARCUS: Well, shall we do what he did? With the Cretan Cleinias and the Spartan Megillus, he discussed political institutions and the ideal legal code on a summer's day, as he describes it,* among the cypress trees and wooded paths of Cnossus, often pausing and sometimes resting. So shall we, as we walk by these tall poplar-trees on the green and shady river-bank and occasionally sit down, discuss these same issues rather more fully than the courts require for their purposes?

16–35. The nature of law must be sought in the nature of man. Man is a single species which has a share in divine reason and is bound together by a partnership in justice

16   ATTICUS: I would certainly like to hear about such things.

MARCUS: And what does Quintus say?

QUINTUS: There's nothing that I'd sooner hear about.

MARCUS: Quite right too; for you may be sure that there is no topic which brings out so clearly* what nature has bestowed on man, how many excellent things the human mind contains, what task we were born and brought into the light to address and accomplish, what sort of factor unites human beings and what natural fellowship exists between them. For these matters must all be clarified before the source of law and justice can be identified.

17   ATTICUS: Does this mean that you consider the science of law to be derived, not from the praetor's edict* (as most authorities hold today), nor from the Twelve Tables* (as our forefathers believed), but from the deepest recesses of philosophy?

MARCUS: That's right, Pomponius. For in this discussion, we are not asking how to frame legally binding conditions or how to answer this and that question for our clients. Let's suppose such problems are important, as indeed they are. They have been handled by many distinguished men in the past, and are now being dealt with by a person* of the greatest expertise and authority. But in our present analysis we have to encompass the entire issue of universal justice and law; what we call civil law will be confined to a small, narrow, corner of it. We must clarify the *nature* of justice, and that has to be deduced from the nature of man. Then we must consider the laws by which states ought to be governed, and finally deal with the laws and enactments which peoples have compiled and written down. There the so-called civil law of our own people too will not be overlooked.

QUINTUS: You certainly *are* going far back, Marcus! Quite 18 rightly, you are tracing the object of our search back to its source. Those who present civil law in a different way are presenting modes of litigation rather than justice.

MARCUS: Not so, Quintus. Ignorance rather than knowledge of the law leads to litigation. But that can wait till later; now let's inspect the first principles of justice.

Well then, the most learned men* have chosen to take law as their starting point. I'm inclined to think they are right, if indeed (as they define it) law is the highest reason, inherent in nature, which enjoins what ought to be done and forbids the opposite. When that reason is fully formed and completed in the human mind, it, too, is law. So they think that law, whose function is to 19 enjoin right action and to forbid wrong-doing, is wisdom. And they believe it received its Greek name* from giving each his own. I think its Latin name* comes from choosing. As they stress the element of fairness in law, we stress that of choice; but in fact each of these is an essential property of law. If this assertion is correct, as on the whole I think it is, the origin of justice must be derived from law. For law is a force of nature, the intelligence and reason of a wise man, and the criterion of justice and injustice. At the same time, as our whole discourse has to do with ordinary ways of thinking, we shall sometimes have to use ordinary language, applying the word 'law' to that which lays down in writing what it wishes to enjoin or forbid. For that's what the man in the street calls law. But in establishing what justice is let us take as our point of departure that highest law which came into being countless centuries before any law was written down or any state was even founded.

20   QUINTUS: Yes, that's more fitting and sensible in view of the method we have chosen for our discussion.

MARCUS: Shall we, then, look for the origin of justice at its source? Once we have found that, we will have a reliable standard for testing our investigations.

QUINTUS: Yes, I think that's the way to proceed.

ATTICUS: Include me, too, in your brother's opinion.

MARCUS: It is our business, then, to maintain and preserve the constitution of that state which Scipio in those six books* proved to be the best. All the laws must be framed to fit that kind of community. Patterns of behaviour are also to be implanted, and not everything is to be laid down in writing. For all these reasons I shall look to nature for the origins of justice. She must be our constant guide as our discussion unfolds.

ATTICUS: Absolutely right. With her as our guide there can be
21   no danger of going astray.

MARCUS: Well then, Pomponius, will you grant me this (for I already know Quintus' view)* that the whole of nature is ruled by the immortal gods, with their force, impetus,* plan, power, sway (or whatever other word may express my meaning more plainly)? If you don't accept that, our argument will have to start on that very point.

ATTICUS: I'll grant it if you insist;* and in fact, because of all this birdsong and the gurgling of the river, I'm not worried that any of my fellow-disciples may overhear.

MARCUS: Ah, but you must be careful! For, like all good men, they are apt to become very angry;* and they won't put up with it if they hear that you've failed to uphold the excellent man's first chapter, where he has written that a god is never concerned* either on his own account or anyone else's.

22   ATTICUS: Please carry on. I'd like to know the relevance of my concession.

MARCUS: I'll be brief; this is the point. The creature of foresight, wisdom, variety, keenness, memory, endowed with reason and judgement, which we call man, was created by the supreme god to enjoy a remarkable status. Of all the types and species of living creatures he is the only one that participates in reason* and reflection, whereas none of the others do. What is there, I will not say in man, but in the whole of heaven and earth, more divine than reason* (a faculty which, when it has developed and become complete, is rightly called wisdom)?

Since, then, there is nothing better than reason, and reason is 23 present in both man and God, there is a primordial partnership in reason between man and God. But those who share reason also share right reason; and since that is law, we men must also be thought of as partners with the gods in law. Furthermore, those who share law share justice. Now those who share all these things must be regarded as belonging to the same state; and much the more so if they obey the same powers and authorities. And they do in fact obey this celestial system, the divine mind, and the all-powerful god. Hence this whole universe must be thought of as a single community shared by gods and men.* Now in communities there is a system (which I shall describe at the appropriate point) whereby differences of status within families are determined by blood-relationships.* In the context of the cosmos the same applies on a much vaster and more splendid scale, establishing ties of blood between men and gods.

In debates on the nature of man it is usually maintained, doubt- 24 less correctly, that in the course of the continuous circuits and revolutions of the heavens the right moment arrived for sowing the human race;* that after being scattered and sown in the earth it was further endowed with the divine gift of mind; that whereas men derived the other elements in their make-up from their mortal nature—elements which are fragile and transitory—their mind was implanted in them by God. Hence we have what can truly be called a lineage, origin, or stock in common with the gods. That is why, out of so many species, no creature apart from man has any conception of God; and why, within mankind itself, there is no tribe so civilized or so savage as not to know that it should believe in a god, even if it is mistaken about the *kind* of god it should believe in. As a result, man recognizes God in as much as 25 he, as it were, remembers his place of origin.* Again, the same moral excellence resides in man and in God, and in no other species besides. And moral excellence is nothing other than the completion and perfection of nature.

There is, therefore, a similarity between man and God. Since that is so, what kinship, I ask you, can be closer or firmer? Nature has lavished such a wealth of things on men for their use and convenience that every growing thing seems to have been given to us on purpose; it does not come into existence by chance. And I don't mean just what shoots forth from the fertile earth, but also domes-
26 tic animals; for they were obviously created for man's use* or his enjoyment* or his food. Again, countless skills have been discovered thanks to nature's teaching. By copying her,* reason has cleverly acquired the necessities of life.

Nature, too, has not only equipped man with mental agility; she has provided him with senses which act as his servants and messengers.* She has given him, as a preliminary outline, dim and not fully developed perceptions of very many things, which form a foundation, as it were, of knowledge. And she has blest him with a versatile physique in keeping with the human mind. For whereas nature made other animals stoop down to feed, she made man alone erect,* encouraging him to gaze at the heavens as being,
27 so to speak, akin to him and his original home. She also shaped his facial features so as to express his innermost character. Our eyes tell our emotional state very clearly; and what we call the expression, which cannot exist in any creature except in man, indicates our character. (The Greeks know what the word means but have no equivalent* at all.) I need not mention the faculties and abilities of the rest of the body, such as the control of the voice and the power of speech, which is above all else the promoter of human fellowship.* For not everything is germane to our present discussion, and I think Scipio has dealt adequately with this topic in the books which you have read.* Since, then, God has created and equipped man in this way, intending him to take precedence over everything else, this point should be clear (not to go into every detail) that nature on her own account goes further. Without any teacher, starting from the sort of things she apprehended through that original rudimentary perception, she herself strengthens and completes human reason.

28 ATTICUS: Good Lord! You're certainly going a long way back in your search for the basis of justice. For that reason I shan't hurry you on to the discussion of civil law which I was hoping for. I would gladly have you spend the whole day on this subject.

For these points that you are bringing in, as ancillary perhaps to other matters, are actually more important than the things which they serve to introduce.

MARCUS: Yes, the points which I am now briefly touching on *are* important. But of all the issues dealt with in philosophical debates surely nothing is more vital than the clear realization that we are born for justice, and that what is just is based, not on opinion, but on nature.* This will at once become clear if you examine the society of men and their relations to one another.

Now there is no single thing that is so similar to, so like, any- 29 thing else as all of us are like one another. If corrupt habits and foolish opinions did not twist and turn aside our feeble minds from their original paths, no individual would be more like himself than everyone would be like everyone else. Thus, however one defines man, the same definition applies to us all. This is suf- 30 ficient proof that there is no essential difference within mankind. If there were, the same definition would not cover everyone. Reason in fact—the one thing in which we are superior to the beasts, which enables us to make valid deductions, to argue, refute our opponents, debate, solve problems, draw conclusions—that certainly is common to us all. While it may vary in what it teaches, it is constant in its ability to learn. For the same things are grasped by the senses of all, and those things that act on the senses act on the senses of all alike; and those rudimentary perceptions that are impressed on the mind (the perceptions I mentioned above) are impressed alike on *all* minds. Speech, which interprets the mind, uses different languages but expresses the same ideas. Nor is there any member of any nation who cannot attain moral excellence by using nature as his guide.

The similarity between human beings is evident in their vices as 31 well as their virtues. They are all beguiled by pleasure, which, though it leads on to vice, bears some resemblance to what is na- turally good; for it gives delight by its lightness and charm, and so, through an error of judgement, is accepted as something ben- eficial. Owing to a similar misconception death is shunned as though it involved the extinction of our true nature, while life is sought because it preserves us in the condition in which we were born. Pain is counted as one of the greatest evils, because it is harsh in itself and apparently leads to the dissolution* of our

32 nature. Again, because good character and good reputation look alike, those who receive public honours are regarded as blessed, and the obscure are objects of pity. Troubles and joys, desires and fears, haunt the minds of all alike; and if men differ in their opinions it does not follow that those who worship a dog or a cat* as divine are not afflicted by the same superstition as other nations. What community does not love friendliness, generosity, and an appreciative mind which remembers acts of kindness? What community does not reject the arrogant, the wicked, the cruel, and the ungrateful—yes, and hate them too? So, since the whole human race is seen to be knit together, the final conclusion is that the principles of right living make everyone a better person. If you agree with this, let us move on to the rest of our discussion; but if you have any questions we should clear them up first.

ATTICUS: No, we have nothing to raise, if I may answer for us both.

33 MARCUS: The next point, then, is that we have been made by nature to share justice amongst ourselves and to impart it to one another. I should add that in the whole of this discussion I want it to be understood that what I call 'justice' comes from nature, but that the corruption brought by bad habits is so great that it extinguishes, so to speak, the sparks given by nature and allows the corresponding vices to spring up and flourish. If human beings believed in their hearts what is in fact the case, namely that, in the poet's words, 'nothing human is alien to them',* then justice would be respected equally by all. For those who have been endowed by nature with reason have also been endowed with right reason, and hence with law, which is right reason in commanding and forbidding; but if with law, then with justice too. But reason has been bestowed on everybody; therefore the same applies to justice. And Socrates was right to curse* the man who first separated self-interest from justice; for that, he complained,

34 was the source of everything pernicious. Hence that famous saying of Pythagoras* . . . [*There is a gap in the text here*]

It is clear, then, that when a wise man shows this goodwill, which ranges so far and wide, to someone endowed with equal moral excellence, an effect is produced which some people* think incredible though it is actually inevitable, namely that he loves the other person as much as he loves himself. For what difference can there be when everything is equal? If there could be some distinction, however tiny, in a friendship, the name of friendship would already have gone; for the essential feature of friendship is that, the moment one partner prefers to have something for himself rather than for the other, it vanishes.

All these arguments provide a firm basis for the rest of our discussion and debate, for they help to show that justice is founded on nature. When I have said a little more about this point, I will come to civil law, the subject from which this whole discourse began.

QUINTUS: Yes, you need add very little. From what you've said 35 it certainly seems to me that justice is derived from nature. I don't know whether Atticus agrees.

ATTICUS: How could I fail to agree when you have proved first that we are, as it were, equipped and arrayed with the gifts of the gods, and secondly that men have a single way of living with one another which is shared equally by everyone, and finally that all are held together by a natural goodwill and kindliness and also by a fellowship in justice? Since we have agreed (rightly, I think) that these assertions are true, how can we now dissociate law and justice from nature?

36–52. The foregoing principles will be supported by all who hold that the virtues are to be sought for their own sake

MARCUS: Quite right; that's how things are. But in the proce- 36 dure of philosophers (I don't mean the older lot,* but those who have set up what might be called philosophical factories*) things that were once expressed in large general terms are now presented separately, point by point. They think that the subject which we now have in hand cannot be adequately dealt with unless this particular proposition (i.e. that justice is derived from nature) is examined on its own.

ATTICUS: I suppose you have lost your freedom of expression; or perhaps you are one of those people who, in arguing a case, defer to the authority of others instead of following their own judgement!

37   MARCUS: Not invariably, Titus. But you see the direction which
this discussion is taking. My whole thesis aims to bring stability
to states, steadiness to cities, and well-being to communities. So I
am anxious not to make a mistake by laying down first principles
which have not been well considered and carefully examined.
Mind you, I do not mean that they should be proved to everyone's satisfaction (that can't be done), but to the satisfaction of
those who believe that everything right and honourable should be
desired for its own sake,* and that things which are not praiseworthy in their own right should not be counted among good
things at all, or at least that nothing should be regarded as a great

38   good if it cannot truly be praised for its own sake. To all these
thinkers—whether they have remained in the Old Academy* like
Speusippus, Xenocrates, and Polemo, or whether they have followed Aristotle* and Theophrastus (who agree with the former
group in fact though differing slightly in their style of presentation), or whether, as Zeno used to do, they have changed their
terms without changing the substance of their beliefs, or whether
they have even followed the austere and difficult school of Aristo,
now refuted and discredited, in considering all else as wholly indif-
ferent except for virtues and vices—to all these thinkers what I
have said should be acceptable.

39   As for those who go in for self-indulgence and are slaves of their
own bodies—people who measure everything that they should
seek and avoid in life by the yardstick of pleasure and pain—even
if they are right (and there is no need to take issue with them here)
let us tell them to preach in their own little gardens,* and let us
ask them to keep away for a little while from any participation in
public life, an area of which they know nothing and have never
wished to know anything. Then there is the Academy, which has
spread confusion in all these issues (I mean the recent Academy
dating from Arcesilaus and Carneades). Let us ask it to keep
quiet;* for if it intervenes in these questions, which seem to us to
have been quite neatly presented and settled, it will cause too
much destruction. At the same time I would like to pacify that
school, and I wouldn't dare to push it away . . .

[*There is a gap here in the manuscript—a gap in which Cicero
seems to have spoken of venial sins. They can be expiated.*]

40   . . . But when it comes to acts of wickedness against men, and sac-

rilege against the gods, no expiation is possible. So the offenders pay the penalty, not necessarily imposed by the courts (which once did not exist anywhere, still do not exist in many places, and where they do exist are often unsound), but they are chased and hounded by the Furies, not with burning firebrands as in the plays,* but with the torment of their conscience and the agony of their guilt. If on the other hand men ought to be kept from wrongdoing by punishment rather than by nature, why on earth should the wicked have anything to worry about if the danger of punishment were removed? Yet no villain has ever been so brazen as not to deny that he has perpetrated a crime, or else fabricate a reason to justify his anger, or seek a defence for his crime in some provision of natural justice. If the wicked dare to invoke such principles, just think how resolutely they will be observed by the good! If, however, it is punishment or the fear of retribution, and not wickedness itself, that deters people from a life of crime and villainy, then no one is unjust; instead, the worthless should be called careless. By the same token, those of us who are persuaded to be 41 good not by probity itself but by some advantage or benefit,* are not good but crafty. How will a man behave in the dark if his only fear is a witness and a judge? What if he comes across someone in a deserted place—someone alone and helpless who can be robbed of a lot of money? Our naturally good and just man will talk to him, help him, and put him on the right road. But the fellow who does nothing for anyone else, and measures everything by his own advantage—you see, I fancy, what *he* will do! Even if he denies that he will murder the man and abscond with his money, he will not deny it because he regards the act as intrinsically evil but because he is afraid it may leak out, that is, that he may suffer as a result. What an attitude! It's enough to make not just a philosopher but even a peasant blush.

Most foolish of all is the belief that everything decreed by the 42 institutions or laws of a particular country is just. What if the laws are the laws of tyrants? If the notorious Thirty* had wished to impose their laws on Athens, even if the entire population of Athens welcomed the tyrants' laws, should those laws on that account be considered just? No more, in my opinion, should that law be considered just which our interrex* passed, allowing the Dictator to execute with impunity any citizen he wished, even

without trial. There is one, single, justice. It binds together human society and has been established by one, single, law. That law is right reason in commanding and forbidding. A man who does not acknowledge this law is unjust, whether it has been written down anywhere or not. If justice is a matter of obeying the written laws and customs of particular communities, and if, as our opponents* allege, everything is to be measured by self-interest, then a person will ignore and break the laws when he can, if he thinks it will be to his own advantage. That is why justice is completely non-existent if it is not derived from nature, and if that kind of justice which is established to serve self-interest is wrecked by that same
43 self-interest. And that is why every virtue is abolished if nature is not going to support justice.

What room will there be for liberality, patriotism, and devotion; or for the wish to serve others or to show gratitude? These virtues are rooted in the fact that we are inclined by nature to have a regard for others; and that is the basis of justice. Moreover, not just our services to other men, but also ceremonies and rituals in honour of the gods will be abolished—practices which, in my view, should be retained, not out of fear, but in consequence of the association between man and God. If on the other hand laws were validated by the orders of peoples, the enactments of politicians, and the verdicts of judges, then it would be just to rob, just to commit adultery, just to introduce forged wills, provided those things were approved by the votes or decrees of the populace.

44 If there is such power in the decisions and decrees of foolish people that they can overturn the nature of things by their votes, why do they not enact that things wicked and destructive should be deemed good and wholesome? And why is it that, if a law can make what is unjust just, it cannot turn evil into good? But in fact we can distinguish a good law from a bad one solely by the criterion of nature. And not only justice and injustice are differentiated by nature,* but all things without exception that are honourable and dishonourable. For nature has created perceptions which we have in common, and has sketched them in our minds in such a way that we classify honourable things as virtues and dishonourable things as vices.

45 It is insane to suppose that these things are matters of opinion

and not grounded in nature. The so-called 'virtue'* of a tree or a horse* (which is actually a misuse of the word) does not depend on opinion but on nature. If that is so, then honourable and dishonourable things too must be distinguished by nature. If moral excellence as a whole were certified by opinion, the same would apply to its parts. In that case who would judge a wise and, shall we say, shrewd man, not on the basis of his natural character but of some external factor? No, moral excellence is reason fully developed, and that is certainly grounded in nature; the same goes for everything that is honourable. Just as true and false, logical and illogical, are judged in their own terms and not by some external criterion, so a consistent mode of life (which is right) and likewise inconsistency (which is wrong) will be tested by their own nature. Or shall we judge the quality of a tree or a horse by nature 46 and not likewise the qualities of young men?* Or should character be judged by nature, and yet the virtues and vices which come from character be judged in some other way? If they are judged in the *same* way, will it not be necessary to judge what is honourable* and what is dishonourable by nature too? Every praiseworthy good must have within itself something to be praised. Goodness itself is good not because of people's opinions but because of nature. If that were not the case, happy people would be happy too because of opinion; and what could be sillier than that? Since, then, good and bad are judged to be so on the basis of nature, and they are fundamental principles of nature, surely things which are honourable and dishonourable must also be judged by the same method and assessed by the standard of nature.

Yet we are confused by the variety and incompatibility of men's 47 opinions;* and because the same disagreement does not occur in regard to the senses, we think the senses are reliable by nature whereas we brand as illusory those ideas that vary from one person to another and do not always remain consistent within the same person. This distinction is far from the truth. In the case of our senses no parent or nurse or teacher or poet or stage-show distorts them, nor does popular opinion lead them astray. For our minds, however, all kinds of traps are laid, either by the people just mentioned, who on receiving young untrained minds stain them and twist them as they please, or else by that power which

lurks within, entwined with every one of our senses, namely pleasure, which masquerades as goodness but is in fact the mother of
all ills. Seduced by her charms, our minds fail to see clearly enough
the things that are naturally good, because those things lack the
sweetness and the exciting itch of pleasure.

48   To bring this whole discourse of mine to an end—the conclusion is obvious from what has been said, namely that one should
strive after justice and every moral virtue for their own sake. All
good men love what is fair in itself and what is right in itself. It
is not in character for a good man to make the mistake of loving
what is not intrinsically lovable; therefore what is right should be
sought and cultivated for itself. If this applies to what is right, it
also applies to justice; and if it applies to justice, then the other
virtues, too, should be cultivated for themselves. What about generosity? Is it free or for profit? When a person is open-handed
without reward, it's free; when he's looking for a profit, it's an
investment. There is no doubt that a person who is called generous and open-handed has duty* in mind, not gain. So likewise
justice looks for no prize and no price; it is sought for itself, and
is at once the cause and meaning of all the virtues.

49   Furthermore, if goodness is sought for its advantages, not for
itself,* then there will be one virtue only; and that will most properly be called selfishness. For where each person measures his
actions totally by his own advantage, to that extent he totally falls
short of being a good man. Hence to those who estimate goodness by its rewards selfishness is the only admirable quality. Where
is a generous person to be found if no one acts kindly for the sake
of another? What becomes of gratitude if people are not seen to
be grateful* to the person to whom they owe thanks? Where is
that holy thing, friendship,* if no one loves a friend wholeheart-
edly, as they say, for his own sake? Why, a friend must be cast off
and abandoned if he offers no hope of profit and reward; and
what can be more barbaric than that? If friendship is to be cher-
ished for its own sake, then human fellowship and fairness and
justice are also to be sought for their own sake. If that is not so,
there is no such thing as justice at all. For the worst kind of injustice is to look for profit from justice.

50   What are we to say of restraint, temperance, and self-control?
What of modesty, decency, and chastity? Do people avoid vice for

fear of disgrace or of laws and lawcourts? Are they innocent and decent in order to be well spoken of? Do they blush in order to win a good reputation? I am ashamed to talk about the sense of shame, ashamed to speak of those philosophers who think it is honourable* to aim at avoiding condemnation without avoiding the vice itself. Well then, can we call those people pure who are 51 deterred from lechery by the fear of disgrace, when that very disgrace reflects the vileness of the thing itself? What can be properly praised or blamed if you ignore the essential nature of what you think should be praised or blamed? Are physical defects, if they are very noticeable, to cause some degree of aversion, while the deformities of the soul are not? A soul's ugliness can easily be inferred from its vices. What can be called more revolting than greed, more bestial than lust, more despicable than cowardice, more abject than dullness and stupidity? What then? Take those people who are conspicuous for one (or more than one) vice. Do we call them wretched because of the losses or damages or pain they suffer, or because of the power and ugliness of their vices? Conversely, the same point can be made positively in the case of goodness.

Finally, if goodness is pursued for the sake of other things, there 52 must be something better than goodness. So is it money or high office or beauty or health? Such things, even when present, are not significant; and how long they are going to *remain* present is quite unknowable. Or is it pleasure (a most disgraceful suggestion)? But it is in scorning and rejecting pleasure that goodness is most convincingly revealed.

You see how long the series of topics and arguments is, and how each is linked to the one before? Indeed I would have run on much longer had I not restrained myself.

52–7. Definitions of the Highest Good

QUINTUS: In what direction, may I ask? For, as far as your talk is concerned, I would gladly run on with you.

MARCUS: Towards the ultimate good,* which is the standard and goal of every action. It is a matter of lively controversy and disagreement among the best thinkers; yet at long last one must come to a decision about it.

53   ATTICUS: How can that be done now that Lucius Gellius is no longer alive?

MARCUS: What on earth has that to do with it?

ATTICUS: I remember hearing in Athens from my dear Phaedrus that your friend Gellius, when he went to Greece as proconsul after his praetorship, brought together all the philosophers who were then in Athens and urged them with great earnestness to put an end to their controversies; if they genuinely wished to stop wasting their lives in futile squabbles, agreement could be reached; at the same time he promised to lend them his assistance in the hope of achieving that end.

MARCUS: Yes, that was a joke, Pomponius, and it has caused many a laugh. But I'd be more than happy to serve as an arbitrator* between the Old Academy* and Zeno.

ATTICUS: How do you mean?

MARCUS: Because they differ about one thing only; on everything else they agree wonderfully.

ATTICUS: You don't say! Is there really just one point of dispute?

54   MARCUS: Well, only one *relevant* point. Whereas the Old Academy held that everything in conformity with nature that helped us in life was good, Zeno thought that nothing was good unless it was honourable.

ATTICUS: Well, that's no small disagreement, even if it's not the sort to cause a total breach.

MARCUS: You would be right if their disagreement were one of substance rather than words.

ATTICUS: So you agree with my friend Antiochus* (I do not presume to call him my teacher). I once lived with him, and he almost dragged me out of our garden and brought me to within a few short steps of the Academy.

MARCUS: He was certainly a wise and sharp man, and of his type a consummate thinker; he was also, as you know, a friend of mine. Whether I agree with him in everything or not is a matter which I shall consider presently. All I am saying now is that this whole dispute can be settled.

55   ATTICUS: How do you make *that* out?

MARCUS: If, like Aristo of Chios, Zeno had said that only the honourable was good and only the base was bad, and that all other things were entirely neutral, and that it didn't make the slightest difference whether they were present or not, then he would have been in serious dispute with Xenocrates, Aristotle, and the whole Platonic school; and they would have differed on a crucial issue affecting the whole theory of ethics. But as it is, while the Old Academy called what is honourable the highest good, Zeno calls it the only good. Likewise they called disgrace the worst evil, he calls it the only one. He classifies riches, health, and beauty as advantageous things,* not as good things, and poverty, ill-health, and pain as disadvantageous things, not as evils. In this he believes the same as Xenocrates and Aristotle but uses different terms. Yet from this disagreement (which is one of words, not of substance) a dispute has arisen about ultimate ends.* In this dispute, since the Twelve Tables do not permit squatters to obtain the rights of possessors* within five feet* of a boundary, we will not allow the ancient possessions of the Academy to be grazed on by this clever man, and we shall determine the ends in question not as a single judge according to the Mamilian Law* but as a Board of Three in accordance with the Twelve Tables.

ATTICUS: So what verdict do we bring in?

56

MARCUS: We find that the markers laid down by Socrates* should be sought out and respected.

QUINTUS: You are already using the terms of civil law and statutes most effectively, Marcus—a subject on which I look forward to hearing your exposition. The decision you have made is indeed important, as I have often heard you say. But there is no doubt about it: the highest good* is either to live according to nature (i.e. to enjoy a life of moderation governed by moral excellence) or to follow nature and live, so to speak, by her law (i.e. as far as possible to omit nothing in order to achieve what nature requires, which means the same as this:* to live, as it were, by the code of moral excellence). Hence I'm inclined to think that this question [*about ends*] can never be decided—certainly not in our present discussion, if we are to complete what we set out to do.

MARCUS: I was following that detour quite happily!

57

QUINTUS: There'll be another opportunity. Now let's get on with what we started, especially as it's not affected by this dispute about ultimate good and evil.

MARCUS: A very sensible suggestion, Quintus. What I've said up to now . . . [*In the lost portion Cicero is apparently asked to apply what has been said about justice to moral theory.*]

QUINTUS: . . . ⟨I am not asking⟩ you to discuss the laws of Lycurgus or Solon or Charondas or Zaleucus, or those of our own Twelve Tables, or the resolutions of the people; but I expect you, in what you say today, to provide a code of living and a system of training for nations and individuals alike.

58–63. Philosophy enables men to know themselves and their place in the natural order

58   MARCUS: What you are looking for, Quintus, is certainly within the scope of this discussion; I wish it were also within my powers! There is no doubt that, as the law should correct wickedness and promote goodness, a code of conduct may be derived from it. That is why wisdom is the mother of all good things; the love of her gives us the word 'philosophy' from the Greek. Of all the gifts which the immortal gods have bestowed on human life none is richer or more abundant or more desirable. In addition to everything else, she alone taught us this most difficult lesson, namely to know ourselves—a precept of such power and significance that it was ascribed, not to any mortal, but to the god of Delphi.

59   The person who knows himself will first of all realize that he possesses something divine, and he will compare his own inner nature to a kind of holy image placed within a temple. His thoughts and actions will always be worthy of that priceless gift of the gods; and when he inspects and tests himself thoroughly he will see how well he has been equipped by nature on entering life, and what implements he has for acquiring and obtaining wisdom. At the beginning he will have conceived in his mind and spirit dim perceptions, so to speak, of everything. When these have been illuminated with the guidance of wisdom, he now realizes that he has the makings of a good man, and for that very reason a happy one.*

60   Once the mind, on perceiving and recognizing the virtues, has ceased to serve and gratify the body, and has expunged pleasure like a kind of discreditable stain; and once it has put behind it all

fear of pain and death, and entered a loving fellowship with its own kind, regarding as its own kind all who are akin to it by nature; and once it has begun to worship the gods in a pure form of religion, and has sharpened the edge of the moral judgement, like that of the eyes, so that it can choose the good and reject its opposite (a virtue which is called prudence from pro-vision)— what can be described or conceived as more blessed than such a mind?

And when that same mind examines the heavens, the earth, the 61 sea, and the nature of all things, and perceives where those things have come from and to where they will return, when and how they are due to die, what part of them is mortal and perishable, and what is divine and everlasting; and when it almost apprehends the very god who governs and rules them, and realizes that it itself is not a resident in some particular locality surrounded by man-made walls, but a citizen of the whole world* as though it were a single city; then, in the majesty of these surroundings, in this contemplation and comprehension of nature, great God! how well it will know itself, as the Pythian Apollo commanded, how it will disdain, despise, and count as nothing* those things that are commonly deemed so precious!

Moreover, it will surround all these things with a kind of stock- 62 ade* consisting of verbal reasoning, expertise in judging what is true and false, and the art, as it were, of understanding the logical consequences of everything and what objections it encounters. And when it realizes that it has been born to join a fellowship of citizens, it will decide to use, not just that subtle method of arguing, but also a more expansive and continuous style* of speech. With such an instrument it will rule nations, reinforce laws, castigate the wicked, protect the good, praise eminent men, issue instructions for security and prestige in language which will persuade fellow-citizens; it will be able to inspire them to honourable actions and restrain them from disgrace; to console the afflicted, and to hand on the deeds and counsels of brave and wise men, along with the infamy of the wicked, in words that will last for ever. Those are the powers, so manifold and so momentous, that can be discerned in a human being by those who wish to know themselves. And the parent and nurse of those powers is wisdom.

ATTICUS: All you say in her honour is impressive and true; but what is the object of all this?

63 MARCUS: First of all, Pomponius, it has a bearing on the subjects which we are now about to deal with, and which we regard as profoundly important. For they will not have that importance unless they are seen to derive from truths of the most far-reaching kind. Secondly, I take pleasure in praising philosophy, and I hope I am right in refusing to pass over in silence a subject which I study devotedly and which has made me whatever I am.

ATTICUS: Quite right. Your tribute was well deserved and from the heart; and, as you say, it was right to include it in this discussion.

BOOK 2

1–7. The scene is set

ATTICUS: Well, we've walked far enough now; and you have to 1 start another section of your talk. So shall we have a change of scene and find somewhere to sit down on that island in the Fibrenus (I believe that's what the other river is called)? Then we can turn our attention to the rest of the discussion.

MARCUS: By all means. That place is a favourite haunt of mine, whether I'm reading, writing, or just thinking.

ATTICUS: As far as I'm concerned, I can't get too much of it, 2 especially now that it's summer. I think nothing of splendid villas with their marble floors and coffered ceilings. As for the artificial channels which our friends call 'Niles' or 'Euripuses',* you can't help laughing at them when faced with scenery like this. A little while ago, when you were talking about law and justice, you saw nature as the key to everything. Similarly, nature is queen of all those places ,where we go in search of mental relaxation and delight. I used to wonder (for I thought there was nothing here except rocks* and mountains, and indeed your speeches and poems gave me that impression)—I used, as I say, to wonder why you were so fond of this place; now, however, I wonder why, when you're out of town, you go anywhere else.

MARCUS: Yes, when it's possible to get away for more than a 3 day or two, especially at this time of year, I head for this beautiful and healthy spot. Unfortunately, it rarely *is* possible. But I suppose I love it for another reason too—one which will not weigh with you, Titus.

ATTICUS: Really? What's that?

MARCUS: Well, to tell you the truth, this is the actual country where I, and my brother here, were born. Yes, we come from a very old local family; we are associated with the place by religious and ancestral ties; and there are many traces of our forebears in the district. Why, I need go no further than that villa. You see how it is now. It was rebuilt, thanks to my father's enthusiasm, on a more lavish scale. As he was in poor health, he spent most of his time here among his books. I was born in this very place, you know, when my grandfather was alive and the house was a small one in the old-fashioned style, like Curius' home in the Sabine country. So there's something deep in my heart and soul which gives me, perhaps, a special affection for the spot. As you will recall, that eminently sensible man* is said to have refused immortality so that he might see Ithaca once again.

4   ATTICUS: That's a good reason, I think, for being fond of the place and coming here in preference to anywhere else. I myself have now become more attached to that house—yes, really—and indeed to the whole locality in which you were born and bred. For we are in some way moved by places associated with those whom we love and respect. Why even in my beloved Athens I do not enjoy the splendid buildings and the superb works of ancient art as much as the recollection of those outstanding men—where they each used to live and sit and conduct their discussions. I even gaze at their tombs with reverence. So from now on I shall think more kindly of this place because you were born here.

MARCUS: Well I'm glad that I've shown you what is virtually my cradle.

5   ATTICUS: And I'm glad to have seen it. But what did you mean by saying a few moments ago that this place, by which I assume you mean Arpinum, is your actual country? Have you *two* countries? Surely we all have just one? Or can it be that the country of Cato, that fount of wisdom, was not Rome but Tusculum?*

MARCUS: Yes, I maintain that he and all people from small towns have two countries, one by nature and the other by citizenship. By being born in Tusculum Cato was admitted to Roman citizenship. So he was a Tusculan by birth and a Roman by citizenship. One of his countries was local, the other legal. Your Attic friends, before Theseus ordered them all to leave the countryside and move into the city (or the *astu*, as it is called) belonged both to their own towns and to Attica. In the same way we think of our country both as our place of birth and as the one which admitted us to citizenship. But the one which takes its name from the state as a whole should have first place in our affections. That is the country for which we should be willing to die, to which we should devote ourselves heart and soul, and on whose altar we should dedicate and consecrate all that is ours. Yet the one which gave us birth is dear to us in a way not very different from that which took us in. And so I shall always insist that this is my country, even though the other is greater and includes this within it.*

ATTICUS: So our friend Pompey the Great was right when, 6 during his defence of Ampius (which he shared with you) he stated in court, in my hearing, that our country owed an enormous debt of gratitude to this town, in that her two saviours* had come from it. So I think I am now persuaded that this place which gave you birth is also your mother-country.

But we're now on the island. What could be more delightful? Like the bow of a ship, it cuts through the Fibrenus, dividing the river into two streams of equal width, which lap against its sides. Then, flowing quickly by, they soon come together again, enclosing an area large enough for a fair-sized wrestling-place. After that, as if its duty and function were to provide us with a venue for our debate, it immediately tumbles into the Liris, losing its less famous name as though it were joining an aristocratic family, and making the Liris much colder. Though I've visited many rivers, I've never come across one colder than this. I can hardly bear to dip my foot in it, as Socrates does in Plato's *Phaedrus*.*

MARCUS: That's right. But I imagine that your Tyamis* in 7 Epirus, which Quintus often speaks of, is in no way inferior in beauty.

QUINTUS: Yes indeed. You mustn't assume that anything is more impressive than our friend Atticus' Amaltheum* with its plane trees. But if no one objects, let's sit down here in the shade and resume our discussion at the point where we left off.

MARCUS: You're quite right to dun me, Quintus, though I thought I had escaped. You won't allow any debts to remain outstanding!

QUINTUS: Make a start, then; we're giving you the whole of the day.

7–17. Recapitulation of natural law

MARCUS: 'With Jupiter the Muse begins . . .' as I said at the opening of my version of Aratus' poem.*

QUINTUS: What's the point of that?

MARCUS: Because I too must now begin this enterprise with Jupiter and the other deathless gods.

8   QUINTUS: Yes, Marcus. That's very appropriate, and it's what you ought to do.

MARCUS: Well then, before we come to individual laws, let us look once more at the significance and nature of law. Since everything we say must be guided by that concept, we have to ensure that we don't occasionally go astray through a misuse of language and forget the importance of reason, on which our laws must be founded.

QUINTUS: Yes, that seems the right way of developing your thesis.

MARCUS: I note, then, that according to the opinion of the best authorities* law was not thought up by the intelligence of human beings, nor is it some kind of resolution passed by communities, but rather an eternal force* which rules the world by the wisdom of its commands and prohibitions. In their judgement, that original and final law is the intelligence of God, who ordains or forbids everything by reason. Hence that law which the gods have given to the human race is rightly praised, for it represents the reason and intelligence of a wise man directed to issuing commands and prohibitions.

9   QUINTUS: You have touched on that subject on a number of previous occasions. But before you come to the laws of human communities, would you please explain the significance of that divine law. That will save us from being swept along and dragged by the tide of custom into the manner of everyday speech.

MARCUS: Since our childhood, Quintus, we have been taught to call 'If [*plaintiff*] summon [*defendant*] to court',* and other things of that kind, laws. But one must understand that this and other orders and prohibitions issued by communities have the power of encouraging people to right actions and deterring them from wrongdoing. That power is not only older than the existence of communities and states; it is coeval with that god who watches
10   over and rules heaven and earth. The divine mind cannot be without reason, and divine reason must have this power to decide on good and evil actions. Even though it was nowhere laid down that one man should stand on the bridge against the whole of the

enemy's army and should order the bridge to be cut down behind him, we will continue to think that the famous Cocles performed that great deed according to the commands and dictates of bravery. And even if in the reign of Lucius Tarquinius there was no written law at Rome against acts of rape, nonetheless Sextus Tarquinius contravened that eternal law in violating Lucretia the daughter of Tricipitinus. For reason existed—reason derived from the nature of the universe, impelling people to right actions and restraining them from wrong. That reason did not first become law when it was written down, but rather when it came into being. And it came into being at the same time as the divine mind. Therefore the authentic original law, whose function is to command and forbid, is the right reason of Jupiter, Lord of all.

QUINTUS: I agree, Marcus, that what is right and true is also 11 eternal, and does not come into force or lapse with the letters in which enactments are written down.

MARCUS: Well then, as the divine mind is the highest law, so, in the case of a human being, when reason is fully developed, that is law; and it *is* fully developed in the mind of the wise man. Those laws, however, which have been formulated in various terms to meet the temporary needs of communities, enjoy the name of laws thanks to popular approval rather than actual fact. We are taught that every law (or at least those which are properly entitled to the name) is praiseworthy by arguments such as these: it is agreed, of course, that laws were devised to ensure the safety of citizens, the security of states, and the peaceful happy life of human beings; and that those who first passed such enactments showed their communities that they meant to frame and enact measures which, when accepted and adopted, would allow them to live happy and honourable lives; provisions composed and endorsed in this way would, of course, be given the name of laws. From this it is reasonable to infer that those who framed harmful and unjust rules for their communities, acting in a way quite contrary to their claims and promises, introduced measures which were anything but laws. So when it comes to interpreting the word, it is clear that inherent in the very name of law is the sense and idea of choosing* what is just and right.

So I ask you, Quintus, as those gentlemen* are wont to do: if 12 a state lacks a certain element, and if precisely because of that lack it does not deserve to be called a state, is that element to be regarded as a good thing?

QUINTUS: Yes, a very good thing.

MARCUS: And if a state lacks law, does it deserve to lose the name of state?

QUINTUS: It certainly does.

MARCUS: So law must be reckoned a good thing.

QUINTUS: I quite agree.

13   MARCUS: What of the fact that many harmful and pernicious measures are passed in human communities—measures which come no closer to the name of laws than if a gang of criminals agreed to make some rules? If ignorant unqualified people prescribe a lethal, instead of a healing, treatment, that treatment cannot properly be called 'medical'. In a community a law of just any kind will not be a law, even if the people (in spite of its harmful character) have accepted it. Therefore law means drawing a distinction between just and unjust, formulated in accordance with that most ancient and most important of all things—nature; by her, human laws are guided in punishing the wicked and defending and protecting the good.

QUINTUS: I quite understand. I now think that no other kind should be given the status or even the name of law.

14   MARCUS: So you think that the laws of Titius and Apuleius were really non-laws?

QUINTUS: Quite. And I think the same applies to those of Livius.

MARCUS: Right—especially as they were rescinded by the Senate in one brief phrase without any waste of time. But the law whose dynamic nature I have explained cannot be rescinded or repealed.

QUINTUS: So you, I suppose, will introduce laws of a kind that can never be repealed.

MARCUS: Certainly—provided they are accepted by the two of you! But I think I must follow the precedent of Plato, that most learned man and most weighty of thinkers. He first wrote about the state and later added a separate work about the laws. Before setting out the legal code itself, I shall say some words in praise of it. I notice that Zaleucus and Charondas did the same when they framed laws for their states, not just for the sake of interest and pleasure, but for the benefit of their communities. Obviously Plato was copying them when he maintained that this, too, was a property of law, that it should obtain a measure of consent* instead of imposing everything by threats of violence.

QUINTUS: What about the fact that Timaeus denies that your 15 Zaleucus ever existed?

MARCUS: But Theophrastus says he did exist; and he, in my view, is just as good an authority (many consider him better). Why our own fellow-citizens, the Locrians, who are my clients, cherish his memory. But whether he existed or not doesn't matter. I'm talking about tradition.

So the citizens should first of all be convinced of this, that the gods are lords and masters of everything; that what is done is done by their decision and authority; that they are, moreover, great benefactors of mankind and observe what kind of person everyone is—his actions and misdemeanours, his attitude and devotion to religious duties—and take note of the pious and the impious. Minds imbued with these facts will surely not deviate from true 16 and wholesome ideas. What can be more certain than this, that no one should be so stupid and so arrogant as to believe that reason and intelligence are present in him but not in the heavens and the world? Or that those things which are barely understood by the highest intellectual reasoning are kept in motion without any intelligence at all? As for the person who is not impelled to give thanks for the procession of the stars,* the alternation of day and night, the regular succession of the seasons, and the fruits which are produced for our enjoyment—how can such a person be counted as human at all? Since everything that possesses intelligence is superior to what lacks intelligence, and since it would be impious to claim that anything was superior to universal nature, it has to be admitted* that universal nature possesses intelligence. Who would deny that these ideas were useful, bearing in mind how many contracts are strengthened by the swearing of oaths, how valuable religious scruples are for guaranteeing treaties, how many people are restrained from crime by the fear of divine retribution, and how sacred a thing a partnership of citizens is when the immortal gods are admitted to that company as judges or witnesses?

There you are. That is what Plato calls the preamble to the legal code.*

17 QUINTUS: Thank you for presenting it, Marcus. I am very pleased that you are concerned with different issues and different ideas from Plato's. What you said earlier was quite unlike his approach, and the same is true of this introduction about the gods. As far as I can see, the only thing you imitate is his literary style.

MARCUS: *Wish* to imitate, perhaps. For no one is, or ever will be, able to imitate that. It is very easy to render the ideas; I would do that if I were not determined to be myself. But what challenge is there in presenting the same thoughts in an almost literal translation?

QUINTUS: I do agree. I would rather you remained yourself, as you've just said. But now, if you will, please set out those laws about religion.

18–22. Religious laws

18 MARCUS: I'll do the best I can; and although our discussion and its setting are private,* I shall present the laws in the voice of the laws.

QUINTUS: And what, may I ask, is that?

MARCUS: There are certain legal phrases, Quintus, which, though not as old as those in the ancient Twelve Tables and Sacred Laws,* are yet somewhat older than the style of our present conversation so as to carry greater authority. I shall follow that manner, with its brevity, as best I can. The laws which I shall promulgate will not be complete in detail (that would be an endless task), but will present the gist and sense of the provisions.

QUINTUS: I'm sure that's the only way to proceed. Let's hear
19 them, then.

MARCUS: They shall approach the gods in purity; they shall adopt a spirit of holiness; they shall set aside wealth. God himself will punish whoever does otherwise.

No one shall have gods of his own, whether new or foreign, unless they have been officially brought in. In private they shall worship those gods whose worship has been handed down in its proper form by their forefathers.

In the cities they shall have shrines; in the countryside they shall have groves and abodes for their tutelary gods.

They shall preserve the rituals of their family and fathers.

They shall worship as gods those who have always been considered divine and those whose services have secured them a place in heaven—Hercules, Liber,* Aesculapius, Castor, Pollux, Quirinus—and also those qualities on whose account human beings are allowed to ascend to heaven—Good Sense, Moral Excellence, Devotion, Good Faith. In their honour there shall be shrines, but none in honour of vices.

They shall observe the established rites.

On holidays they shall abstain from lawsuits, and they shall hold these holidays in the company of* their slaves when their tasks have been finished; and so that it may occur thus let it be arranged at recurrent intervals throughout the year. The priests shall offer in public certain crops and certain fruits—this according to fixed rites and on fixed days. Likewise they shall keep for 20 other days an abundance of milk and young; and to ensure that this be not transgressed the priests shall lay down the procedure and the annual sequence for that sacrifice; and they shall decide which victims are appropriate and welcome to each divinity.

Different divinities shall have different priests; all together shall have pontiffs; individually they shall have *flamines*.* And in the city the Vestal Virgins shall watch over the undying fire on the public hearth.

Those who are unfamiliar with the methods and rituals for conducting these private and public ceremonies shall seek guidance from the public priests. Of these there shall be three kinds: one to preside over ceremonies and sacred rites, and another to interpret the strange utterances of prophets and seers which the Senate and people have accepted. In addition, the interpreters of Jupiter the Best and Greatest, that is, the public augurs, shall divine the future by means of signs and omens and maintain their art. And the 21 priests shall pay attention to vineyards and patches of withies* and the safety of the people.* They shall give prior warning about omens to those who are engaged in the business of war or state, and those groups shall take heed of them. They shall foresee the anger of the gods and react appropriately. They shall take measures to neutralise flashes of lightning in fixed quarters of the sky,* and they shall keep the city and the countryside and their ancestral fields of observation mapped out and free of obstruction. And whatever an augur shall pronounce unjust, unholy, harmful, or ill-omened shall be null and void. And if anyone fails to obey, that shall be a capital offence.

The fetial priests* shall act as judges in the name of the people* concerning the ratification of treaties, peace, war, and truces; and they shall decide about questions of war.

Prodigies and portents shall, if the senate so decrees, be referred to Etruscan soothsayers,* and Etruria shall instruct her leading men in that art. They shall sacrifice in expiation to whatever gods they think fit, and they shall also make atonement in response to flashes of lightning and to the striking of certain places.

No nocturnal sacrifices shall be conducted by women except those which shall take place in due form on behalf of the people;* and they shall initiate no one into any mysteries, except those of Ceres* through the Greek rite, as custom allows.

22   An act of sacrilege* which cannot be expiated shall be deemed to have been impiously committed; that which can be expiated* shall be expiated by the official priests.

At public games, where there is no chariot-racing and no athletic competitions, they shall make provision* for the people's joy by singing, accompanied by strings and pipes, and they shall associate that pleasure with the honour of the gods.*

Of ancestral rites they shall observe the best.*

Except for the slaves of the Idaean Mother* (and in their case only on specially appointed days) no one shall take up collections.

Anyone who steals or makes away with a sacred object or an object lodged in a sacred place shall be deemed a parricide.*

The divine punishment of perjury* is death, the human punishment disgrace.

The priests shall inflict the ultimate penalty on a person found guilty of incest.*

Let not an impious man dare to placate the gods' anger with gifts.

Let them be scrupulous in fulfilling their vows; there shall be a penalty for breaking a promise.

No one shall consecrate a field.* Let there be moderation* in dedicating gold, silver, and ivory.

Private religious observances* shall be continued in perpetuity. The rights of the spirits of the dead shall be holy. Good men who have died shall be held to be gods. The money spent on them, and the mourning* over them, shall be kept small.

23–69. Comments on the foregoing laws

QUINTUS: How little time it has taken you, Marcus, to cover 23 this large body of law! But as far as I can see, this set of religious regulations is not very different from the laws of Numa and the customs of our country.

MARCUS: Well, Africanus apparently established in the books on the Republic that of all forms of government our old Roman one was the best. So don't you think we are bound to provide laws which are in keeping with the best constitution?

QUINTUS: Why yes; I think we are.

MARCUS: In that case you should expect laws which will maintain that superior type of government. And if I happen to propose some measures today which do not exist in our state and never have, they will nevertheless figure as a rule in our ancestors' tradition, which at that time had the force of law.

ATTICUS: Well then, would you please argue in support of your 24 body of law, so that I may be able to say 'as you propose'.*

MARCUS: Really, Atticus? Are you not going to speak against it?

ATTICUS: I shall certainly not vote against you on any major issue.

MARCUS: On smaller matters,* if you wish, I shall let you off* agreeing with me!

QUINTUS: Yes, I take the same view as Atticus.

MARCUS: Mind now, this may take some time!

ATTICUS: I hope it will. There's nothing we'd rather be doing.

MARCUS: The law bids us approach the gods 'in purity', that is, with a pure heart. That embraces everything. It does not dispense with the need for bodily purity, but one has to understand that since the heart is far superior to the body, and since care is generally taken to make the body clean when it approaches the gods, purity must be much more scrupulously observed in the case of the heart. The body's impurity is removed with a sprinkling of water or by the lapse of time, whereas impurity of heart cannot fade with time, nor can it be washed away by any river.

25   As for 'adopting a spirit of holiness' and 'setting aside wealth', that means that goodness of character is pleasing to God, and that extravagance should be given no place. After all, we would like poverty to be on an equal footing with wealth even among men; so why should we make it impossible for poverty to approach the gods by making extravagance a feature of our ceremonies, especially as nothing is likely to be less pleasing to God himself than that the path to appeasing and worshipping him should not be open to all. Moreover, the fact that god himself, not some judge, is appointed to inflict punishment clearly reinforces religion by the fear of retribution.

That an individual's 'own gods, whether new or foreign'* should be worshipped causes confusion among religions and
26   introduces rites which are unfamiliar to our priests. It is resolved that 'those gods whose worship has been handed down by their fathers' should be worshipped, provided that their fathers themselves have obeyed this command.

I hold that there should be 'shrines in the cities'. I do not follow the Persian priests* on whose advice Xerxes is said to have burnt the temples of Greece on the grounds that they enclosed within their walls gods for whom every place should be open and free, and whose temple and home consisted of the entire world. The Greeks and our ancestors had a sounder idea. To promote piety towards the gods, they wished them to inhabit the same cities as we do. This belief fosters a religion which is advantageous to states, if that most learned man, Pythagoras, was right when he said* that piety and religion are uppermost in our minds when we are attending to divine observances. Thales, too, who was the wisest of the Seven Sages, said* that people should believe that everything they saw was full of gods; then everyone would be more pure in heart, just as people are when they are in the most sacred temples. For we have, according to common opinion,* a visual as well as a mental conception of the gods. That is also the point of having 'groves in the countryside'.*

27   Again, the worship of the Lares* handed down by our fore-

fathers, established for master and slave alike within sight of the farm and villa, is not abandoned. 'To preserve the rituals of their family and fathers': that is, to retain the religion handed down, as it were, by the gods, since the further back one goes in time the nearer one gets to the gods.

That the law enjoins the worship of deified human beings like Hercules and others indicates that, while the souls of all are immortal, those of the brave and good are divine.* It is right that 28 'Good Sense,* Devotion,* Moral Excellence,* and Good Faith'* should be deified; and in Rome temples have long been publicly dedicated* to those qualities, so that those who possess them (and all good people do) should believe that actual gods have been set up within their souls. At Athens, after atoning for the crime against Cylon, on the advice of the Cretan Epimenides they built a shrine to Insult and Shamelessness.* That was a misguided act; for virtues, not vices, should be deified. The ancient altar to Fever* on the Palatine, and the other to Evil Fortune* on the Esquiline must be refused recognition, and all things of that kind are to be rejected. If we have to devise names, we should choose rather ones like Conquering Power and Protectress, and titles like Jove the Stopper* and the Invincible, and names of desirable things like Safety, Honour, Help, and Victory. Because the spirit is raised by the expectation of good things, Hope* was rightly deified by Calatinus. And let Today's Fortune* be acknowledged as a deity, for it has influence over every day, or Fortune the Heedful,* that she may send help, or Chance Fortune* in cases where uncertain events are particularly indicated, or First-born Fortune* from giving birth.

Next, the system of holidays and festivals involves, in the case 29 of free men, a respite from lawsuits and disputes; in the case of slaves, a rest from work and toil. The official who draws up the calendar must have regard to the completion of various agricultural tasks. As for the dates, careful account should be taken of intercalation* to ensure that the offerings of first fruits and young, as mentioned in the law, are maintained. That practice was wisely introduced by Numa, but has now lapsed owing to the negligence of later pontiffs. The rule laid down by the pontiffs and sooth-sayers should not be changed—I mean the rule governing which animals should be sacrificed to which god (which god should receive larger victims, which unweaned victims, which male, which female). The custom of having a number of priests for 'all the gods together' and separate priests for each facilitates the interpretation of the law and the discharge of religious duties. Since Vesta,* as she is called—a name derived from the Greek, which we retain almost in its Greek form without translating it— takes into her protective embrace, so to speak, the hearth of the city, six virgins should be in charge of her worship, so that a more efficient watch may be kept on the maintenance of the fire, and so that women may be aware that their sex is capable of practis- ing strict chastity.

30   The next measure has to do not only with religion but also with the state of the country. It is to the effect that people cannot ade- quately attend to religion in the home without the guidance of the officials who are in charge of public ceremonies. The people's con- tinual need of the advice and authority of the aristocracy holds the state together.

The classification of priests* takes account of every legitimate kind of religion. Some are appointed to appease the gods by taking charge of regular religious rites; others to interpret the utterances of seers (though not of many, for that would be an endless busi- ness; also care must be taken that no one outside the priestly college should know the particular prophecies that have been offi-

31 cially recognized). The greatest and most prestigious power in the state is that of the augurs, combined, as it is, with political author- ity. I don't say this because I'm an augur myself* but simply because one cannot think otherwise. If we consider their official rights, what is more impressive than the ability to dismiss assem- blies and meetings called by magistrates (with or without *imperium*), or, when they have already taken place, to cancel their decisions? What is more momentous than the abortion of a process already begun, if one augur says 'On another day'? What is more majestic than the right to decide that consuls should resign their office? What is more awesome than the power to grant or withhold the right to do political business with the people or plebs? Or than quashing laws illegally approved, as when the Titian Law* was annulled by the decree of the college, or when the Livian Laws* were cancelled on the recommendation of Philip- pus who was both consul and augur? Or than the fact that nothing

done by any official at home or in the field can receive the approval of any body without their permission?

ATTICUS: Well now, I see and admit that such powers are con- 32 siderable. But in your college there is a serious disagreement* between Marcellus and Appius, both excellent augurs. (I know, because I came across their books.) One contends that auspices were invented to serve the practical purposes of the state; the other believes that your art can, as it were, predict the future. Tell me, what do you think about that question?

MARCUS: What do I think? Well, I think that divination, which the Greeks call *mantike*, exists, and that the particular area which has to do with birds and other signs comes within the scope of our art. For if we grant that the gods exist, that the world is ruled by their will, that they also care for the welfare of mankind, and are able to show us signs of future events, I don't see why I should deny the existence of divination. The assumptions I have made are 33 true; so the conclusion that I want follows from them, and is, indeed, necessary. Furthermore, our country, like every kingdom, every community, and every nation, is full of numerous instances in which many an augur's prediction has come true, despite all the odds. The names of Polyidus, Melampus, Mopsus, Amphiaraus, Calchas, and Helenus could never have become so famous, nor would so many nations have retained their reputation to the present day (e.g. the Phrygians, Lycaonians, Cilicians, and especially the Pisidians), had not antiquity shown that such things were true. Nor would our own Romulus have founded the city by means of augury, nor would the name of Attus Navius have survived so long and so vigorously in people's memory, had not all these men uttered many predictions which were surprisingly confirmed by events.

Yet there is no doubt that the art and skill have now vanished as the result of age and neglect. So I do not agree* with the man who denies that this skill ever existed in our college, nor with the one who thinks it is still alive today. Among our ancestors it had, I think, a dual function, i.e. it occasionally played a role in times of national crisis, but most often it influenced practical decisions.

ATTICUS: I absolutely agree,* and I think your account is the 34 most convincing. But let us have the rest.

MARCUS: I shall indeed, as briefly as I can. We next come to the law governing war.* In my law I have enacted that in beginning, waging, and ending ·a war justice and good faith should be the most influential factors, and that there should be official spokesmen in connection with such matters. As for the soothsayers' rites, expiations, and atonements, I think they have been set down clearly enough in the law itself.

ATTICUS: I agree; all the pronouncements in question have to do with religion.

MARCUS: But I do wonder, Titus, how you can agree with what comes next, or how I can refute you.

35   ATTICUS: And what, may I ask, is that?

MARCUS: The provision about women's nocturnal sacrifices.

ATTICUS: But I do agree with that, especially as in the law itself you make an exception of the regular official sacrifices.

MARCUS: What, then, will become of our Iacchus and Eumolpidae* and their solemn mysteries if we abolish nocturnal rites? For we are framing laws, not just for the Roman people, but for all good and stable communities.

36   ATTICUS: I take it you make an exception of those rites into which we ourselves have been initiated.

MARCUS: Yes, I shall do so. For I think your beloved Athens has brought to birth, and contributed to human life, many outstanding and divine creations, and nothing better than those mysteries. Thanks to them we have become mild and cultivated, moving from a rough and savage life to a state of civilization; we have learned from so-called 'initiations' things which are in fact the first principles of life, and we have been taught a way of living happily and also of dying with brighter hopes. What I dislike about nocturnal festivals is illustrated by the comic poets.* Had such licence existed in Rome, what, one wonders, would that fellow* have done—the one who, with lustful intentions, intruded on a sacrifice where not even an involuntary glance was permitted?

ATTICUS: By all means bring in such a ban for Rome, but do not take our ⟨Athenian⟩ laws away from us.

37   MARCUS: I return, then, to mine. We must certainly take great care to ensure that the good name of women is safeguarded by the clear light of day when many eyes are upon them, and that they shall be initiated into the mysteries of Ceres according to

those rites which are practised in Rome. Our ancestors' strictness
in such matters is shown by the old senatorial resolution about
the Bacchanalia,* and by the consuls' inquiry and punishments,
supported by military force. In case we may perhaps seem rather
harsh, the Theban Diagondas in central Greece suppressed all nocturnal rituals by law in perpetuity. Strange gods, and the ceremonies in their honour which turned night into day, were satirized
by Aristophanes, the wittiest poet of the Old Comedy. In his
work* Sabazius and other foreign deities were prosecuted and
banished from the state.

To resume: an unintentional infringement must be carefully
atoned for; in this way the official priest should relieve the
offender from anxiety. But he should condemn and denounce as
sacrilege ⟨outrageous and deliberate breaches of religious law⟩.

Next, as the public games are divided between theatre and race-
course, athletic contests should take place on the race-course in
running, boxing, and wrestling, and also in chariot-racing until
undisputed winners emerge. The theatre should be alive with song,
accompanied by strings and pipes, provided such performances
are kept within due bounds as the law requires. I agree with Plato*
that nothing can so easily influence young and impressionable
minds as the variety of vocal sounds. One can hardly express what
an enormous power that exerts for better or worse. It animates
the sluggish and calms the excited; now it relaxes the emotions,
now it makes them tense. In Greece many states would have benefited from retaining the old-fashioned manner of singing. As it
was, their characters changed along with their singing and degen-
erated into effeminacy. Either they were corrupted, as some think,
by the sweet seductiveness of the music, or, after their sternness
had been subverted by other vices, their ears and souls became
changed, leaving room for this musical change too.

That is why Greece's greatest thinker and by far her most
learned scholar was very worried about this deadly infection. He
maintains that the laws of music* cannot be changed without
bringing a change in the laws of the state. I myself do not think
the phenomenon is so alarming, nor yet do I think it should simply
be waved aside. I do notice how in theatres which once used to
be filled with the agreeable plainness of Livius' and Naevius' tunes
audiences now rock to and fro jerking their necks and eyes in time

with the inflexions of the singer's voice. Ancient Greece used to punish that sort of thing severely. It foresaw far in advance that the deadly plague, gradually creeping into the citizens' minds and infecting them with pernicious crazes and pernicious ideas, would suddenly bring about the collapse of entire states—if, indeed, it is true that Sparta, which was famed for its severity, ordered every string which Timotheus had on his instrument beyond the number seven to be cut out.

40   Next in the body of law is the provision that 'the best of the ancestral rites' should be observed. When the Athenians consulted Pythian Apollo* about what ceremonies in particular they should retain, the following reply was given: 'those which were customary amongst your ancestors'. When they returned, saying that their ancestral custom had often changed, and asking what custom out of the many they should choose to follow, they were told 'the best'. It is certainly true that whatever is best should be considered the oldest and the nearest to God.

I have abolished all collections except the one which is devoted specifically to the Idaean Mother and lasts just a few days.* Such practices fill a man's mind with superstition and empty his pocket.

41   A person who commits sacrilege is liable to punishment. This means not only one who has stolen 'a sacred object' but also one who has stolen 'an object lodged in a sacred place'. Nowadays too deposits are frequently made in temples. When in Cilicia, Alexander* is supposed to have put money in a shrine at Soli. And they say that the eminent Athenian, Cleisthenes,* when he was apprehensive about his fortunes, placed his daughters' dowries in the care of Juno at Samos.

As for perjury and incest, I assume there is no need for any comment here.

Impious men are not 'to dare to placate the gods with gifts'. They should pay attention to Plato,* who forbids anyone to doubt what God's reaction to this will be; after all, no good *man* is prepared to accept gifts from a villain.

Enough has been said in the law about the need to be scrupulous in fulfilling vows. ⟨For nothing is more binding than⟩ the contract by which we are tied to God by vows. There is surely no justified objection to the penalty imposed* for breaking a holy promise. I need not adduce here examples of wicked men;

tragedies are full of them. Instead I shall mention briefly actual events of which everyone is aware. I suspect that the instance which I am about to recall may seem to lie beyond the scale of an ordinary person's experience; still, since I am talking to *you*, I shall reveal everything in the hope that what I say will seem welcome to the immortal gods rather than objectionable to men.

On my departure* all the laws of religion were sullied by vile 42 and criminal citizens. My domestic gods were cast down; in their place a temple of Licence* was erected; the man who had watched over their shrines was expelled. Consider for a moment (there is no point in mentioning names) the results which ensued. When all my property had been seized and destroyed, I refused to allow the deity who was the guardian of the city* to be desecrated by unholy men; I conveyed her from my house to the house of the Father himself. For doing so I won from the Senate, from Italy, and from every nation in the world the verdict that I had saved my country. And what more splendid experience than that could a man have? As for those who by their crimes cast down and trampled on religion, some of them are broken up and scattered in obscurity. The ringleaders in those crimes, who outdid the rest in the profanation of all that was sacred, suffered every kind of agony and disgrace in their lives, and in addition were deprived of a burial and of proper funeral rites.

QUINTUS: Yes, I'm aware of all this, Marcus; and I'm duly 43 grateful to the gods. Yet all too often we see things turning out rather differently.

MARCUS: That is because we have false notions, Quintus, about the nature of divine punishment. We lapse into common misconceptions and fail to notice the truth. We gauge human unhappiness by death, or physical pain, or mental suffering, or an adverse verdict. I grant that these are normal human experiences which have happened to many good men. But crime involves a grim retribution—one which is intrinsically of the utmost severity over and above the legal consequences. I have seen men who would never have been my enemies had they not loathed their country, consumed by greed or fear, or the guilty knowledge of what they were doing, at one moment fearing, at another despising, religion and the courts which they had also subverted by bribing not gods but men.

44 I shall stop there and not pursue the indictment further, especially as I have obtained a greater revenge than I sought. I shall just put the matter briefly in this way: divine punishment is twofold; it involves harassing the minds of the guilty during life and, when they are dead, attaching such infamy to them that the living not only accept but also rejoice at their destruction.

45 Fields are not to be consecrated. I entirely agree with Plato, who uses roughly the following language, if I can translate him: 'The earth, then, like a domestic hearth, is sacred to all the gods; so no one should consecrate it twice over. Gold and silver in cities, whether in private houses or temples, arouse envy. Again, ivory, taken as it is from an animal's carcass, is not sufficiently clean for a god. Bronze and iron are the paraphernalia of war, not of a temple. Whatever wooden object one wishes, however, may be dedicated in public temples, provided it is made of a single piece of wood; a stone object is also permissible, and so is a piece of textile, provided it has not taken more than a month's work on the part of a woman. White is the colour most appropriate to a god in all offerings, and especially in the case of textiles. Dyed material should be avoided except for military insignia. The most holy gifts are birds, and pictures painted by one artist in a single day. Other gifts, too, should be along similar lines.' Those are Plato's wishes.* But in general I do not prescribe such narrow rules, for I make concessions to people's shortcomings and the resources available in our day. And I suspect that agriculture will decline if any superstition develops in regard to the use of the land and its subjection to the ploughshare.

ATTICUS: I've grasped all that. It now remains for you to deal with 'perpetual observances' and 'the rights of the spirits of the dead'.

MARCUS: What an astonishing memory you've got, Pomponius! I'd forgotten those points.

46 ATTICUS: No doubt you had; but I remember them and I'm waiting to hear them discussed, especially because they have to do with both pontifical and civil law.

MARCUS: That's true. Great experts have delivered many oral and written opinions about these matters. During this talk I mean to take up as best I can what our civil law says about every branch of law to which our discussion leads me. But I shall only go so far as to clarify the point on which each part of the law is based. In this way it will not be difficult (at least for anyone of normal intelligence) to grasp the law governing whatever new case or problem occurs, because he will know under what heading to look it up.

But legal experts, whether to cause confusion and so give the 47 appearance of having a wider and deeper knowledge than they do, or (more probably) through their incompetence at putting the subject across (for an art is not just a matter of knowing something; it is also a matter of communication) often endlessly subdivide a thing which is based on a single idea. In the case of this very subject, for example, how vast it is made by the two Scaevolas, both of whom are pontiffs and at the same time experts in law! Publius' son* says, 'I often heard my father maintain that no one makes a good pontiff unless he knows civil law.' The *whole* of civil law? Why so? What has a pontiff to do with regulations about party-walls or the water supply or anything else except what is concerned with religion? And think how small an area that is. It is confined, I take it, to rituals, vows, festivals, graves, and other such things. Why, then, do we make so much of this topic, when all the other related matters are so very small, and when even the area of ritual, which is of wider consequence, is covered by one provision, namely that these ceremonies should be preserved for ever and handed down within families generation by generation, and, in the words of my law, 'should be continued in perpetuity'? These regulations decreed by the pontiffs ensure 48 that the observances should not be forgotten when the father of a family dies; for they require that such observances should be continued by those who have benefited financially from the father's death.

When this simple rule had been laid down—a rule which is quite adequate for understanding the system—countless others appeared, filling the books of the legal experts. An attempt has been made to determine who should be obliged to carry out the rites. In the case of heirs,* the answer is entirely reasonable, for they are the deceased's immediate next of kin. Then comes the person who, as a result of the man's death or will, receives as much as all the heirs put together. He, too, should accept the obligation, for that is in line with the intention of the rule. In the third place, if there is no heir, the duty devolves upon the man who has acquired by possession the greatest amount of the deceased's property at the time of his death. Fourthly, if no one has acquired anything, the duty falls on the creditor who retains the largest part 49 of the estate. Last of all is the person who owed money to the deceased and did not repay it to anyone; he should be treated as if he had received that money from the estate.

We have learned these categories from Scaevola. The ancients distinguished them differently. They presented the law in these terms: the obligation to conduct rites is imposed in three ways— by inheritance, or by receiving the greater part of the property, or, if the greater part of the property has been distributed in bequests, by receiving anything from that source. But let us 50 follow the pontiff.* You notice that everything is based on one principle, namely the pontiffs' wish that the rites should go with the deceased's property, and their opinion that holidays and rites should be held by the same people. The Scaevolas add that, when an estate is divided, if no deductions have been stipulated* in the will, and the legatees have voluntarily received less than has been left to all the heirs together, they should not be obliged to perform the rites. In the case of a gift* they interpret the rule in a different way. Where a gift has been made by a person who is under the authority of the head of the family, that gift is valid if made with the approval of the latter. If it was made without his knowledge, it is not valid, unless he gives his retrospective approval.

51   From these provisions many minor problems arise. But surely an intelligent person will easily see his way through them if he bears in mind the fundamental principle. Suppose, for instance, a man accepted* less to avoid the obligation of performing the rites, and later one of this man's heirs collected on his own account the sum which had been waived by the man whose heir he was; and suppose that this sum, combined with the earlier sum acquired, came to no less than had been left to all the other heirs together, then the man who had collected the money would be bound to perform the rites on his own, without his co-heirs. The authorities have even provided that, where someone has received a larger bequest than he can accept without incurring religious duties, he should formally declare* through bronze and balance that the

heirs' obligations under the will have been discharged. In that situation the estate has been freed from liability to pay, and it is as though there had never been a legacy in the first place.

Regarding this situation and many others, I would like to ask   52
the Scaevolas, who were supreme pontiffs and, in my view, extremely shrewd men: why do you want to add a command of civil law to a knowledge of the law of the pontiffs? By the former you tend to cancel out the latter. Rites go with the deceased's property by the authority of the pontiffs, not by any law. So if you were only pontiffs, the pontiffs' authority would be upheld; but being at the same time great experts in civil law, you use this knowledge to circumvent that authority. It was the opinion of the supreme pontiffs Publius Scaevola and Tiberius Coruncanius, and of the others too, that those who received bequests of as large an amount as all the heirs put together should be obliged to perform the rites. I grasp the pontiffs' ruling. What is added from the   53
sphere of civil law? The section on the division of the estate has been carefully drafted to allow the deduction of one hundred *nummi*;* thus a device was discovered for relieving the estate of the burden of performing the rites. As if the testator had not wished to forestall such a manœuvre, this legal expert, Mucius himself, who is also the supreme pontiff, advises the legatee to accept less than the sum left to all the heirs. They always used to say* that the legatee was bound to perform the rites, whatever he received. Once again, such men are freed from that obligation.

This other thing has nothing to do with pontifical law, and is taken over directly from civil law—the device whereby they formally declare the heir free from his obligation to pay the legacy by means of bronze and balance. The situation is then the same as if the money had never been bequeathed at all, provided that the legatee has obtained a formal promise of payment in respect of the amount bequeathed, so that it is owed to him under the terms of a contract and not as the result of ⟨a legacy⟩ . . . [*In the lost part of the MS, Cicero completed his discussion of domestic rites and moved on to the obligations owed to the spirits of the dead. See the end of section 22 above.*]

. . . a learned man, with whom Accius was on very friendly   54
terms. But he [Decimus Brutus], I believe, followed the tradition that December was the last month of the year,* whereas to the

ancients the last month was February. Moreover, he thought it was a sacred duty to offer the largest type of animal to the dead.

55   So much religious awe surrounds a grave that it is considered sacrilege to inter anyone who does not belong to the clan or share its rites. That was the decision made by Aulus Torquatus in the case of the Popilian clan in the age of our forefathers. Nor would the days of purification [*denicales*], whose name is derived from death* [*nex*] because they are observed in connection with the dead, be counted as holidays along with the rest-days of the other gods had not our ancestors intended that those who had departed this life should be included among the gods. The law requires that these days of purification should be fitted into the religious calendar in such a way that they do not clash with other private or public holidays. The whole manner in which this pontifical law is put together manifests great reverence and veneration. I need not specify how long a family should remain in mourning, what details should be observed in offering gelded rams to the household god,* what procedure should be followed in burying the severed bone,* what obligations are involved in connection with the sow, or at what point in time the burial place becomes a sacred inviolable grave.

56   I myself believe that the most ancient form of burial was that which, according to Xenophon,* was decreed by Cyrus for himself. The corpse is consigned to the earth, placed and laid out as if it were covered by its mother's blanket. We are told that our own King Numa was buried in the same fashion in that grave which is not far from the altar of Fons; and we know that the Cornelian clan has employed this type of burial up to our own time. The remains of Gaius Marius, which were resting in peace, were scattered on the waters of the Anio on the instructions of the victorious Sulla. If he had been as wise as he was fierce, he 57 would not have been incensed with such bitter hatred. I'm inclined to think it was for fear that this might happen to himself that Sulla was the first of the patrician Cornelii to instruct that his body be cremated.

Writing of Africanus, Ennius asserts* 'Here lies he . . .' Rightly, for those who are buried are said to lie. Yet their place of burial is not called a grave until the rites have been conducted and the pig has been slain.* The expression which has now come into general use in regard to all who have been buried (i.e. that they are 'interred') was then specifically used of those who had been covered by having earth thrown over them. Pontifical law testifies to that custom; for until a piece of earth is thrown upon the bone, the place where a body has been cremated has no element of sanctity. Once the earth has been thrown, the person is said to be interred, and the place is called a grave. At that point it becomes entitled to many religious rites. In the case of a man who has been killed on board ship and then thrown into the sea, Publius Mucius decided that the family was free from pollution because his bones did not remain above the earth. Yet the duty of sacrificing a sow was laid upon his heir, a three-day holiday was decreed, and a female pig had to be slaughtered by way of expiation. If the man had drowned, the same procedure would have been prescribed except for the expiatory offering and the holidays.

ATTICUS: I see what's laid down in the pontiffs' rules, but I 58 wonder if there is anything in the laws.

MARCUS: There's not much, admittedly, Titus; and I expect you know it already. Those regulations pertain not so much to religion as to the laws governing tombs. One of the laws of the Twelve Tables* says 'no burial or cremation of a corpse shall take place in the city', presumably because of the risk of fire.* The fact that it adds 'or cremation' indicates that one who is cremated is not buried, but only one who is interred.

ATTICUS: What about those eminent men who have been buried within the city since the Twelve Tables?

MARCUS: I suppose, Titus, there were people like Publicola and Tubertus, who before the law was passed were given this privilege on account of their valour*—a privilege legitimately retained by their descendants; or else there were men like Gaius Fabricius, who obtained this honour because they were exempted from the law on account of their valour. But just as the law forbids burial within the city, so it has been ruled by the college of pontiffs that it is illegal for a tomb to be built in a public place. You know the temple of Honour* outside the Colline gate. Tradition has it that there was once an altar on that site. When a metal plaque was discovered nearby (a plaque inscribed with the words 'To Honour'), this led to the dedication of the temple. But since many burials were on that site, they were dug up; for the pontiffs decreed that a public place could not be made subject to the obligations associated with private religion.

59   There are other regulations in the Twelve Tables for reducing expense and lamentation at funerals. These were in the main imported from the laws of Solon. The law says 'Do no more than this:* do not smooth the pyre with a trowel'. You know the rest. As boys we learned the Twelve Tables as a compulsory recitation. No one learns them now. After limiting the expense, then, to three veils, a small purple tunic, and ten pipers, the law goes on to do away with lamentation: 'Women shall not scratch their cheeks* or have a *lessus* on the occasion of a funeral.' The old interpreters, Sextus Aelius and Lucius Acilius, said they were not sure what this meant, but suspected it was some kind of funeral garment. Lucius Aelius takes *lessus* to be a mournful wailing, as the word itself suggests.* I tend to believe this second explanation, since that is the very thing that Solon's law forbids.* The rules are commendable, and in general they are as relevant to the rich as to the poor. It is entirely in keeping with nature that differences in fortune should be abolished in death.

60   Other funeral customs, too, which tend to intensify grief were abolished by the Twelve Tables. 'One shall not gather* the bones of a dead man in order to have a funeral later.' The law makes an exception of a man who has died on active service or in a foreign land. The following rules are also in the laws: 'Anointing by slaves is abolished, as is every kind of drinking bout.'* Such practices are rightly abolished; and they would not have been abolished had they not existed. 'There is to be no expensive sprinkling (of wine on the pyre), no festoons,* no censers'—let us leave those requirements aside. The important point is that decorations awarded as a mark of honour do belong to the dead; for the law ordains that a chaplet earned by courage* should be placed on the man who earned it and on his father without incurring any penalty. I suppose it was because holding more than one funeral and preparing more than one bier for a single individual had become customary that these practices, too, were forbidden by law. The same law contained the clause 'And no one shall add gold'. Notice how civilized an exception is made to this by another law: 'But in the case of one whose teeth are fastened by gold,* a person shall not incur a penalty by burying or burning the corpse without extract-

ing the gold.' Notice at the same time that burial and cremation are held to be different things.

There are, moreover, two laws about tombs. One protects 61 private houses, the other the tombs themselves. The former forbids any new pyre or mound to be constructed within sixty feet of another's house without his consent, in view of the risk of serious fire. The other, by forbidding the 'forum' (i.e. the entrance chamber of a tomb) or the mound to be acquired by possession, safeguards the rights of tombs.

These provisions, which we find in the Twelve Tables, are certainly in accordance with nature, which is the criterion of law. The rest are based on custom: that public notice should be given of a funeral if any entertainment is to take place, that the person in 62 charge of the funeral should have the services of an attendant and lictors, that where the deceased has held public office a speech in his honour should be delivered at a public meeting, and this encomium should be followed by a song accompanied by a piper. Such a song is called a *nenia*, a term also applied to mournful songs in Greece.*

ATTICUS: I am glad that our laws are being made to conform to nature, and quite delighted by the good sense of our ancestors. But I don't find any limit placed on the cost of tombs,* as there is in the case of other expenditure.

MARCUS: Yes, you're right. I suppose you have seen in the case of Gaius Figulus' tomb the lengths to which such extravagance has now gone. There was once very little desire for such ostentation, as is shown by many examples from the time of our forefathers. The interpreters of our law, in regard to the clause in which they are instructed to eliminate expense and lamentation from the rites of the dead, are supposed to understand this to mean primarily that the magnificence of tombs is to be reduced. Such measures have not been overlooked by the wisest lawgivers. In Athens 63 too, they say, the present burial law goes back to Cecrops their first king.* When the next of kin had performed the ritual, and the body had been covered with earth, seeds of corn were sown, so that while the bosom and lap of the mother, as it were, might be given to the dead, the soil might be purified by the corn and returned to the living. A feast then took place, attended by the relatives wearing garlands. In their presence a speech was deliv-

ered in praise of the deceased (but it had to be true,* for it was
64 considered blasphemous to utter falsehoods). That concluded the
ceremony. The man of Phalerum* writes that later, when funerals
and mourning became extravagant, such excesses were forbidden
by one of Solon's laws—a law which our Committee of Ten
included almost verbatim in the tenth table. The clause about the
three veils* and most of those provisions are taken from Solon.
What he said about lamentations has been translated literally:
'Women shall not scratch their cheeks or have a *lessus* on the
occasion of a funeral.'

About tombs, however, there is nothing in Solon apart from 'no
one shall destroy them or bury an outsider within them.' And
there is a penalty 'if anyone damages, breaks, or knocks down a
burial mound' (for I think that is what is meant by *tumbos*) 'or a
monument or a column'. But later on, because of the enormous
size of the tombs which we now see in the Ceramicus, it was
enacted that 'no one should build a tomb which it took ten men
65 longer than three days to complete'. It was forbidden to decorate
a tomb with stucco-work and to set up what they call *herms*.*
Encomiums, too, were forbidden, except in the case of public
funerals; and even then the speech had to be delivered by a person
officially appointed for the purpose. To reduce the amount of
lamentation, throngs of men and women were not allowed to
66 attend; for a crowd intensifies feelings of grief. That is why Pittacus allows no one at all to attend a funeral from outside the family.
But Demetrius also says that elaborate funerals and tombs once
again became common, reaching much the same level of extravagance as we see in Rome today. He himself passed a law to reduce
the practice. He was, as you know, a highly learned man; but he
was also a most conscientious citizen, highly expert in safeguard-
ing the interests of his country. Anyhow, he reduced extravagance,
not only by imposing penalties but also by prescribing the acceptable time of day; he insisted that funerals should be conducted
before dawn. He also fixed a limit with regard to new tombs, forbidding anything to be placed over the mound of earth except a
pillar (which had to be no higher than three cubits) or a table or
a small bowl. And he appointed a special official to see that these
laws were observed.
67   These, then, were the laws of your Athenian rulers. But let us

consult Plato, who refers funerary rituals to experts on religious ceremonies, a practice which we have retained. Now about tombs he says this:* he forbids any piece of cultivated or cultivable ground to be used for a tomb; but he insists that the sort of land which is capable of accommodating the bodies of the dead without harm to the living should be filled to the maximum extent. Land capable of bearing crops and providing food like a mother should not be diminished by anyone, living or dead.

He also forbids the construction of a tomb higher than five men 68 could build in five days. Nor is any stone object to be erected or placed in position larger than is needed to contain an inscription in honour of the deceased running to four heroic lines,* of the sort that Ennius calls 'long'. So we have the weighty opinion of this exceptional man about tombs. He also limits the amount of money to be spent on funerals to something between one and five *minae*,* depending on the person's wealth. After that, he writes those words about the immortality of the soul, the restful existence which will be enjoyed by the good after death, and the punishments that lie in store for the wicked.

So there, I think, you have an account of the whole section on 69 religious observances.

QUINTUS: Indeed we do, Marcus—and in great detail. Please move on to the rest.

MARCUS: Yes I shall. And since you've been kind enough to encourage me, I shall finish it in today's discussion. I hope so, anyhow, as it's such a beautiful day. I notice that Plato did the same, and that the whole of his talk about the laws was concluded in one summer day.* So that's what I shall do, and I shall speak about magistrates. For, once matters of religion have been settled, magistrates are surely the most important element in the structure of the state.

ATTICUS: Carry on, then, and follow the scheme with which you began.

BOOK 3

1–11. Introduction, followed by the proposed laws

1   MARCUS: Well then, I'll follow, as I have from the start, the lead of that inspired man whom I praise more often, perhaps, than is necessary, because I regard him with something like veneration.

ATTICUS: No doubt you mean Plato.

MARCUS: The very man.

ATTICUS: Ah no. You will never praise him too warmly or too often. Even our friends,* who don't like to hear anyone praised except their own leader, allow me to be as devoted to him as I please.

MARCUS: And they're quite right. What devotion could be more fitting for a man of your discrimination, who in my view has achieved in both his life and his writings the very difficult feat of combining seriousness with good humour?

ATTICUS: I'm glad I interrupted you, for you've given a splendid proof of your high opinion of me! But carry on as you began.

2   MARCUS: First, then, let us praise the law itself in terms which are both true and appropriate to its nature.

ATTICUS: By all means, just as you did in the case of the law governing religious practices.

MARCUS: You appreciate, then, that a magistrate's function is to take charge and to issue directives which are right, beneficial, and in accordance with the laws. As magistrates are subject to the laws, the people are subject to the magistrates. In fact it is true to say that a magistrate is a speaking law,* and law a silent magis-

3 trate. Nothing is so closely bound up with the decrees and terms of nature (and by that I wish to be understood as meaning law) as authority. Without that, no house or state or clan can survive— no, nor the human race, nor the whole of nature, nor the very universe itself. For the universe obeys God; land and sea abide by the laws of the universe; and human life is subject to the commands of the supreme law.

4   If I may come, now, to matters which are closer to us and more familiar—all ancient peoples were once subject to kings. That kind

of power was originally vested in the wisest and the most just. (And that practice prevailed, for the most part, in our country as long as the kings reigned over it.) Subsequently that power was also entrusted to their descendants in succession, a custom which survives even in contemporary monarchies. Those who were opposed to monarchy wished to obey—not nobody, but not always a single person. However, here I am providing a body of law for free communities; so I will adjust my laws to the type of government which I think best. (In the six earlier books* I presented my views about the best constitution.)

Magistrates,* then, are a necessity. Without their good sense and 5 close attention there can be no state. In fact the whole management of a country depends on the apportionment of their functions. Not only must their authority be clearly delimited; the same applies also to the citizens' duty to obey them. A man who exercises power effectively will at some stage have to obey others, and one who quietly executes orders shows that he deserves, eventually, to wield power himself. So it must be the case that anyone who executes orders will have hopes of holding power at some time himself, while the man at present in charge will bear in mind that before long he will have to obey others. I lay it down, as Charondas does in his laws, that the people should not only obey the magistrates and carry out their instructions, but should also give them honour and esteem. Our friend Plato* held that citizens who oppose the magistrates are descended from the Titans, who themselves opposed the gods. Having cleared the ground, let us now come to the laws themselves, if that's all right with you.

ATTICUS: Yes, it's all right with me, and so is the order in which you are treating the material.

MARCUS: Commands shall be just, and citizens shall obey them 6 quietly and without protest. Magistrates shall punish the guilty and unruly citizen by fine, prison, or flogging, unless an equal or higher authority or the people forbid it. The accused shall have the right of appeal to those quarters. When the magistrate has delivered or pronounced his decision, a trial shall take place before the people* to fix the fine or other penalty. In the field there shall be no appeal* against the decision of the commanding officer; whatever order is given by the officer in charge of the campaign shall be fixed and final. A number of minor magistrates shall be appointed to several areas, each with authority in his own sphere. In the field they shall hold command over those to whom they have been assigned, and be their tribunes. At home they shall watch over public funds,* ensure the security of prisoners, punish capital offences,* coin bronze,* silver, or gold in the public mint, judge cases* brought before them, and carry out whatever the Senate decides.

7   There shall be aediles, who shall look after matters in the city, including the food supply and official entertainments. For them this shall be the first step on the ladder* leading to higher office.

The censors* shall draw up a list of the population, recording ages, children, households and possessions; they shall watch over the city's temples, streets, and aqueducts, and also the treasury and taxes; they shall divide the citizens and assign them to tribes; then they shall divide them according to possessions, age, and rank; they shall distinguish the sons of the cavalry and the infantry; they shall not allow men to remain bachelors; they shall regulate the behaviour of the citizens and not permit a disreputable person to remain in the Senate; they shall be two in number and shall hold office for five years; the other officers shall be annual; the post of censor shall always have occupants.

8   There shall be a legal official, or praetor, to decide civil cases or to give directions for their decision. He shall be the guardian of civil law. Equal to him in power there shall be as many officials as the Senate shall decree or the people command.

There shall be two with royal power;* and from their leading, judging, and consulting they shall be called praetors, judges, and consuls. They shall hold the supreme military power and shall take orders from no one. To them the safety of the people shall be the highest law.

9   No one shall hold the same office again until a period of ten years has elapsed. They shall abide by the ages laid down in the year-law.*

But when a particularly serious war or civil disorder occurs, one man* shall for a period no longer than six months hold power equal to that of the two consuls, if the Senate so decide. After being appointed under favourable auspices he shall be Master of the People. He shall have an officer to command the cavalry* with an authority equal to that of the legal official.*

When there are no consuls and no master of the people there shall be no other magistrates. The auspices shall be in the hands of the Senate, and it shall from its number appoint a member with the power* to arrange for the due election of consuls through the Assembly of Centuries.

Magistrates, with and without *imperium*,* and ambassadors shall leave the city when the Senate shall so decree or the people so command. They shall conduct just wars in a just manner;* they shall treat the allies with consideration; they shall exercise control over themselves and their staff; they shall increase the glory of their country and return home with honour.

No one shall be appointed ambassador* for the sake of conducting his private affairs.

The ten officials whom the plebs shall appoint on its own behalf to protect it from violence shall be its tribunes.* What they forbid and what they enact through the plebs shall be binding. They shall be sacrosanct and shall not leave the plebs without tribunes.

All magistrates shall have the right to take auspices and to 10 conduct trials. The Senate shall be made up of their number. Its decrees shall be binding. But if an authority equal to or higher than [*the presiding magistrate*] shall veto its decrees, those decrees shall be written out and preserved.

The [*senatorial*] order shall be of unblemished behaviour and shall set an example to the rest.

When the people's appointment of magistrates, judicial verdicts, and legislative decisions, positive and negative, have been made by vote, the details shall be disclosed to the aristocracy* and shall reflect the free choice of the people.

But if anything needs to be attended to outside the scope of the magistrates, the people shall appoint someone to attend to it and shall confer on him the authority to do so.

A consul, a praetor, a master of the people, a master of the cavalry, and any official proposed by the Senate for conducting the election of consuls, shall have the right to preside over meetings of the people and the Senate. And the tribunes appointed by the plebs shall have the right to preside over meetings of the Senate; they shall also bring before the plebs whatever is required.

Proceedings with the people and in the Senate shall be conducted with decent restraint.

11   A senator shall have a reason for his absence or else shall be liable to censure. A senator shall speak in his turn and at moderate length. He shall have a grasp of public affairs.

Meetings of the people shall be free from violence. An authority equal to or higher than [*the presiding magistrate*] shall have the power to overrule.* But if any disturbance takes place during the proceedings, the responsibility shall rest with the presiding magistrate. Anyone who blocks a harmful measure shall be deemed a public benefactor.

Presiding magistrates shall observe the auspices and obey the official augur; when bills have been read, they shall keep them on file in the treasury; they shall not take a vote on more than one question at a time;* they shall inform the people about the matter at issue and allow them to be informed by magistrates and private citizens.

They shall not propose laws directed at private individuals.* They shall not propose a motion involving a citizen's life* except through the chief assembly* and those whom the censors have enrolled in the citizen body.

They shall not accept gifts* or give them when seeking or holding or having held office. If a person transgresses any of these rules, the penalty shall fit the crime.

The censors shall preserve the true meaning of the laws. On leaving office, men shall give a report of their acts to the censors; by doing so, however, they shall not be any the less liable to prosecution.

The law has been read. 'Depart* and I shall order voting-tablets to be distributed.'

12–47. Comments on the laws

12   QUINTUS: How succinctly, Marcus, you have drawn up a scheme of all the magistrates for our inspection! But they are almost identical with those of our own country, even if you have introduced a little novelty.

MARCUS: That is a very perceptive point, Quintus. We are, in fact, talking about the harmoniously mixed constitution which Scipio praises in those books and prefers to all others—a type which could not have been achieved without such a system of magistrates. For bear in mind, the state is defined by its magistrates and those who are in charge, and each type of government is identified by the way those officials are organized. Since our constitution was given the most sensible and well-adjusted form by our ancestors, I found little or nothing to change in the laws.

ATTICUS: Well then, will you do the same for us with the magistrates as you did with religious law at my instigation and request—that is, explain why you regard your system as the best?

MARCUS: I'm happy to oblige, Atticus. I'll present the whole 13 topic as it has been investigated and discussed by the most perceptive Greek thinkers. I shall also bring in our laws as I did before.

ATTICUS: That's just the kind of presentation I'm looking for.

MARCUS: Now I said a good deal on this subject in my earlier books, as I had to, since I was trying to discover the best kind of state. But there are some points about magistrates which are relevant to this topic—points examined first by Theophrastus and then, in greater detail, by Diogenes the Stoic.

ATTICUS: Really? Such matters were also handled by the Stoics?

MARCUS: Well no; only by the one I have just named, and 14 subsequently by that great and deeply learned man, Panaetius. The older Stoics supplied perceptive theoretical discussions of the state, but did not offer, as I am doing, a practical guide for communities of citizens. It was rather from the Academy that all those well-known writings derived, starting with Plato's. Then Aristotle in his exposition illuminated the whole area of politics, and so did Heraclides of Pontus, starting likewise from Plato. Theophrastus, a pupil of Aristotle's, spent a great deal of time, as you know, on that kind of subject, and Dicaearchus, another of Aristotle's pupils, gave useful service in this field of study and research. Later, following Theophrastus, Demetrius of Phalerum, whom I mentioned earlier, led political theory in a striking manner out of the quiet seclusion of the scholar's study, not just into the dust and heat of the day, but into the line of battle and the actual conflict. I could mention many great statesmen who were quite learned, and many excellent scholars who were not particularly experienced in politics; but apart from Demetrius, who can easily be found to have excelled in both spheres, being a major figure in scholarly research and also in governing his country?

ATTICUS: I fancy such a man* *can* be found—and from the three of us at that. But do carry on as you began.

15 MARCUS: So then, these thinkers inquired whether there should be just one magistrate in the country who would be obeyed by everyone else. That, I understand, was the view of our ancestors after the expulsion of the kings. But as the monarchical type of state, though once admired, was later rejected, not so much because of monarchy's faults as because of a monarch's,* clearly if one magistrate is to rule over all the others, only the name of king has been abandoned; the institution itself will remain in 16 being. Hence it was not without good reason that in Sparta Theopompus appointed ephors* to oppose the kings, and here we appointed tribunes to oppose the consuls. A consul has the right, laid down in the legal code, that he should be obeyed by all the other magistrates, except a tribune. The latter was appointed subsequently to prevent the recurrence of what had happened before.* The presence of an official who was not to be bound by the consul's authority was the first step in the reduction of consular power. The second was the fact that the tribune lent his support, not only to other magistrates, but also to private individuals who flouted the consul's authority.

17 QUINTUS: What you are talking of was a great calamity. For with the birth of the tribunate the weight of the aristocracy diminished and the sheer force of the masses gathered strength.

MARCUS: Not so, Quintus. Was it not inevitable that the consular power on its own should appear rather arrogant and oppressive? After a moderate and sensible balance had been achieved . . . [*There is a gap in the text here. The fragment from Macrobius printed below apparently belongs to Cicero's comment on the law quoted in section 9 above, namely 'they shall treat the allies with consideration'.*] . . . Who will be in a position to protect the allies if he cannot grasp the distinction between what is in the country's interest and what is not? (Macrobius, *De Differentiis et Societatibus Graeci Latinique Verbi*, in H. Keil, *Grammatici Latini* v. 620, 644.)

18 'They shall return home with honour' [9 above]. Nothing apart from honour should be brought home by sound and honest magistrates from enemies or from allies.

Again, it is surely obvious that nothing is more discreditable than that a man should serve as an ambassador for anything other than the sake of his country. I say nothing about how they have behaved and still behave—those who use the position of ambassador as a means of chasing legacies or debts; for that may be a vice of human nature. But what, I wonder, is actually more disgraceful than a senatorial ambassador without any responsibility, any instructions, or any official duties? As consul I would have abolished such ambassadorial appointments with the support of the full Senate (even though they were clearly to the senators' advantage), had not an irresponsible tribune* of the plebs intervened to stop me. I still managed to reduce the duration of such appointments, which had been unrestricted, to one year. So the abuse remains, even though a time-limit has been imposed.

But now, if you don't mind, let us leave the provinces and return to the capital.

ATTICUS: *We* don't mind, but those who are travelling around in the provinces won't like it at all!

MARCUS: Still, if they obey these laws, Titus, they will find   19 nothing more delightful than the capital and their own homes, and nothing more tedious and stressful than a province.

Next comes a law which endorses the power of the tribunes of the plebs—a law existing in our own state. No need to argue about that.

QUINTUS: But I do wonder, Marcus, what you think of that power. It seems to me pernicious; for it came into being at a time of sedition,* and its effect is to promote sedition. If we care to recall its origin, we see that it was born when the citizens had recourse to arms, and key points in the capital were occupied and placed under siege. It was quickly put to death,* as hideously deformed children* should be, according to the Twelve Tables. But somehow or other it soon came back to life, returning even more ugly and horrible than before. What damage did it not cause! First, in keeping with its unholy nature, it tore away every mark of honour from the Senate; everywhere it made the lowest equal to the highest, causing turmoil and confusion. Even when it had demolished the venerable power of the aristocracy it still did not rest. I say nothing of Gaius Flaminius and events which now seem   20 antiquated because of the lapse of time; but what rights did the tribunate of Tiberius Gracchus leave to the best type of citizen? Five years before that, the plebeian tribune, Gaius Curiatius, the lowest and foulest creature in existence, threw the consuls Decimus Brutus and Publius Scipio,* those great and admirable men, into jail—an outrage without precedent.

Take Gaius Gracchus. Through his tribunate, and through those daggers which he claimed to have tossed into the forum to make the citizens fight like gladiators with one another, did he not over-turn the entire state of the country? I need not mention Saturni-nus,* Sulpicius, and the others, whom the country could not beat

21 off without taking up the sword. But why should I cite things from bygone days which others endured rather than recent examples known to ourselves? Was there ever anyone so audacious and so hostile to us as to aim at subverting our position,* who did not for that purpose sharpen the dagger of some tribune against us? When wicked and desperate men failed to find such a weapon in any household, or indeed in any clan, they felt obliged, in the country's hour of darkness, to cause confusion among the clans.* It was a remarkable fact, which will redound to our eternal credit, that no tribune could be found who was willing, for any bribe, to turn against us, except one who had no right to be a tribune at all.

22 What devastation he caused—devastation which could only have been caused by the madness of a filthy beast lacking any vestige of sense or any prospect of success, and inflamed by the madness of a mob! That is why, in this instance, I strongly approve of Sulla, who by his law stripped the plebeian tribunes of their destructive power,* leaving them only the right to give assistance. As for our friend Pompey, in all other matters I invariably sing his praises, loudly and unstintingly; but I say nothing about his policy on the tribunes' power, for while I am reluctant to criticize, I refuse to praise him.

23 MARCUS: You discern the faults of the tribunate very clearly, Quintus. But in criticizing any institution it is unfair to neglect its good points while picking on and listing its bad points and defects. On that principle even the consulship is open to attack, if you collect the misdemeanours of certain consuls whom I forbear to name. I admit there is an element of evil inherent in the office of tribune; but without that evil we would not have the good which

was the whole purpose of setting it up. 'The plebeian tribunes', you say, 'have too much power.' Who's arguing with that? But the crude power of the people is much more savage and violent. By having a leader it is sometimes milder than if it had none. For the leader knows he is going ahead at his own risk, whereas the surging mass is blind to the risk it is running. 'But sometimes it is whipped up.' Yes, and often it is calmed. What set of officials 24 is so wild that not one in ten has any sense? Why, Tiberius Gracchus himself came to grief because he overrode the vote of a tribune and even had him deposed. What brought about his downfall if not the fact that he removed from office a colleague who was blocking* his programme?

Think of the good sense which our forefathers showed in this matter. After the Senate had conceded that power* to the plebs, the weapons fell from their hands, the rebellion was extinguished, and a compromise was found which enabled lesser folk to imagine that they were equal to the leading men. That alone was what saved the country. 'But', you say, 'there were *two* Gracchi.' Yes, and you could count as many as you like in addition to them. When ten tribunes* are appointed, you will find some dangerous specimens in every age, and perhaps more who are unreliable rather than sound. Still, the highest class is not the target of resentment, and the common people do not engage in dangerous contentions over their rights. That is why either the kings should 25 never have been expelled, or else the plebs had to be given actual, not just nominal, freedom. In fact that freedom was given in such a way that the common people were induced by many excellent regulations to acquiesce in the aristocrats' authority.

My own case, my dear and admirable Quintus, while it came up against the power of the tribunes, involved no quarrel with the tribunate itself. The plebs were not incited* to resent my position; no, the jails were thrown open, slaves were stirred up* against me, and the threat of military force was also employed. What I had to face was not that poisonous wretch but a political crisis of the most serious kind. Had I not given way,* the country would not have enjoyed the benefit of my services for long. This was proved by the sequel; for what free citizen—nay, what slave worthy of freedom, did not have my safety at heart? Nevertheless, if what I 26 did for the safety of the country* had not, in the event, won universal approval, if the hatred of the frenzied mob had been inflamed and thus led to my banishment; and if the power of the tribunes had incited the people against me, as it was incited by Gracchus against Laenas and by Saturninus against Metellus, I would have put up with it, my dear Quintus. I would have been comforted not so much by the philosophers living in Athens whose metier was consolation, as by the eminent men* who, exiled from that city, preferred to be deprived of their ungrateful country rather than to continue living in a place of wickedness.

As for Pompey,* in that one matter you are not so enthusiastic about him. But you're not taking sufficient account, I think, of the fact that he had to decide not just what was best but also what was necessary. He realized that this country could not be deprived of the tribunes' office. Our people had eagerly pressed to have it when it was an unknown quantity; so how could they do without it now that they knew what it was? It was the duty of a sensible citizen, when dealing with a cause which was not intrinsically disastrous* and was too popular to be opposed, not to leave it in the hands of a demagogue. That *would* have been disastrous.

You realize, Quintus, that in a talk of this kind one has to say 'Precisely' or 'Absolutely right' to enable the speaker to pass on to a new topic.

QUINTUS: Well actually I *don't* agree with you; still, I'd like you to move on to the rest of your talk.

MARCUS: So you stand fast and refuse to budge from your previous opinion?

ATTICUS: Well really I must say I take pretty much the same view as Quintus. But let's hear the rest of what you have to say.

27   MARCUS: Next then, all magistrates are granted 'the right to take auspices and to conduct trials' [10]—trials with the proviso that the people should have the power to hear appeals, auspices to allow the adjournment of numerous futile meetings by means of justifiable postponements.* Often the gods have used the auspices* to check a wrongful initiative on the part of the people.

The stipulation that 'the Senate is to be made up of former magistrates' [10] is certainly a democratic measure in that no one can enter the highest body unless he has been elected by the people (for the censors can no longer co-opt). But this defect is immediately mitigated by a confirmation of the Senate's authority, for my

law goes on to say 'Its decrees shall be binding'. The fact is that 28
if the Senate controls public policy, and if everyone supports its
decrees, and if the other orders allow the state to be directed by
the guidance of the highest order, then a constitutional compromise takes place whereby the power is vested in the people, but
authority in the hands of the Senate. As a result of that compromise the moderate and harmonious condition of the state
described earlier is preserved, especially if the next law is
observed, the next law being 'The order shall be of unblemished
behaviour and shall set an example to the rest' [10].

QUINTUS: That's a splendid law, Marcus; but your insistence on
the Senate's unblemished behaviour carries very wide implications
and needs to be interpreted by a censor.

ATTICUS: To be sure, the whole order is behind you and cher- 29
ishes most happy memories of your consulship; but if I may say
so, this law may well exhaust* not just the censors but the whole
company of judges!

MARCUS: No more of that, Atticus! We're not talking about the
present Senate or the men of today but about those of the future—
if, indeed, anyone will be prepared to obey these laws. Since the
law ordains totally unblemished behaviour, no one with any blemishes will even get into that order.* That, of course, is hard to
achieve except through a special kind of education and training.*
On that point I shall perhaps say something later, depending on
time and opportunity.

ATTICUS: The opportunity will certainly be available, since you 30
are going through the laws in order; and the length of the day
provides lots of time. But even if you leave out the bit about education and training, I shall ask you to take it up again.

MARCUS: Very well, Atticus. Bring it up, and the same goes for
anything else that I leave out.

'It shall set an example to the rest' [10]. If we achieve that, we
achieve everything. For just as the whole state is apt to be infected
by the vicious desires of its leaders, so it is healed and set right by
their restraint. When Lucius Lucullus, that great man whom we
all knew, was criticized for the luxury of his villa at Tusculum, he
is supposed to have given a very neat reply. He had, he said, two
neighbours, a Roman knight who lived further up the hill and a
freedman who lived below him. *Their* villas were luxurious; so he

was entitled to have whatever was permitted to his social inferiors. Do you not see, Lucullus, that their greed was inspired by you? They would not have been permitted such indulgence if you 31 hadn't gone in for it yourself. Who would tolerate such people, on seeing their houses crammed with statues and pictures, some of which are public property and others are of a sacred and holy kind? We would all put a stop to their acquisitiveness if it weren't for the fact that those who ought to do so are guilty of the same greed. The vices of the leading citizens are not so serious an evil (though in themselves they *are* a serious evil) as the fact that those men beget a host of imitators.* If you're prepared to go back over the records of history, it is plain that the state has taken its character from that of its foremost men. Whatever changes have taken place in the conduct of its leaders have been reproduced in the 32 lives of the people. That is a much sounder idea than the opinion of our friend Plato,* who maintains that changes in the nature of states follow from changes in the vocal style of its musicians. I believe that changes in the conduct of states mirror changes in the lives and life-style of the aristocracy. Corrupt leaders do a more deadly disservice to their country in that they not only contract vices themselves but also infect the community. They are a menace, not just because they are corrupt themselves but because they corrupt others. They do more damage by their example than by their misdemeanours. Actually this law, which extends to the senatorial order as a whole, could be narrowed in its scope; for few, indeed very few, are so eminent in prestige and position that they can corrupt or correct the moral character of the state.

These observations are enough for now. They have been elaborated in greater detail in that other work.* So let's move on to what remains to be covered.

33   Next comes the matter of votes, which according to my law 'shall be disclosed to the aristocracy and shall reflect the free choice of the people' [10].

ATTICUS: I was listening very carefully, I assure you. Yet I didn't fully understand the meaning of the law or the terms in which you formulated it.

MARCUS: I'll explain it, Titus, and in doing so I'll enter on a difficult question which has been discussed often and at length. In assigning magistracies, judging legal cases, and passing laws and bills, is it better for votes to be registered openly or in secret?

QUINTUS: Is there any doubt about that? I'm afraid I may disagree with you again.

MARCUS: I don't think you will, Quintus. For my opinion is the same as the one which I know you have always held, namely that when it comes to voting nothing could be better than a vocal declaration. But we have to see whether that is practicable.

QUINTUS: If you don't mind my saying so, Marcus, that reser- 34 vation is especially misleading to the man in the street, and inimical to the public interest—I mean when something is said to be right and proper but to be impracticable—in other words that one must give in to the people. The people can be overridden when a strict procedure is adopted; moreover, it is better to be overwhelmed by force when defending a good cause than to acquiesce in a bad one. As everyone knows, the ballot has removed all the aristocracy's power. When the people enjoyed liberty, they never wanted that law. They only clamoured for it when they were ground down by the dominant power of the leading citizens. (That is why among the judgements pronounced on really powerful men, those recorded orally are more adverse than those written on tablets.) Hence the leaders should have been deprived of their excessive licence in putting bad measures to the vote; the people should not have been presented with a subterfuge whereby the tablet ensured the secrecy of a wrong-headed vote thus keeping the aristocracy in the dark about what each man thought. That is why no good man has ever been prevailed on to introduce or support a proposal like yours.

There are four ballot laws* in existence. The first has to do with 35 allotting magistracies, i.e. the Gabinian Law, proposed by a vulgar and insignificant fellow. Two years later came the Cassian Law about people's courts, introduced by Lucius Cassius—a man of high birth but one who (if I may say so without offending his family) left the respectable side and, by his populist policies, went hunting for bits of approving gossip. The third is the law of Carbo about adopting and rejecting measures. He was a wicked troublemaker who, even when he returned to the respectable side, failed to protect himself from its members. Oral voting seemed 36 to survive in only one type of case, which Cassius himself had excluded, namely treason trials. Gaius Coelius introduced the ballot for this type of trial too; yet he regretted as long as he lived that he had damaged the country simply to destroy Gaius Popillius. In this town our grandfather showed remarkable courage throughout his life in resisting Marcus Gratidius, who was proposing a ballot law, even though he was married to Gratidius' sister (our grandmother). Gratidius caused a storm in a teacup,* as they say; (later his son,* Marius, caused a storm in the Aegean sea.*) When the matter was reported to the Senate, the consul Marcus Scaurus said to our grandfather, 'I wish, Marcus Cicero, you had chosen to help me by employing your energy and integrity in the highest councils of the land rather than in a country town.'

37   Therefore, since we are not now merely reviewing the laws of the Roman people, but are either reviving ones that have vanished or writing new ones, I think you should say, not what can be obtained from the present community, but what is best. Your much-admired Scipio bears the blame for the Cassian Law, for it is supposed to have been brought in on his recommendation.* If *you* bring in a ballot law, you yourself will be responsible. I don't like it, nor does our friend Atticus, to judge from his expression.

    ATTICUS: I have never liked any populist measure. I hold that the best government is the type set up by Marcus here when he was consul—the type that is controlled by the aristocracy.

38   MARCUS: Well you, I notice, have thrown out my law without a ballot! Nevertheless, though Scipio made an adequate defence of his position in those other books, here I am giving the people only that amount of freedom which will allow a thriving aristocracy to use its authority. This is the way I have framed the law on voting: 'The details shall be disclosed to the aristocracy and shall reflect the free choice of the people' [10]. This law implies the intention that it should supersede all the laws passed more recently—laws which use every device to conceal the vote, preventing anyone from inspecting a tablet, asking how a person has

39 voted, or soliciting his support. The Marian Law* even made the gangways narrow. If these measures are designed to prevent bribery, as on the whole they are, I do not object to them. If, however, laws will never succeed in eliminating bribery, then by all means let the people have the ballot as a guarantee of liberty, provided the vote is disclosed* and actually displayed to the best and most unimpeachable citizens. In that way liberty will exist

precisely in the sense that the people are given the opportunity to do the aristocracy an honourable favour.

As a result, Quintus, the situation you mentioned a moment ago is now brought about, namely that fewer men will be condemned by the ballot than used to be condemned by the voice, because the people are content to have the constitutional power. Provided they retain that, in other respects their will is handed over to authority and influence. So, leaving aside the corrupt purchase of votes, you see, don't you, that if canvassing is silenced the people will be at a loss, when they come to vote, about what the aristocracy thinks. The consequence is that, thanks to my law, the appearance of liberty is given to the people, the authority of the aristocracy is retained, and the cause of quarrelling is removed.

Next comes a statement about who is to have 'the right to preside over meetings of the people or the Senate' [10]. That is 40 followed by an important, and in my view an admirable, law: 'Proceedings with the people and in the Senate shall be conducted with decent restraint,' that is, in a quiet, disciplined manner. The presiding magistrate controls and shapes not only the attitude and will but almost the facial expression of those over whom he presides. ⟨Exerting this influence*⟩ is not difficult except in the case of the Senate. For a senator is not the sort of man whose mind needs to be directed by the presiding official; he is keen to command attention in his own right. Three things are required of him: that he should be present (for when members are present in force the business acquires an extra importance); that he should speak in his proper turn* (that is, when he is invited to do so), and at moderate length, so as not to run endlessly on [11]. Brevity in expressing one's thoughts is a highly praiseworthy quality, not just in a senator but in any speaker. One ought never to make a long speech,* except when the Senate is going wrong (which happens most frequently as the result of improper influence) and no magistrate is attempting to save the situation (then it is a service to waste the entire day*), or when the issue is so important as to call for abundant eloquence on the part of a speaker to exhort or to inform the house. Our friend Cato is a great expert in both kinds of speech.

The law adds: 'He shall have a grasp of public affairs'* [11]. It 41 is essential for a senator to be familiar with the state of the country (that has wide implications—knowing what it has in the way of troops, how well off it is financially, what allies, friends, and tributaries the country has, what laws, conditions, and treaties apply to each), to understand legislative procedure, and to be aware of traditional precedent. You can now appreciate the whole range of knowledge, application, and memory without which no senator can be properly equipped for his job.

42   Then there are the people's assemblies. Here the first and most important rule is 'there must be no violence' [11]. Nothing is more damaging to a state, nothing so contrary to justice and law, nothing less appropriate to a civilized community, than to force through a measure by violence* where a country has a settled and established constitution. The law further requires that a magistrate imposing a veto should be obeyed. There is nothing more admirable than that; for it is better to obstruct a good proposal than to acquiesce in a bad one [11].

As for my rule that 'The responsibility shall rest with the presiding magistrate' [11], I have taken the whole provision from the opinion expressed by that very judicious man, Crassus.* The Senate followed his advice when the consul Gaius Claudius raised the subject of the disorder fomented by Gnaeus Carbo.* It ruled that disorder could not take place in the people's assembly without the consent of the presiding magistrate; for he had the power to close the meeting as soon as a veto had been exercised and a commotion had begun. Anyone who allows things to go on when no business can be done is inviting violence. By this law he loses his immunity* to prosecution.

43   Then comes the ruling 'Anyone who blocks a harmful measure shall be deemed a public benefactor' [11]. Who would not loyally come to the aid of the state if he knew he would be praised by the voice of such an excellent law?

This is followed by regulations which we also have in the laws and customs of our state: 'They shall observe the auspices and obey the official augur' [11]. It is the duty of a conscientious augur to bear in mind that he must be ready to assist on momentous national occasions, that he has been assigned as an advisor and servant to Jupiter the Best and the Greatest (just as officials have been assigned to him to observe the auspices at his command), and that certain specific areas of the sky have been allotted to him so that he may be able to give frequent assistance to the state from that quarter.

Then come regulations about the reading of bills, the handling of items one at a time, and the right to consult magistrates and private citizens [11].

After that we have two splendid laws taken from the Twelve 44 Tables. One gets rid of legislation directed at private individuals,* the other forbids any motion regarding a citizen's life to be proposed except through the chief assembly [11]. What an excellent provision our ancestors made for future generations, at a time when seditious plebeian tribunes had not been created or even thought of! They refused to allow laws to be passed against individual people (for that is what *privilegium* means). What could be more unjust than such laws when, by definition, a law is something enjoined and binding on everyone? They forbade legislation against individuals unless it was passed by the Assembly of Centuries; for when the people are split up according to wealth, rank, and age, they think more carefully about their votes than when they meet indiscriminately in their tribes. Hence Lucius Cotta, a 45 man of great ability and deep insight, was all the more justified in saying that in my case no legal measure at all had been passed against me. He pointed out that, apart from the fact that those transactions took place in the presence of armed slaves, no valid decision could be taken by the Council of the Plebs about a citizen's life, nor by any assembly against an individual; therefore I did not need a law ⟨to rehabilitate me⟩, because absolutely no legal action had been taken against me.* However, you and other very distinguished men preferred to take the view that the whole of Italy* should make clear its opinion of a man against whom slaves and brigands claimed to have passed a law.

Next comes a regulation about accepting money and offering 46 bribes. Since laws have to be endorsed by court verdicts rather than verbal formulae, I have added 'The penalty shall fit the crime' [11]. In this way each offender is to be paid back in his own coin— violence being punished by death or exile, greed by a fine, improper canvassing by disgrace.

The final laws are not in force in our community, but they are necessary for the good of the state. We have no method of protecting our laws; and so our laws are what our clerks want them

to be. We obtain them from copyists, but have no official record*
confirmed by an official text. The Greeks* used to be more punc-
tilious in this respect. They used to appoint 'Guardians of the
Law', and these men would keep an eye, not just on the text of
laws (that practice was also current among our ancestors), but
also on men's behaviour, and would call them back when they
47 strayed beyond the law. This duty should be discharged by the
censors. (Remember I have enacted that 'the post of censor shall
always have occupants' [11].) Before these same men, outgoing
magistrates are to give a public account of what they have done
during their period of office [11], and the censors are to pronounce
a preliminary judgement on them. In Greece this function is performed by officially appointed accusers. Yet these men cannot be
strict if they are not doing the job voluntarily. So it is better that
the account should be given and the case stated before the censors.
A full hearing, however, should be reserved for a trial, with pros-
ecutor, in a court of law.*

That is all that needs to be said about magistrates, unless you
think I have left something out.

ATTICUS: Well, even if we say nothing, does the point we have
reached not suggest to you what you should deal with next?

MARCUS: Next? I suppose you mean the courts, Pomponius, for
that subject follows on from the magistrates.

48–9. A discussion is adumbrated on the legal powers of magistrates

48 ATTICUS: What? Don't you think something should be said
about the law of the Roman people, as you set out to do?

MARCUS: What, may I ask, do you find wanting at this point?

ATTICUS: Wanting? Why, something which I think it is disgraceful for statesmen not to know about. You said a moment ago
that the text of the laws was obtained from copyists. By the same
token I notice that most magistrates, owing to their ignorance of
their own legal system, know only as much as their clerks wish.
Therefore, if, when you were setting out your laws about religion,
you thought it right to speak about the transference of religious
duties, you should see to it, now that your magistrates have been
duly appointed, that you discuss the legal powers of those in positions of authority.

MARCUS: I shall do so briefly, if I can manage it; for Marcus 49
Junius* wrote a very full account of the matter to your father, who
was a friend of his, and (in my view anyhow) handled it in
an expert and thorough manner. As for us, we should think and
speak independently on the subject of natural law, but on Roman
public law we shall state what has come down to us from earlier
generations.

ATTICUS: That is certainly my view, and I look forward to the
very treatment you indicate . . .

FRAGMENTS OF THE LAWS

1. We should think ourselves lucky that death will bring a state
which is either better, or else no worse, than what we know in
life. For when the mind is active without the body, that kind of
life is divine; but if the mind is devoid of consciousness, we surely
experience no ill (Lactantius, *Divinae Institutiones* 3. 19).

2. Just as one and the same nature holds together and underpins
the universe, and all its parts are in harmony with one another,
so all human beings blend with each other by nature; but because
of their wickedness they are at variance, and they fail to understand that they are blood-relatives and are placed under one and
the same protection. If that point were grasped, there can be no
doubt that men would live the life of gods (Lactantius, *Divinae
Institutiones* 5. 8).

3. Since, then, as we can see, the sun has now moved a little
beyond the zenith, and this whole place is not yet sufficiently
shaded by these young trees, let us, if you agree, go down to the
Liris and carry on the remainder of our discussion in the shade of
those alders (Macrobius, *Saturnalia* 6. 4. 8).

APPENDIX

NOTES ON THE ROMAN CONSTITUTION

Official Bodies

The **Senate** or **Council of Elders** was a body of 300 with ten members from each of thirty voting districts (*curiae*), which in turn were based on the original three tribes. The senators, or fathers of families, represented the richest and most powerful clans. At one time, as a much smaller body, they had advised the king. Under the Republic they advised the magistrates who consulted them, but in virtue of their corporate experience their influence in every area of government was far weightier than that implies.

The *comitia curiata* or **Assembly of Voting Districts**, originally consisting wholly of patricians, ratified the appointment of a new king. It met at the king's behest to pledge loyalty in war or to endorse a death-sentence. It also had some more minor functions, such as witnessing wills and adoptions. Its importance dwindled with the passage of time.

The *comitia centuriata* or **Assembly of Centuries**, which was originally summoned by the king, met in the *Campus Martius* (Field of Mars). Its organization and procedure are described on pp. 47–8, 189–90. The function of the body was to enact laws; to elect consuls, praetors, and censors; to vote in capital cases (i.e. those involving death or exile); and to declare war and peace.

The *comitia tributa* or **Assembly of Tribes**, representing the whole population, was convened by a consul or praetor. It elected quaestors and curule aediles. As it met within the city and was more democratic than the Assembly of Centuries, it gradually increased in importance. Its measures were apparently subject to the approval of Senate until 339.

The *concilium plebis* or **Council of the Plebs**, like the *comitia tributa* was organized by tribes, but was not attended by patricians. It was presided over by a tribune and it elected tribunes and plebeian aediles. It also issued resolutions (*plebiscita*), which after 287 had the status of laws, and heard trials of non-capital offences. The Council drew closer in function to the Assembly of Tribes (which patricians often failed to attend), and frequently the two bodies are not distinguished in our sources.

The plebeian leaders were not members of an impoverished urban proletariat. Their families were squires of substantial means, and when they succeeded in gaining access to the governing class, they soon formed a new nobility which in its turn became exclusive. In the last 150 years of the Republic ten new men reached the consulship. Cicero was the only one to do so between 93 and 48.

In the Senate, members were invited to speak in order of seniority. In the other bodies there was no debate from the floor; members simply voted on the issues presented to them. (At the preliminary meetings, however, officials would vigorously advocate or oppose bills.) Ropes divided the membership according to centuries or tribes. These enclosures were connected to the magistrate's platform by gangways. Each century or tribe produced a majority vote, which was then conveyed to the magistrate. Up to 241 BC new tribes were added for new citizens, but after that the number was fixed at 35: four in the city, sixteen in the immediate vicinity, and fifteen elsewhere, resulting from Rome's expansion in Italy. Thereafter new citizens, in particular the Italians after 84, were distributed through the existing tribes, which consequently ceased to be territorial units.

The **king** wore a purple robe and sat in an ivory chair—the *sella curulis* (derived from *currus* = chariot). He was attended by officials (lictors) carrying the *fasces* (bundles of rods tied round an axe) which symbolized his absolute power. Though head of the state religion, he delegated the performance of rituals and the interpretation of religious law to priests. He appointed arbitrators for civil suits and special officials for cases of treason and homicide. He was in charge of foreign relations, and was responsible for raising and commanding an army. His financial resources came from rents of public domains, customs, licences from the salt trade, and fines.

Magistrates

Consuls were two equal 'colleagues', elected annually by the Assembly of Centuries, and gave their names to the year. They inherited the king's regalia (though the full purple robe was reserved for special occasions), and also his attendants and symbols of power. They were in charge of foreign relations and had command of the army. At home they were the chief magistrates, convening and presiding over the Senate. In 366 the first plebeian became consul; but, as Roman magistrates had no salaries, such men had to be well off.

The **Dictator** or **Master of the People** was appointed only at times of crisis and held office for a maximum of six months. He was not elected by the people, but was nominated by a consul. His decisions were not subject to veto.

The *Magister Equitum* or **Master of the Cavalry** was appointed by the dictator as his assistant and had the rank of a praetor.

From about 443 two **Censors** were elected by the Assembly of Centuries from ex-consuls. They drew up a list of citizens and their property every five years for purposes of taxation. They entered office in the spring and held it for eighteen months; re-election was not allowed. They also revised the roll of the Senate and reviewed the knights, admitting new members and, in cases of disreputable conduct, expelling old ones. After the work was completed there was a public ceremony of purification in the Field of Mars, offering atonement for sin and thanks for blessings received.

Praetors were originally two military leaders (*prae* + *ire*); but at an early stage these came to be called consuls instead. In 366 the name praetor was attached to a newly instituted legal official, who had to be a patrician. He was elected by the Assembly of Centuries. In the middle of the third century the office was doubled, one praetor becoming the 'city praetor', the other (dealing with cases involving outsiders) the 'foreign praetor'. As provinces were acquired the numbers rose to four (with Sicily and Sardinia) and then to six (with Nearer and Further Spain). Sulla raised the number to eight, to provide chairmen for his courts of inquiry. There were sixteen under Caesar.

In the early fifth century the **Aediles** were two plebeian officials, elected by the Council of the Plebs, who managed the temple (*aedes*) of Ceres and Liber on the Aventine Hill and looked after its archives. Gradually their responsibilities were widened to cover the administration of the city (streets, public buildings, markets, water- and food-supply, public order). In 367 two curule aediles (initially patrician) were added to share these duties. They were elected by the Assembly of Tribes. The aediles also shared the task of organizing public games.

The **Quaestors** were two legal and financial assistants to the consuls, elected after 447 by the Assembly of Tribes. In 421 the number was raised to four, and plebeians were admitted. As a result of Rome's increasing power in Italy four more were added *c.*267. Eventually Sulla raised the number to twenty and decided that the post should give automatic entry to the Senate. In the second century their duties became mainly financial. They included the supervision of treasury records, the collection of taxes and fines, and the sale of property acquired by conquest.

By 449 the number of **Tribunes of the Plebs** had risen to ten. Their duty was to intervene on behalf of plebeians in trouble with the law.

The plebeians, in turn, swore to obey and protect them. They presided at the Council of the Plebs, and referred grievances to the consuls and Senate. By 216 they could convene and preside over meetings of the Senate. Because the tribunes had the right of veto, they were used by the senatorial authorities as a way of blocking unwelcome legislation.

Priests

Roman religion was a matter of ritual rather than doctrine. The priesthoods, which were held by secular magistrates, were retained by the patricians until 300. Then four plebeian **pontiffs** and five plebeian **augurs** were added, bringing the numbers up to eight and nine respectively. There was a special group of priests who consulted the Sibylline oracles when instructed to do so by the Senate. Their number was raised from two to ten in 367, and then to fifteen in the time of Sulla. Mention should also be made of the **fetiales** who carried out the rituals concerned with war and treaties.

Down to the third century pontiffs and augurs were appointed by their own colleges; after that they were elected by seventeen out of the thirty-five tribes, chosen by lot. The college of pontiffs also included the three major **flamens**, those of Jupiter, Mars, and Quirinus (there were fifteen in all, appointed from patrician families). As well as supervising the state cult, the *pontifex maximus* (chief pontiff) was in charge of the calendar. This involved the periodic intercalation of a month to bring the Roman lunar year into line with the sun. At the start of every year the *pontifex maximus* would post a list of forthcoming events on a board outside his residence. Both pontiffs and augurs were standing committees of the Senate, but the augurs acquired greater political influence from the custom of taking auspices. By searching the sky for signs they attempted to ascertain the will of the gods. Since no public action could be taken without divine approval, the authorities regularly persuaded the augurs to obstruct unwelcome decisions by discovering adverse omens. The whole system depended on the credulity of the masses and (at least) the double-think of the aristocracy. For a table of priests and their functions see Beard and North 20–1.

The Equites

An additional note is called for on the **equites** or **knights**. These men originally constituted the cavalry of the Roman army and had their horses supplied at public expense. They usually belonged to important families in the country towns, and had to possess fortunes of at least

400,000 sesterces. If they wished, they might gain entry to the lower ranks of the Senate; but, given the restrictions on the commercial activities of senators, many of them preferred to engage in business, which often involved the lucrative activity of letting contracts, including the right to collect taxes in the provinces. Between the time of Gaius Gracchus and Cicero (except for a short period under Sulla) the knights supplied at least a third of the court which tried cases of extortion. This gave them considerable political influence. Socially they mixed with senatorial families, with whom they formed a narrow upper-class band of the population.

EXPLANATORY NOTES

THE REPUBLIC

BOOK I

The missing portion of the preface will have contained, at least, an address to the dedicatee of the work, probably Cicero's brother Quintus, and an announcement of the subject, doubtless with some reference to Cicero's own position at the time of writing (the preface to *De Oratore* may be read for comparison).

Abstention from public life was recommended principally by the Epicureans, though this was subject to qualification (1. 10 below), and in fact many members of the Roman ruling class combined an interest in Epicurean philosophy with an active political career. At the point where our text begins, Cicero is using a familiar argument from the exploits of Roman patriots, a type of argument which he employed also in different philosophical contexts (*Paradoxa* 1. 12, *Tusculan Disputations* 1. 39, *Cato Maior* 75).

3 *the two Scipios*: Gnaeus and Publius: the latter was the father of Scipio Africanus the elder.

   Publius Africanus: Scipio Africanus the elder.

   Cato: Cato the Elder, for whom Cicero had particular admiration as a 'new man' like himself; cf. *R.* 2. 1. Cato remained active in politics until his death in 149 BC, at the age of 85. His political career was indeed stormy; he is said to have survived 44 prosecutions.

   Tusculum: now Frascati. This Latin community had received full Roman citizenship in 323 BC; cf. *L* 2. 5.

4 *moral excellence (virtus)*: see Note on the Translation. Cicero here touches on a question that was much discussed in ancient ethics; Socrates in Plato's dialogues constantly draws the analogy between moral virtues and practical skills or branches of knowledge (such as medicine or carpentry), and the Stoics, taking over the Socratic principle that virtue is a kind of knowledge, maintained that the truly wise and virtuous man was good at everything, including politics, regardless of whether he ever put his knowledge into practice. Cicero here maintains the common-sense (and Peripatetic) view that only the practical display of virtue qualifies a person to be called morally excellent.

   most important field of practice . . . is in the government of a state: cf. *R.* 6. 13 (in the Dream of Scipio).

statesman: Latin *civis*, literally 'citizen', but Cicero when using this word always envisages a leading member of a community who will take responsibility for governing it; cf. 1. 45 'a great citizen' and the phrase *optimus civis* 'best citizen', alias the *rector rei publicae* 'ruler', 'statesman' (see Introd. p. xxii).

in wisdom itself: the word *sapientia* 'wisdom' was often used to refer to philosophy without further qualification, although it equally often referred to practical wisdom and common sense. Cicero's argument here plays on the two meanings.

5 *Camillus' exile, etc.*: the first two of these examples belong to earlier Roman history; the others all belong to the turbulent period since the Gracchi. Nasica was the killer of Tiberius Gracchus: cf. on 6. 8.

murder of his chief supporters: something appears to be missing from the text after *C. Mari clades*. We have assumed that Cicero is speaking only of the massacre of Marians by Sulla. It is clear from Appian *Bella Civilia* 1. 71 ff. that Marius gave as good as he got, but Cicero was loyal to his fellow-townsman. For a similar context (possibly of relevance for the reconstruction of the text here) cf. *De Oratore* 3. 2. 8.

6 *that the state had been saved*: Cicero was prevented by the tribune Metellus Nepos from making a speech on laying down his office as consul at the end of 63 BC; so he merely took the customary oath, adding to it the words that he had 'saved the state' (referring to his defeat of the Catilinarian conspiracy). Evidently the public, or such of it as was present on the occasion, approved. Cf. *Fam.* 5. 2. 7 (letter to Metellus Nepos' brother, Metellus Celer), *In Pisonem* 6.

maintenance: normally owed by children to their parents, in the absence of old-age pensions. The image is as old as Aeschylus, *Seven against Thebes* 477 θανὼν τροφεῖα πληρώσει χθονί; cf. also Lysias 2. 70, Plato, *Republic* 520b.

excuses: in *De Officiis* 1. 71, Cicero in a more reflective mood admits two classes of persons who need not take part in politics: (*a*) those with uncertain health (he was perhaps thinking of his own father, cf. *L.* 2. 3), and (*b*) 'those with outstanding intellect who have devoted themselves to learning'; but in the case of others he reiterates the arguments here advanced.

7 *proviso*: this was the Epicurean doctrine. Cicero's objection to it is telling, and this paragraph establishes the idea, important for the rest of the argument, that politics is a career or profession involving specific skills, training, and experience.

8 *men who enjoy a very great authority*: Plato and Aristotle.

Seven Wise Men: the usual list was: Thales, Pittacus, Bias, Solon, Cleobulus, Periander, and Chilon (though there were many variants).

Thales is the only one who was not a leading politician and the only one who is now counted as a philosopher.

preserving: this echoes Cicero's own claim to have 'saved' the state.

Since I have had the good fortune . . .: cf. *L*. 3. 14.

⟨I am not unqualified . . .⟩: there is clearly a gap in the text; the insertion necessary for the sense is here made before *auctores*, following Keyes (NB full details of modern sources are given in the Bibliography).

to you and me: Cicero is in all probability addressing his brother Quintus. The alleged reporting of the conversation by Rutilius Rufus is a transparent but plausible fiction. Rutilius had been an associate of Scipio and his circle; he was in exile in Asia Minor from 92 BC until his death in 77, and Cicero and his brother visited him there during their tour of Greece and the East in 78–77 BC (cf. *Brutus* 83). Rutilius was something of a historian of his own times and Cicero doubtless learned from his writings as well as from his conversation.

this whole matter: reading *ad rationem omnium ⟨harum⟩ rerum* with Ziegler.

consulship of Tuditanus and Aquilius: 129 BC, the year in which Scipio Aemilianus died.

Latin holidays: the *Feriae Latinae* commemorated the alliance between Rome and the Latins and traditionally marked the beginning of the campaigning season; all the magistrates left Rome to offer sacrifice on the Alban Mount together with the leaders of other Latin communities. Scipio and his friends, not being magistrates in that year, could treat the period of the festival simply as a holiday. It was a 'moveable feast', the date being fixed by the consuls on entering office. In the earlier period of the Republic it took place in the spring, but from 153 BC the beginning of the consular year was changed to coincide with the beginning of the civil year on 1 January (cf. note on *L*. 2. 54; see Michels 97–9) and the Latin festival was apparently moved earlier; in the present dialogue it is still winter (1. 18), though a fine day.

9 *a second sun*: this portent is referred to by Cicero also at *De Natura Deorum* 2. 14 and there is no reason to doubt that the report of it came from historical records; similar occurrences are mentioned from time to time, e.g. Cic. *De Divinatione* 1. 97, Livy 28. 11. 3, 41. 21. 13, Pliny, *Natural History* 2. 99. In the passage from *De Natura Deorum* it is taken to foreshadow the death of Scipio Aemilianus; if this was the usual interpretation there would be a dramatic irony in making Scipio and his friends discuss it here with such rational confidence. The phenomenon is a well-recognized natural one, and there is no need either to suppose that the portent was mere invention or hallucination, or to invoke literary precedents like the distressing experience of Pentheus in Euripides, *Bacchae* 918. Images of the sun may

appear in different parts of the sky, caused by reflection and/or refraction of light by ice crystals in the atmosphere. The commonest such phenomenon is the *parhelion* or 'sun-dog', which occurs to one side of the sun itself; there may be two, one on either side. Parhelia appear significantly smaller and fainter than the sun; they are not round but usually appear the shape of a tear-drop with the narrow end pointing away from the sun; and they show rainbow-like colour effects due to refraction of light. A parhelion may have been thought of as a second sun, but a more likely candidate is the *anthelion* or counter-sun, which appears at the same altitude as the sun but opposite to it in the sky. It is not so often observed, but descriptions indicate that it appears about the same size, shape and colour as the sun, although significantly fainter. Being uncoloured it is assumed to arise from reflection alone, not refraction. (The fact that the anthelion appears opposite the sun would also enhance its status as a symbol of political confrontation.) Ancient scientists were well aware of these phenomena. Aristotle, *Meteorologica* 3. 2. 6. 372ᵃ gives a brief account; Seneca, *Naturales Quaestiones* 1. 11. 2–3 refers to the double or triple suns reported as omens, and explains them as parhelia, the cause of which he gets approximately right; cf. also Pliny, *Natural History* 2. 99. For a modern meteorological account see Geddes, 326–31. We are most grateful to Dr David Jones of the Chemistry Department, University of Newcastle upon Tyne, for information on this subject.

Plato: this passage provides one of the most explicit pieces of ancient evidence on the relation of the views expressed by 'Socrates' in Plato's dialogues to those of the historical Socrates—or at least on how it was regarded in Cicero's time. On the reported journeys of Plato see Riginos; the evidence for a journey to Egypt is regarded as suspect, though the Italian voyages are generally accepted as historical.

10 *Numantia*: this Spanish fortress was captured by Scipio in 133 BC, thus bringing to an end the war in Spain.

Laelius: on the friendship of Scipio and Laelius see further Powell (1) 9.

old enough to have been quaestors: on Fannius and Scaevola, see note on *Laelius* 3, Powell (1) 77–8.

11 *universe*: the idea that the whole universe is our home is a Stoic one; cf. *L.* 1. 23, *De Finibus* 3. 64, *De Natura Deorum* 2. 154, Seneca, *De Otio* 4. 1.

some decree: Manilius was an eminent lawyer, and this passage (like many in Cicero) makes facetious use of very precise Roman legal terminology. The decree referred to is the *interdictum uti possidetis*, which was the first step in a procedure used in cases of disputed possession of land. The Roman law of actions required that one party should be in actual possession and the other should bring the action; the onus of proof lay with the bringer of the action. It was therefore

necessary first to determine who actually had possession. The inter-
dict, granted by the praetor, prohibited either party from disturbing
the other's possession while the preliminary issue of fact was decided.
See Gaius 4. 160; Justinian, *Institutiones* 4. 15. 4; *Digest* 43. 17. 1;
Jolowicz 273–4.

Sulpicius Galus: his astronomical interests are mentioned also by
Cicero in *Cato Maior* 50. His demonstration with the globe was in
fact quite irrelevant to the phenomenon of the double sun, except in
so far as it established the principle that celestial phenomena in general
could be explained rationally.

12 *globe*: this passage gives us most of the information we have on the
'Archimedean sphere', which was evidently a mechanism for demon-
strating the movements of the heavenly bodies, similar to what has in
modern times been called an 'orrery', although the exact details of its
construction remain somewhat obscure. It could well have been as
mechanically sophisticated as the first-century BC clockwork calendar
of which remains were discovered in a shipwreck off the island of
Antikythera (see Peterson 21–32). According to Cicero, *De Natura
Deorum* 1. 88 the philosopher Poseidonius also had such a sphere. In
what follows it must be remembered that Archimedes' model of the
solar system would have been geocentric.

temple of Valour (Virtus): near the Porta Capena at the southern
entrance to Rome; vowed by M. Marcellus after his triumph over the
Gauls in 222, and dedicated by his son seventeen years later (Livy 29.
11. 13).

that other globe: presumably an ordinary geographical globe, made to
demonstrate the sphericity of the earth; Eudoxus will have made a
celestial globe marked with the constellations (showing the sky inside
out, as it were), whereas Archimedes' 'sphere' or 'globe' was presumably not solid but based on a framework of interlocking rings or bands
(what is called an armillary sphere).

cone-shaped shadow: causing an eclipse of the moon; this is quite
correct astronomically as regards the relative positions of sun, moon
and earth. To demonstrate this properly, the Archimedean sphere
would have needed to incorporate a lamp to represent the sun, which
would cast a shadow on the other side of the globe that represented
the earth. An eclipse of the sun, at new moon, is often followed two
weeks later by an eclipse of the moon, because both happen when the
moon's orbit is in the same plane as the earth's. Cf. Cic. *De Divinatione* 2. 17; Pliny, *Natural History* 2. 7.

13 *in the great war . . . between Athens and Sparta*: this eclipse happened
on 3 August 431 BC; Bickerman 87; cf. Thucydides 2. 28; Plutarch,
Pericles 35. 2.

the moon and night: this phrase, odd-looking at first sight, is in fact
appropriate, as the eclipse referred to took place at sunset (Skutsch

ad loc.). By our reckoning it was apparently on 21 June 399 BC.

Major Annals: the *Annales Maximi* were a chronological record of official events, based on the archives of the Pontifex Maximus. Their style was apparently laconic (cf. *L.* 1. 6). Events such as eclipses, which were thought to be of religious significance, were naturally included in them. Cf. *De Oratore* 2. 52; Cornell 13–15; Frier.

July the seventh in the reign of Romulus: it seems that this eclipse has not been identified with certainty; not surprisingly, since the dates of Romulus' reign are purely legendary and it is impossible to identify the year or to determine the degree of inaccuracy in the calendar at that time.

Romulus: the deification of Romulus is here treated in a rationalistic manner; cf. 2. 17–20; in the Dream of Scipio, however, we learn that the souls of all good statesmen ascend to heaven (6. 13, 6. 16). There is a gap in the text here, but it is possible to see roughly what the train of thought must have been. Tubero remarks that Scipio appears to have changed his mind (presumably from 1. 15). Scipio will then have responded that he did not mean to disparage scientific study (cf. 1. 30 below). On the speech which follows see Powell (4); Zetzel 117. The ideas derive from philosophical 'protreptic', i.e. exhortations to philosophical study.

14 *citizen's . . . right (Ius Quiritium)*: the legal term for civil-law ownership as opposed to mere possession. Cicero plays on the technical language of Roman law.

necessary rather than desirable things: cf. Plato, *Republic* 347c–d (Lee's translation): 'That [the prospect of being governed by someone worse than themselves] is what, I believe, frightens honest men into accepting power, and they approach it not as if it were something desirable out of which they were going to do well, but as if it were something unavoidable, which they cannot find anyone better or equally qualified to undertake.'

doing nothing: i.e. not taking part in public business; this is the language of the Roman senator for whom even the busiest people were living a life of 'leisure' (*otium*) if they were not involved in politics and warfare.

15 *him*: Q. *Aelius* Tubero, here assumed to be related to Sextus *Aelius* Paetus Catus.

Iphigenia: by Ennius (Jocelyn fr. 95, pp. 108, 324–8), based on Euripides' *Iphigenia in Aulis*.

16 *Zethus*: the debate between the warrior Zethus and his brother Amphion the musician in the *Antiope* of Euripides (on which Pacuvius' play of the same name was based) is mentioned by Plato in his *Gorgias*; cf. *De Oratore* 2. 155.

three commissioners: the commission set up under Tiberius Gracchus'

law to reassign the public land, dispossessing the Italian landowners
in favour of poorer Roman citizens. The issue split both the Senate
and the people, as is made clear here. Scipio supported the *status quo*
and the interests of the Italian landed classes ('allies and Latins'). This
whole passage is written (not surprisingly) from the point of view of
the supporters of Scipio and opponents of Gracchus; after all, it is
Scipio's greatest friend who is talking; but Cicero himself also took
very much the same line.

17 *Panaetius . . . Polybius*: both men were recipients of Scipio's patronage. The reference to them here has tended to be taken as a coded
message that Cicero is about to make detailed use of some work of
Panaetius or Polybius or both, but this goes beyond what may legitimately be deduced from the text. It is clear that Cicero's political
theory and account of the Roman constitution has much in common
with that of Polybius, but there are also considerable differences (see
Zetzel 22–4), and definite influence from Panaetius is difficult to detect.
The mention of the two names here is, more than anything else, a piece
of imaginative scene-setting.

craftsman: the Socratic analogy (cf. above, note on 1. 2 'moral excellence'); Cicero again insists that politics is an art. His emphasis here
on the hereditary duties of the Roman ruling class is worth reflecting
on: Cicero himself was not born into the Roman senatorial order but
made his own way into it.

18 *toga-wearing people*: 'The Romans, lords of the world, the toga-
wearing nation', as Virgil (*Aeneid* 1. 282) was later to put it. We are
not to think here of the toga as symbol of civilian as opposed to military life, but as a symbol of nationhood.

the meaning of the name: to begin with definitions is a familiar technique in philosophical expositions, doubtless inspired by the habits of
Socrates in Plato's dialogues; cf. *De Finibus* 1. 29.

initial union: Greek philosophical accounts of politics tended to do just
this; e.g. Aristotle, *Politics* 1252ᵃ.

19 *property of the public (res populi)*: the word 'republic', *res publica*,
literally means 'public property' (although *res* has a wider meaning,
embracing also at least 'affairs', 'business'). *Res publica* approximately
represents Greek πόλις and πολιτεία, but the definition given here is
based on the etymology of the Latin term: see M. Schofield, 'Cicero's
Definition of *Res Publica*', in Powell (3).

not every kind of human gathering: cf. Aristotle, *Politics* 7. 1328ᵇ, the
polis must be self-sufficient; the Stoics (quoted by Dio Chrysostom 36.
20) included law in the definition.

weakness: the explanation of the origin of society as a contract for
mutual protection was familiar in antiquity. It was associated particularly with the Epicureans (cf. Lucretius 5); Polybius also believed
it, and in 6. 5. 7 actually cites 'weakness' as the reason for the

development of societies. Cicero here rejects this view in favour of the Aristotelian and Stoic line that it is part of human nature to form communities regardless of utility.

decision-making process: the word used here, *consilium*, means both 'policy' (cf. 'counsel') and 'deliberative body' (cf. 'council'; the English spelling is influenced by a mistaken connection with another Latin word *concilium* 'assembly, gathering').

20 *aristocracy (optimates)*: see Note on the Translation.

nod and wish: we have accepted Castiglioni's conjecture *nutu ac (voluntate; eodem) modo*.

depraved version: it was standard in Greek political theorizing since Plato to divide the possible constitutions into good and bad versions, the bad sometimes being seen as the result of corruption of the good, but sometimes as arising in other ways. Thus tyranny is seen as the perversion of monarchy, oligarchy as that of aristocracy, and mob rule as that of democracy.

21 *cruelly capricious*: we retain *ad immutandi animi licentiam* and take it as adverbial, qualifying *crudelissimus*.

cycles: the concept of cycles of political change was prominent in Plato's *Republic* and, in a more elaborate form, was an important element in Polybius' constitutional theory: see Walbank 131–2, 139–46. For the development of this theme see below, 1. 64–8, 2. 45.

mixture: this is the first mention of the 'mixed' constitution, which is to be a key concept in the ensuing discussion. The theory of the mixed constitution is again associated especially with Polybius: for his version and its antecedents see Walbank 132, 135–7. However, Cicero first deals with the question of whether any of the simple constitutions, monarchy, aristocracy and democracy, is to be preferred to the others. Scipio successively presents the arguments for democracy and aristocracy in the section that follows. He does not endorse these arguments himself; still less should we assume that Cicero endorsed them.

22 *Rhodian*: the constitution of Rhodes was more purely democratic even than that of Athens: Cicero describes it below at 3. 48.

Ennius: this quotation is used by Cicero also in *De Officiis* 1. 26, but there is no information as to its original context: Jocelyn fr. 169, p. 141.

50: this section almost certainly comes from the democrats' speech. Büchner and others have attempted to show that it comes instead from a lost speech in favour of monarchy; but the content of this section would hardly fit an expression of monarchist views, since the argument is that *all* kings are equivalent to tyrants.

23 *a royal family*: Sparta had a dual kingship; one of the kings always came from the family of the Agids, the other from the Eurypontids.

chosen by lot: many of the Athenian officials were appointed by lot, considered a more 'democratic' procedure than popular election, although the choice of candidates was made in such a way as to prevent the appointment of anyone thoroughly unsuitable.

25 *But what about yourself, Scipio?*: pressed further by Laelius, Scipio now puts the arguments for monarchy in his own person. There are six arguments: (1) Jupiter rules the universe; (2) Rome had kings not long ago; (3) monarchy is like the domination of reason over the passions; (4) it is common practice to have a single individual in charge of an estate or a household, etc.; (5) the Romans in time of crisis commit the state to the power of a single dictator; (6) a just king such as Romulus leaves nothing to be desired. However, Scipio is presented as approving of monarchy only in theory and by comparison with the other two simple forms, not unconditionally (cf. more clearly still 2. 47–8); note also that Scipio in this passage does not elicit full agreement from the other speakers. It is made quite clear that he regards monarchy as a dangerous form of government because of the ease with which it can turn into despotism, whereas the mixed constitution offers safeguards against this contingency.

Aratus: his poem began in Cicero's version with the words *Ab Iove Musarum primordia*; this opening formula was adapted by other poets including Virgil (*Eclogues* 3. 60).

26 *Homer's words*: Iliad 1. 530.

57: some editors here insert fr. 1 (printed at the end of Book 1), but others place it in the gap at section 34. It seems impossible to determine which placing is right. The speaker is probably Laelius.

a proud one: alluding to the name of Tarquinius Superbus, 'Tarquin the Proud'.

A very just one: Servius Tullius (cf. 2. 38).

Greece was already growing old: an exaggeration; Romulus supposedly lived in the eighth century BC.

28 *ship's captain and doctor*: these analogies were so familiar from Plato that Cicero passes over them lightly here.

29 *dictator*: see Appendix: Notes on the Roman Constitution. It is peculiar that Cicero ignores the obvious derivation of *dictator* as 'one who dictates', and instead concentrates on the fact that the dictator 'is appointed' (*dicitur*).

our augurs' books: Scipio addresses Laelius as a fellow-member of the augural college, of which Cicero himself became a member in 53 BC (while he was writing the *Republic*). These books were manuals of procedure; their extent and availability to those outside the college is uncertain.

As Ennius says: on the quotation from Ennius see Skutsch 105–9.

30 *Plato*: Republic 8. 562c ff.

32 *something else*: retaining MS reading *aliud*.

33 *two dangers*: Carthage and Numantia.

   you yourself: reading *ipse*, Watt's conjecture for MS *esse* (the two
   words sounded similar or identical in late Latin pronunciation; cf.
   Italian *esso* from *ipsum*).

   Fr. 1: see on 1. 57 above.

34 *Fr. 3*: attributed to Book 1, but its placing is quite uncertain.

BOOK 2

Most of what survives of the second book is taken up with an account of
the development of the Roman constitution. The purpose is not mere anti-
quarianism, although there appears to be an element of that in some of the
details (as Cicero makes Scipio virtually acknowledge in 2. 55). As Scipio
says several times in the dialogue, the aim is to provide an actual historical
example both of what is meant by the mixed constitution in its best form,
and of the various changes that can take place in the government of a state,
instead of discussing these matters in purely theoretical terms or, as Plato
did, with reference to an imaginary ideal state. The early history of Rome,
as understood by Cicero, provides him with examples of (*a*) pure monarchy (the reign of Romulus), which nevertheless soon acquired aristocratic
and democratic elements; (*b*) tyranny (Tarquinius Superbus, and the subsequent attempts of Sp. Cassius, Sp. Maelius, M. Manlius to gain control of
the state); (*c*) pure aristocracy (the decemvirate) which within a very short
time was corrupted into oligarchy (the second set of decemvirs); (*d*) if not
pure democracy, at any rate a period in which the people demanded more
rights for itself (immediately after the expulsion of the kings) and two
popular revolts (the two Secessions of the Plebs); (*e*) an imperfect version
of the mixed constitution parallel to that of Sparta or Carthage (the constitution of Servius Tullius); and (*f*) the fully-fledged republican constitution, a better version of the mixed constitution than any other yet devised.
As soon as (*f*) is reached, the narrative ends. This does not mean that Cicero
saw the republican constitution of 449 BC as ideal or perfect, merely that,
granted the conceptual framework of Greek political theory, no further significant and radical changes took place thereafter. Although, therefore, this
account happens to be the earliest surviving narrative of the regal period
and the beginnings of the Republic, it has no pretensions to completeness;
little is said, for example, of the 'struggle of the orders' or of Rome's rise
as a Mediterranean power. It is clear that Cicero was reasonably careful
with his historical research, but much of the material came not from authentic records but from tradition and legend, or else from antiquarian attempts
to explain the origins of existing institutions. Cicero's main point of reference, in fact, was the Roman constitution as it existed in his own time. His
account may be compared with our other main sources for the period, Livy
and Dionysius of Halicarnassus, both of whom wrote somewhat later but
give much fuller historical narratives. See further Cornell; E. Rawson (1)
36–7; Ferrary (3); Hathaway. On the problem of Cicero's relation to Polybius see Walbank 147–8.

35 *two fathers*: Scipio's real father, L. Aemilius Paulus, and his adoptive
father, P. Cornelius Scipio (son of Scipio Africanus).

no genius of such magnitude: the style of this passage is ponderous in
the Latin, probably reflecting Cato's own style. Scipio prefaces his narrative with the observation that the Roman constitution is the result
of gradual evolution, and is better that way: an implicit condemnation
of suggestions for radical change.

'origin': Cato's historical work was entitled *Origines*; the first part of
it did indeed deal with the origins of Rome and the other communities of Italy (Nepos, *Cato* 3. 3). It is possible, though unprovable, that
Cicero drew on this work as a source.

36 *Romulus*: the Romulus story here appears in a simplified form, without
the murder of Remus, which, whatever its true significance, was
irrelevant to Cicero's purposes here. The she-wolf appears merely as
'an animal from the forest'; Cicero distances himself from folk-tale.

augury: cf. 2. 16 below. According to the legend, Romulus and Remus
took auspices to find out which of them should be king. Remus
ascended the Aventine and saw six vultures; Romulus ascended the
Palatine and saw twelve. This decided the issue in Romulus' favour.
Cicero again omits the element of competition with Remus, and
regards Romulus as the founder of the Roman institution of augury,
an institution which (as an augur himself) he constantly praises,
although he had philosophical difficulties with the concept of divination (cf. *L*. 2. 31 ff., and *De Divinatione* 2).

a colony: Ostia; cf. 2. 33.

coastal sites were not particularly suitable: the Greeks debated whether
cities should be founded near the sea: cf. Plato, *Laws* 704a–705b, Aristotle, *Politics* 7. 6. Livy very probably recalls this passage in 5. 54. 4
(the speech of Camillus persuading the Romans not to abandon the
city).

37 *Carthage and Corinth*: both ruthlessly destroyed by Rome in the mid-
second century BC. Carthage was, of course, destroyed by the Scipio
who speaks here; Corinth, by L. Mummius, brother of the Spurius
Mummius who is a minor character in this dialogue. Cf. Purcell.

apart from Phlius . . . : Cicero discusses this passage in a letter to
Atticus (6. 2. 3). Atticus had queried the statement that all Peloponnesian communities had a sea-coast: what about Arcadia? Cicero
replied that he had himself been surprised to find it in a work of
Dicaearchus, a careful researcher who himself lived in the Peloponnese, but had consulted his learned slave Dionysius, who was at first
equally puzzled but then pointed out that Arcadia had an outlet to the
sea at Lepreon, and that some other apparently landlocked communities were late foundations. 'So', says Cicero, 'I transferred the passage
in so many words from Dicaearchus.' Phlius is in the north-east
Peloponnese.

Dorians: not in the wider sense of speakers of the Doric dialect, but in the narrower sense of inhabitants of the area called Doris in northern Greece.

38 *a novel and somewhat crude plan*: for the Rape of the Sabines cf. Livy 1. 9–13.

39 *'Fathers'*: the senators were called *patres* or 'fathers' in certain contexts. 'Patricians' were supposedly descendants of the senators of the regal period (2. 23 below).

three tribes: the Roman citizen body was anciently divided into three tribes called *Ramnes*, *Tities*, and *Luceres* (cf. 2. 36 below); the present context provides an explanation (philologically rather implausible) for these names. They may reflect early ethnic divisions (Latin, Sabine, Etruscan). Each tribe was divided into ten 'voting-districts' or *curiae*. The assembly of the Roman people thus divided was called the *comitia curiata* (cf. Appendix). These divisions still existed for ceremonial purposes in the late Republic, but the three ancient tribes had long been superseded for all practical functions by a newer system of thirty-five tribes (Cornell 173; Staveley 122–3; Taylor (2) 3–5).

Sparta: the parallel was often drawn between the Roman 'Senate' and the Spartan 'Gerousia': both words mean 'assembly of elders'; cf. 2. 50 below.

explained later: not in the extant parts of the text. On the client system see Cornell 289–92.

40 *livestock etc.*: Cicero is right in deriving the word *pecunia* 'money' from *pecus* 'cattle'. The same semantic shift is apparent in the English word 'fee'; cf. German *Vieh* 'cattle', from a Germanic root cognate with *pecus*. 'Cattle' went the opposite way; it originally meant 'property' generally, cf. 'chattels', 'capital'.

eclipse of the sun: cf. above, 1. 25.

second year of the seventh Olympiad: the first Olympiad began in 776/5 BC; the date given here is therefore 751/0, which is also the date given by Polybius (cf. 2. 27 below). The now conventional date of 753 was established by Cicero's friend Atticus; its popularization by Varro leads to its modern designation as the 'Varronian' dating. See Zetzel 175–6; Bickerman 76–8.

confusion over the name: another Lycurgus, king of Elis, was supposed to have founded the Olympic games.

sometimes clumsily conceived: the rest of this paragraph is absent from the MS but is preserved by St Augustine. The missing portion will have contained a mention of the poet Hesiod who was supposed to be the grandfather of Stesichorus.

41 *doyen of writers*: Plato.

best men (optimates): cf. Introd. n. 14.

42 *'Patricians'*: cf. above, note on 2. 14.

interregnum: under the Republic, the consuls had responsibility for conducting the election of their successors. If both consulships were vacant, the Senate appointed an official known as *interrex* (lit. 'between-king') who held office for five days only. Successive *interreges* were appointed until the elections could be held; the period during which *interreges* held office was known as an *interregnum*. The Romans believed, as indeed the name of the office implies, that this procedure went back to the regal period.

Assembly of Voting Districts: see Appendix and 2. 14 above. Cicero's point here is that the appointment of the king was in two stages. First the king was chosen by the *comitia curiata*; then the same body formally passed a law to confer the regal power on him. This statute was called *lex curiata*. Under the Republic, the election of the higher magistrates was no longer in the hands of the *comitia curiata* but in those of the *comitia centuriata*, on which see below, 2. 39 ff., but their position was still formally confirmed by a *lex curiata*. The *lex curiata* had been the subject of controversy from time to time during Cicero's career. It is very unclear precisely what it enabled a magistrate to do that he could not, in practice, do without it. At one point Cicero implies that it concerned the right to command an army (*De Lege Agraria* 2. 30). In 54 BC, at the time when Cicero was conceiving the plan of the *Republic*, there was apparently obstruction of the normal procedure in connection with the appointment of Appius Claudius to govern the province of Cilicia. Appius declared that he would go to his province even without the law, at his own expense (*Fam.* 1. 9. 25, *Att.* 4. 18. 4, *Q. fr.* 3. 2. 3). However, it is not clear that Cicero is here alluding directly to these political squabbles. It is more likely that he has in mind a general concern for legitimacy, and that his purpose is to trace democratic elements in the Roman constitution right from the beginning, and to highlight the function of the popular assembly as the legal source of political power. He mentions the *lex curiata* again in connection with each of the four succeeding kings, Tullus Hostilius, Ancus Marcius, Tarquinius Priscus, and Servius Tullius.

divided . . . the territory: conquered territory was, in the first instance, public property (*ager publicus populi Romani*). Two things could be done with it: it could be leased to tenants who would pay a rent to the treasury, or it could be divided up and allocated to private owners. In historical times, as most notably in the case of the Gracchi, such allocations always stirred up violent controversy, because they invariably involved land that had already been leased, and thus entailed both dispossession of existing landholders and loss of state revenue. Cicero himself was strongly opposed to such measures (cf. Introd. pp. xviii–xix). But here he envisages an ideal, primitive situation, in which the land is simply lying unused and may be allocated to individuals without offending anyone, as happened in the case of some early Greek colonies.

priests: the pontifices; see Appendix.

laws: the so-called *leges regiae* or royal laws, regulating religious procedures, were supposed to derive from the reign of Numa.

43 *Salii*: a highly aristocratic religious fraternity responsible for certain rituals connected with Mars, including ceremonial war-dances, whence the name (*salire* = to jump or dance).

rituals: ritual formulae had to be recited with absolute precision; if a mistake was made, the whole ritual had to be repeated from the beginning, together with an expiatory sacrifice.

44 *senate house*: the senate-house of the Republic was called the *Curia Hostilia* and was supposed to have been built by Tullus Hostilius. The present building on the site dates from the reign of Diocletian.

place for the people's assembly: the Comitium, the open area in front of the senate-house.

fetials: priests responsible for the rituals of declaring war and concluding treaties; cf. *L. 2. 21.*

lictors: attendants who walked before the king or, in republican times, the higher magistrates, carrying the *fasces* (bundles of rods) which symbolized regal or magisterial power. Consuls in the Republic were entitled to twelve lictors, as the kings were supposed to have been.

46 *greater families, lesser families*: on the rather shadowy distinction between the 'greater' and 'lesser' patrician families, see R. E. Mitchell, 134 n. 11 and 153–4.

knights: see Appendix.

I notice, incidentally, that . . . maintaining them: this parenthesis explains the origin (via Tarquinius Priscus' Corinthian father) of a Roman custom of supporting the cavalry by means of a tax on the childless and on unmarried women, doubtless to compensate for the fact that they were not providing manpower (though others take *orborum et viduarum* to mean 'widows and orphans': Nicolet 36–45). But Livy 1. 43. 9 attributes the introduction of this tax (on *viduae* alone) to Servius Tullius, not Tarquinius Priscus, and the present passage in Cicero is the only evidence that such a tax existed at Corinth. In addition to its possibly dubious content, the sentence breaks up the narrative so abruptly as to suggest that it may be an interpolation; see Nicolet 29–31.

twelve hundred: there is doubt about the number; in Livy 1. 36. 7, which deals with the same event, the number appears in some manuscripts as 1,800, in others as 1,300. Clearly 1,300 is wrong, as the number must be divisible into six equal 'centuries'. 1,200 is written in our MS as ∞ACCC, i.e. *M ac* (= 'and') *CC*. A correction to ∞DCCC (1,800) would be very easy, but since the reading in Livy is not absolutely certain either, we have retained the MS reading.

Roman Games: the *Ludi Romani* lasted a fortnight in September.

Jupiter Optimus Maximus: the temple of Jupiter 'Best and Greatest' on the Capitol was the destination of triumphal processions, where captured spoils were dedicated. The letters 'D.O.M.' (*Deo Optimo Maximo*) in Christian dedicatory inscriptions represent a Renaissance classicizing revival.

a slave: there may be a connection between the name Servius and the word *servus*, a slave; cf. Cornell 131–2.

47 *official fabrication*: cf. Livy 1. 41, according to whom this episode was masterminded by the queen, Tanaquil.

39: this section is an account of the institution of the *comitia centuriata*, the assembly which elected the higher magistrates throughout the republican period. Cicero clearly brings out the main point in connection with this assembly: '*the preponderance of votes should be in the hands, not of the masses, but of the wealthy.*' The population was divided into 'classes' on the basis of individual wealth, as assessed at the five-yearly census. Each 'class' contained a certain number of 'centuries', each with one vote, but the centuries of the poor were much larger than those of the rich, and the individual votes of the poorer citizens counted for relatively little. The highest class of all was that of the equestrians. To the original six centuries of publicly endowed cavalry established by Tarquinius Priscus (cf. 2. 36) Servius Tullius was supposed to have added twelve more, making eighteen (the number in historical times). The rest of the people, originally the infantry, were divided into five classes. The first class comprised citizens with property valued at 100,000 sesterces or more. According to Livy and Dionysius there were originally eighty centuries in the first class, but in the third century BC this was reduced to seventy, to produce a correlation with the new system of thirty-five tribes. It is the newer system that Cicero describes here. The vote of each century was announced openly as it was cast; voting was in descending order of wealth, and stopped as soon as a majority (i.e. 97 centuries out of 193) was reached. Cicero here envisages a situation, apparently not uncommon, in which the first class together with the equestrians and 'carpenters' all voted the same way. In such a case, only eight more centuries were needed to secure a majority. The effect was that whenever there was near-unanimity among the rich, the mass of the poorer citizens did not get the chance to vote at all. The centuriate assembly was not only based originally on military organization, but was actually referred to formally as *exercitus* (the army); it met in the Campus Martius, the traditional parade-ground of the Roman people (though civilian dress was worn). The preponderance given to wealth may astound a modern democrat: the Roman argument was that in matters of war and peace, which were originally the main business of this assembly, the views of those with most to gain or lose should carry the greatest weight. Cf. Livy 1. 43; Dion. Hal. 4. 16–18; Cornell 179–97; Staveley 123–9; Taylor (2) 85–106.

original six: the *sex suffragia* (lit. 'six votes') representing the six orig- inal equestrian centuries established by Tarquinius Priscus.

carpenters (fabri tignarii): they were allotted a separate century, doubt- less owing to their special function in the army; it voted with the first class of propertied citizens. Some sources speak of a second century of *fabri* (perhaps metalworkers). There were also special centuries for *accensi* (reservists, who acted as servants when not called for military duties), trumpeters and horn-players, cf. 2. 40 below, but these voted after the fifth class and before the 'proletarians'.

the total is eighty-nine: the number 89 must be correct. The manu- script originally read VIIII but the correcting hand added LXXX above the line. It is probable that the word *octoginta* dropped out after the previous word, *data*; the scribe's eye will have slipped from one word ending in *-ta* to the next.

⟨*have no say . . . mass of the people*⟩: the construction changes abruptly here, and a gap in the text seems likely; we have supplied a likely restoration of the sense.

assidui: the word is the same as the ordinary Latin word *assiduus* (whence our 'assiduous') and means 'settled'; but Cicero offers an implausible etymology connecting it with *as*, the name of a coin.

48 *proletarii*: the 'proletarians', i.e. all citizens with no property (Cicero's etymology is right in this case: *proles* 'children'), were all grouped together in a single 'century', which voted last of all (and therefore only when the votes of the previous 192 centuries produced a tie).

Fr. 1 (printed at the end of Book 2) may belong here.

Sparta, and Carthage: standard examples of the mixed constitution from Aristotle's *Politics* onwards.

without balance: the Latin word is *temperata*, 'tempered' or 'con- trolled' (cf. 2. 65 and the musical image in 2. 69). It is not clear that Cicero here has a fully developed theory of constitutional 'checks and balances', though something more like it emerges in the discussion of tribunes at 2. 57–9 below; and he is certainly not talking about con- stitutional monarchy in the modern British sense. The main difference between a king like Servius Tullius and a Republican magistrate is the latter's limited term of office. The Servian constitution could still be subverted by a bad king (as it was by Tarquinius Superbus).

49 *cycle*: cf. above, 1. 45; 1. 64–8.

50 *men who have tried to seize despotic power*: named in the next section. It is almost certain that Tiberius Gracchus was the target of censure in the lost passage that follows. Cf. *Laelius* 36 ff.

Presumably the argument here is that distribution of power to Senate and people is not in itself enough to prevent a monarchy from turning into a tyranny.

51 *the other figure*: in view of the fragmentary state of the text it is not

altogether clear whether this 'figure' is specifically meant to be Brutus (as Zetzel takes it) or is merely a type of the wise statesman, the opposite of a tyrant. Either way, it is used as the means whereby the concept of the ideal statesman is introduced for the first time. As the context makes clear, there was no adequate word for 'statesman' in Latin before, and Cicero had recourse to a number of different images (helmsman, guardian, etc.) to convey the idea. Cf. Powell (2).

52: the gap will have contained a summing-up of the regal period. Fr. 2 (printed at the end of Book 2) may belong here, or in the next gap; others place it at 2. 43.

52 *that law*: owing to the gap in the text, it is not at all clear what law is referred to.

'the people's friend': Publicola, Valerius' surname.

appeal: the right of appeal (*provocatio*) to the popular assembly against the decision of a magistrate was a vital element of the Roman citizen's rights. Cicero here argues that the right had existed already in the regal period, although it was embodied explicitly in Valerius Publicola's law as well as in the later *lex Valeria Horatia* and *leges Porciae*. On *provocatio* in general see Lintott (2) 226–67.

axes to be removed: the *fasces* (2. 34 above) in historical times contained axes only when the magistrate was exercising his authority outside the walls of Rome.

53 *alternate months*: during the Republic the consuls took it in turns to be attended by the twelve lictors for a month at a time; the consul who came top of the poll usually had the first turn.

54 *Remember . . . authority of the consuls*: these two sentences (one in Latin) interrupt the narrative, and the phrase 'on so tight a rein' is puzzling in context. An interpolation may be suspected.

because of one man's sadistic lust: this refers to the event described by Livy, 8. 28. The old custom in cases of insolvency was *nexum*, i.e. debt bondage. One Lucius Papirius so maltreated a youth bonded to him on account of an inherited debt that the Senate resolved to abolish the system.

burden: reading *oneri* (Moser) for MS *generi*.

fines and forfeits: cf. 2. 16 above.

55 *ten men*: the *decemviri* appointed to draw up the laws of the Twelve (originally Ten) Tables; Cornell 272–6.

Gaius Julius: Cicero clearly thinks Julius was one of the second set of Decemviri, although Livy (3. 33) places him in the first.

63: a gap of a mere four leaves is left for the end of Scipio's historical narrative (p. 56). He must have said that the Roman republican constitution reached more or less its present form after the fall of the Decemvirs. This is in tune with Polybius' statement (6. 11. 1) that the

Roman state was 'well managed' from 449 BC. There is no reason to assume that Cicero's account depends in detail on a lost portion of Polybius (cf. Walbank 147–8); both writers justifiably took the fall of the Decemvirate as the beginning of continuous republican government. Neither Cicero nor Polybius implies that no improvements could take place thereafter; Polybius explicitly says that the Roman system reached its full perfection only at the time of the Hannibalic War.

57 *model presented by nature*: it is not in the least clear what this image was; speculation is fruitless.

wild beast: the elephant.

58 *Just as with string instruments . . .* : the musical image comes from Plato, *Republic* 443d; the reader should note that 'harmony' in ancient musical terminology means what we mean by 'tuning', there being no well-developed system of 'harmony' in our sense in ancient music. The passage (including some lines that are missing from our MS) is quoted by Augustine, *De Civitate Dei* 2. 21, who also provides a summary of the context; the notion of justice as harmony in the state (similar to Plato's concept of justice in his *Republic*) provided the transition from the theory of constitutions to the debate on justice in the next book.

BOOK 3

60 *3*: part of the preface to the second pair of books. Cicero (speaking in his own person) is discussing the origins of civilization, culminating in the development of the art of politics.

changeless and eternal: this reflects Platonic conceptions of mathematical entities as belonging to the eternal realm of Ideas.

62 *8*: this section introduces the debate on justice between Philus and Laelius. On the reconstruction of the arguments of the two speeches see Ferrary (1) and (2).

you needn't worry: reading *verendum ⟨non⟩ est* (Leopardi).

your habit of arguing both sides of a case: this, if taken at its dramatic face value, implies that Philus followed Academic methods of disputation; whether he did or not, Cicero certainly did.

Carneades: this refers to the notable deputation of three Greek philosophers to Rome in 155 BC. Carneades the Academic, Critolaus the Peripatetic, and Diogenes of Babylon, the Stoic, were chosen to plead on behalf of the Athenians for remission of a fine imposed for ill-treatment of the neighbouring community of Oropus. As well as conducting the official business, Carneades also gave public lectures. On one day he argued that justice was indispensable in government; on the following day he argued the contrary case that government was necessarily based on injustice (this second speech, especially coming from an official ambassador, naturally shocked traditionally-minded Romans). This is the inspiration for Cicero's pair of opposing speeches here, but Cicero has reversed the order so that the case for justice is seen to be the stronger: Cicero's first speech (that of Philus) is based on Carneades' second, and Laelius then rebuts the arguments of Philus.

63 *chariot of winged snakes*: Medea's chariot (Pacuvius, fr. 242 in Warmington, *ROL* iii).

Xerxes: Herodotus' account of the Persian capture of Athens (8. 50–5) makes no mention of this alleged justification.

64 *Lex Voconia*: Manilius' age is relevant here as well as his legal expertise: he was already a qualified jurisconsult by the date when the *Lex Voconia* was passed (probably 169 BC, forty years before the dramatic date of the dialogue). This law, in full *Lex Voconia de mulierum hereditatibus*, provided (*a*) that a woman could not be made an heir to an estate of more than 100,000 sesterces, (*b*) that a woman could be a legatee, but that no single legatee could take more than the heirs; the effect of these two provisions together was that a woman could not inherit more than half of any substantial estate; (*c*) that of female relatives only a mother, a daughter, or a sister could inherit in cases of intestacy. It is notable that Cicero, at least, was quite aware of the injustice to women involved in these arrangements.

possess money of her own: a woman was not *sui iuris* in Roman law and her property was legally the property of her father or guardian.

vestal virgin: vestals were, alone of Roman women, allowed to make a will.

Pythagoras and Empedocles: Pythagoreans (of whom Empedocles was one) in general adhered to vegetarianism as a consequence of their belief that human souls could be reincarnated in animals.

66 *decree from the hand of justice*: presumably that all lands conquered by force should be restored to their original owners. The Athenians and Arcadians claimed to be 'autochthonous', i.e. the first and original inhabitants of their respective territories.

group of thinkers: the Epicureans.

67 28: cf. Plato, *Rep*. 2. 361a–362c.

68 29: see Index of Names for Pompeius and Mancinus. Philus here omits to mention that the Numantines refused to do Mancinus any harm.

33: on the natural law doctrine see further *Laws* 1 and Introd. pp. xxvii–xxxi.

72 *Attic orators*: e.g. Demosthenes, Lysias, or Isocrates.

43: Scipio now carries on the argument. It has been agreed that justice is necessary in a state; Scipio draws the conclusion that an unjust state is no state at all, recalling his own definition of *res publica* as the property of the public.

74 *we think at once of a bad king*: this was the Roman reaction to the words *rex* and *regnum*: cf. above, 2. 52.

Fr. 1: this fragment comes from a story of an encounter between Alexander the Great and a pirate (cf. Augustine, *De Civitate Dei* 4. 4. 8) and may well belong in Philus' speech.

Frr. 2–3: probably from Laelius' speech.

75 *Fr. 4*: attributed by editors to the conversation after the end of Laelius' speech: Laelius is elsewhere compared with Isocrates in similar terms (*De Oratore* 2. 10, 3. 28).

BOOK 4

77 *Polybius*: the passage is not preserved.

cadets: those undergoing the *ephebeia*, a two-year period of military training at Athens (for ages 18–20).

Eleans and Thebans: cf. Plato, *Symposium* 182b (Pausanias' speech).

everything should be held in common: Plato, *Republic* 416d. In fact, the common ownership of property in Plato's ideal state was not to apply to all the citizens, but only to the ruling Guardians and the military class.

festooned with garlands: Plato, *Republic* 398a. The Platonic passage in fact mentions only poets in general, not Homer by name, although there has been a good deal of criticism of Homer in what precedes.

78 *8*: this fragment presumably refers to the Athenian commanders who were put to death after the battle of Arginusae (406 BC) for failing to pick up those who were shipwrecked: Xenophon, *Hellenica* 1. 7. 4. This was the occasion when Socrates alone refused to support the illegal proposal to have the generals tried all together.

9: the criticism of dramatists here also recalls the third book of Plato's *Republic* (cf. above, 3. 5).

10: on the status of actors see Beare (3rd edn.), 166–7. Roman law deprived actors of civil rights: *Digest* 3. 2. 1. Section 13 below appears to argue that acting was more respectable among the Greeks, although Demosthenes treats Aeschines' association with the stage as a slur on his character.

79 *Naevius*: there was, at any rate in later times, a persistent tradition to the effect that Naevius did in fact compose libellous verses. Gellius 3. 3. 15 states that he was imprisoned for constant attacks on the nobility, and while in prison wrote two plays which brought him back into favour. A late commentator on one of Cicero's speeches adds a story about Naevius' brush with the aristocratic Metelli; and Gellius (7. 8. 5–6) further reports that certain lines by Naevius were believed to have been a disguised attack on Scipio Africanus. It may be that Cicero was unaware or incredulous of these traditions, but the conflict of evidence is peculiar nevertheless. See Beare (3rd edn.), 40–1.

BOOK 5

81 *the poet*: Ennius: the reference is to *Annals* 156 Skutsch.

Manilius: the surviving text does not indicate the identity of the speaker here; the attribution to Manilius suits the legal subject-matter.

83 *The aim*: cf. Introd. p. xxii.

Nothing in a state: this fragment is not specifically attributed to *R.*, but the placing here is likely.

84 *Fr.* 1: probably belongs to the discussion of which part is preserved in 5. 5 above.

BOOK 6

85 *Gracchus*: Tiberius Gracchus, father of the famous brothers, censor in 169 BC with C. Claudius Pulcher; for the context see Livy 43. 16.

this writer: Xenophanes of Colophon (fl. *c*.530 BC). The Greek text is preserved by Athenaeus, 12, 526a (Freeman p. 21). Xenophanes is satirizing his fellow-citizens of Colophon for adopting luxurious habits from their Lydian neighbours. The context in Cicero is not known.

Laelius' speech: this is presumably the speech referred to in *De Natura Deorum* 3. 43: 'I have gained better instruction on how to worship the immortal gods, guided by pontifical law and ancestral custom, from those miniature sacrificial bowls [*capedunculis*, diminutive form of the word used here], bequeathed to us by Numa and described by Laelius in his little speech which is pure gold, than from the explanations of the Stoics' (tr. P. G. Walsh). Compare also *De Natura Deorum* 3. 5, *Brutus* 83, *Laelius de Amicitia* 96. Apparently (if all these passages refer to the same speech) the occasion was a proposal to open the priestly colleges to popular election, which Laelius opposed. One can only speculate about the relevance to that issue of this fragment, which seems rather to be concerned with the simplicity and inexpensiveness of the equipment needed for Roman ritual (cf. *R.* 2. 27).

86 8: the context leading up to the Dream of Scipio is given by Macrobius in his *Commentary on the Dream of Scipio* (for which see Stahl).

Favonius Eulogius: an orator of Carthage and pupil of St Augustine, who *c*. AD 390–410 wrote a 'disputation' on the Dream of Scipio, concerned largely with numerology and the Music of the Spheres.

The Dream of Scipio: the Dream is pure fiction, of a kind rare enough in classical Latin prose literature. It is modelled on the 'myths' of Plato's dialogues, and especially on the Myth of Er at the end of his *Republic* (614b–621d). In that passage, Socrates told the story of Er the Pamphylian, who was found apparently dead on a battlefield, and was taken home for cremation. Er came back to life as he lay on the funeral pyre, and described his vision of the fate of the soul after death. Cicero replaces this story with a somewhat more plausible account of a dream attributed to Scipio himself, the main speaker of the dialogue. As regards content, the Dream of Scipio owes less to the Myth of Er than to two other works of Plato, the cosmological dialogue *Timaeus* (which Cicero himself translated at least in part, although it is not clear whether the translation was made before or after he wrote the *Republic*), and the *Phaedo*, which narrates Socrates' last conversation on the nature of the soul. As in the *Timaeus*, the abode of the blessed dead is placed not in the mythical Elysian Fields but in the actual universe, among the stars. Cicero has also added details from the accepted astronomical and geographical doctrines of his time.

The Dream has survived detached from its original context, but it should never be forgotten that it is the concluding section of the *Republic* and that its main rhetorical function is as an exhortation to patriotism. It may devalue worldly fame and success in comparison with the rewards of immortality, but it certainly does not devalue political activity as such, which (according to Africanus' ghost) is the chief arena for the display of human excellence and the surest way to achieve happiness after death. For more detailed commentary and bibliography see Powell (1) and (4).

served in Africa: at the outbreak of the Third Punic War, 149 BC.

87 *Ennius*: at the beginning of his *Annals* (fragments 2–11 Skutsch), Ennius recounted a dream in which Homer had appeared to him.

Africanus: Scipio Africanus the elder, adoptive grandfather of the Scipio of this dialogue.

cannot remain at peace: a tendentious remark: in fact Carthage was reluctant to go to war in 149.

a very great war: Scipio was elected consul for the second time for the year 134, in order to finish the war in Spain (in which several Roman commanders had been unsuccessful: cf. *R.* 3. 29). This ended with the siege and capture of Numantia in 133, the year of Tiberius Gracchus' tribunate. Scipio returned to Rome for his second triumph ('riding in a chariot to the Capitol') in 132.

my grandson's: Tiberius Gracchus (son of Cornelia, daughter of Scipio the elder).

eight times seven revolutions: this portentous prophecy alludes to the fact that Scipio was 56 years old in 129 BC, the dramatic date of this dialogue and the year of his death.

to assume the dictatorship: he never did, nor is there any evidence outside this passage that it was even proposed; see note on 1. 63 above and Geiger.

88 *unholy hands of your relatives*: Cicero appears to have believed firmly that Scipio was murdered for political reasons by his own relatives,

although his death may well have been natural and was announced as such at the time. Cf. Powell (1) 82–3.

set out from this place: alludes to the Platonic doctrine of the pre-existence of the soul: see esp. *Phaedo* 70c–77a and *Timaeus* 41d–42d; cf. Cicero, *Timaeus* 42–46.

15: the prohibition of suicide derives principally from Plato's *Phaedo*, 61d–62c.

custody: Reproduces the ambiguity of the Latin and of Plato's Greek: is the soul 'on guard' (life being envisaged as a sort of military duty) or 'under guard' (imprisoned in the body, perhaps as a punishment)? See Powell (1) 153–4.

89 *smallest star*: the moon; the word 'star' covers the planets (wandering stars) as well as the 'fixed' stars.

nine circles: this is the standard Platonic and Aristotelian view of the cosmos, with the earth in the centre, surrounded by the orbits of the sun, moon, and planets, and enclosed by the sphere of the fixed stars. The order of the planets given here by Cicero is the correct one (in terms of distance from the earth). This image of the cosmos persisted through the Middle Ages and Renaissance (see Lewis 23–8).

contrary motion: the sun, moon, and planets do indeed (in general) appear to move slowly round the Zodiac from west to east, the opposite direction to the apparent daily motion of the heavens caused by the rotation of the earth.

90 *sound*: the famous doctrine of the Music of the Spheres, of Pythagorean origin: see Powell (1) 159–60. Cf. Shakespeare, *Merchant of Venice* v. i. 54–65.

Catadoupa: one of the cataracts on the Nile. The story of the deaf tribe is not only false in itself but is not even a good analogy; we who are allegedly deafened by the Music of the Spheres can hear plenty of other things.

91 *some people stand at a different angle*: it is to be noted that the spherical shape of the earth is taken for granted. It was a prevalent ancient view that the Southern Hemisphere could not be reached.

belts: the Greek word *zone* meant both literally a belt (the article of clothing) and a 'zone' or 'belt' in the geographical sense; the Latin *cingulum* or *-us* in general has only the former meaning. The theory of the five zones (two frigid, two temperate, and one torrid) approximately represents reality.

narrow from north to south: Cicero underestimates the size of Africa, following the common ancient view that it extended only as far as the branch of 'Ocean' which was erroneously supposed to flow all round the earth at the Equator.

92 *year*: the doctrine of the 'Great Year', explained here, derives from Plato, *Timaeus* 39d; cf. Cicero, *Timaeus* 33.

Romulus: cf. 1. 25.

Goodness . . . by her own enticements: Cicero may have in mind the story of the Choice of Hercules, Xenophon, *Memorabilia* 2. 1. 21 ff.

my father: i.e. Aemilius Paulus.

A man's true self is his mind: this idea was part of Platonic doctrine, or at any rate part of the popular view of it; it is most clearly stated in a Platonic dialogue whose authenticity has been disputed, the *First Alcibiades* (130b).

93 *Whatever is in constant motion . . .* : this paragraph is translated verbatim from a passage of Plato's *Phaedrus*, 245c–e. An acknowledgement of the source would clearly have been inappropriate here: Africanus' ghost must know these things at first hand.

94 *I awoke from sleep*: probably the end of the dialogue. What more could Laelius and the rest have said after this?

Fr. 2: the quotation is from an epigram of Ennius in which these words were put in the mouth of Scipio Africanus (see Warmington, *ROL* i. 400).

THE LAWS

BOOK 1

97 *this oak*: according to Cicero's poem, *Marius*, which was probably written about 57 BC in honour of his fellow-townsman, Marius saw an eagle rise from an oak tree, fight a serpent, and then fly off to the east—an omen of military success. The relevant passage is quoted in Cicero, *De Divinatione* 1. 106.

to solicit support for yourself: Quintus was also a poet; he had written a number of tragedies.

Scaevola: probably Scaevola (4) in the Index of Names. The phrase is a pentameter, and no doubt belongs to an epigram of the kind represented by Catullus 95.

the olive tree: Athena competed with Poseidon for control over Athens. She gave the city an olive tree; he gave it a salt-water spring (Herodotus 8. 55).

Ulysses: in *Odyssey* 6. 162 ff. Odysseus addresses Nausicaa, saying that the only sight of comparable perfection he has seen is 'the fresh young palm tree shooting up by the altar of Apollo on the island of Delos'.

'acorn-laden oak' . . . *'tawny messenger . . .'*: quotations from *Marius*.

98 *not far from your house*: in Rome Atticus lived on the Quirinal Hill; he also had a house in Athens.

Aquilo . . . Orithyia: in Plato, *Phaedrus* 229b Socrates is asked whether he believes the story of the north wind carrying off Orithyia.

the standard of truth: elsewhere Cicero calls history 'the witness of the times, the light of truth, the life of memory, the teacher of life, the messenger from the past' (*De Oratore* 2. 36). See Brunt (2). On occasions, however, he was prepared to condone a degree of embroidery; cf. *Fam.* 5. 12.

so closely akin to oratory: several pupils of the orator Isocrates (436–338) became historians, e.g. Ephorus and Theopompus. Cicero held that history should supply instances (*exempla*) which could be used by orators, and that rhetoric (especially the rhetoric of display) could show historians how to compose vivid descriptions. Cf. *De Oratore* 2. 62–4; *Orator* 38 f., 66.

99 *the Annals of the Pontifex Maximus*: the Chief Priest displayed a board each year with information about public (including religious) events. About 130, the surviving material of this kind was published in eighty volumes, thus laying the foundations for the Roman genre of annalistic historiography. Such chronicles had no stylistic pretensions. The

early historians, like Cato, Fabius Pictor, and Calpurnius Piso, left bare records of dates, names, and events; they did not grasp, we are told, how style could be embellished, and thought that brevity and intelligibility were all that mattered; cf. *De Oratore* 2. 52–3. This judgement would seem to be over-harsh. Cato, certainly, was capable of stylistic embellishment; see Aulus Gellius, 13. 25. 12–15.

Gellius: a conjectural emendation for the corrupt *belli*.

Latin hacks: these were teachers of rhetoric in Latin. Cicero speaks of them as intellectually superficial; politically they were suspected of fostering populist ideas. Lucius Crassus and his colleague in the censorship closed the school in 92. In *De Oratore* 3. 94 Crassus refers to it as 'a school of impertinence'.

a good deal . . . lack of propriety: reading *multa sed inepta elatio, summa impudentia* with Mommsen.

those who have not yet published their work: one such writer may have been Julius Caesar, whose *Commentaries* are mentioned in Cic. *Brutus* 262.

the glorious and unforgettable year: 63 BC.

100 *a diplomatic mission*: as Atticus hints, a so-called 'free mission', for which senatorial permission was needed, entailed no official duties; it was, in effect, a period of leave abroad. In *L.* 3. 9 and 18 Cicero disapproves of the custom.

the sung passages: there were three formal elements in Roman comedy: spoken verse, recitative, and lyric. Cicero is probably referring to the last two, which were accompanied by the pipe and called for greater vocal effort.

calm philosophical discourse: the style which Cicero has in mind is described at greater length in *Orator* 64.

101 *Scaevola's consultations*: Atticus and Cicero attended the consultations of Scaevola (2), the Augur. See also Nepos, *Atticus* 1. 4. On Scaevola's death in 87, Cicero studied with Scaevola (3), the Pontifex (*De Amicitia* 1. 1).

102 *party walls*: a neighbour might not demolish a party wall.

gutters: rain-water might be directed on to a neighbour's land.

as he describes it: Plato, *Laws* 625 (Penguin trans. p. 46).

so clearly: reading *tam manifesto* with Watt (1) 265.

the praetor's edict: Each year, when the chief legal magistrate took office, he published an edict, setting out the principles on which he intended to administer justice. His successor would take over the edict, making whatever changes and additions were necessary. Thus a body of law grew up, supporting or complementing the code of civil law.

the Twelve Tables: c.450 a Committee of Ten had codified Roman civil and criminal law in the Twelve Tables. See *ROL* iv; Crawford, 555–721.

103 *a person*: thought to be Servius Sulpicius Rufus (consul 51), who was the leading jurist of his age; cf. Cic. *Brutus* 152.

the most learned men: in particular, the Stoics. 'Zeno holds that the law of nature is divine, and that it has the function of commanding what is right and forbidding the opposite' (Cic. *De Natura Deorum* 1. 36; for parallels see Pease's note). 'The law of all things . . . is that which commands men, who are by nature political animals, to do the things which ought to be done and forbids them to do what ought not to be done' (Chrysippus, *SVF* 3. 314).

its Greek name: *nomos* is the Greek for law; *nemo* means 'I assign' or 'distribute'.

its Latin name: Cicero, rather unconvincingly, connects *lex* (law) with *lego* (I choose, i.e. I choose what is just and right; cf. *L.* 2. 11). The actual derivation is uncertain.

104 *those six books*: i.e. *The Republic*.

Quintus' view: Quintus seems to have believed in providence (*De Divinatione* 1. 10). In *De Finibus* 5. 96 he endorses the position of Antiochus as expounded by Piso.

impetus: reading *motu* with Watt (1) 266.

I'll grant it if you insist: as an Epicurean, Atticus did not believe that the gods ruled the world; but he makes the concession for the sake of the argument. Hence the teasing tone of what follows.

they . . . become very angry: according to Epicurus, good men did *not* become angry.

god is never concerned: see Epicurus in D.L. 10. 139: 'A blessed and immortal being has no trouble itself and causes no trouble to anyone else. Hence it is devoid of anger or favour.'

105 *the only one that participates in reason*: recent studies of animal behaviour make it clear that most of the ancients seriously underestimated the reasoning power of many species. See Sorabji.

What is there . . . more divine than reason?: the saying is attributed to the Stoic Cleanthes in Cic. *De Natura Deorum* 1. 37.

a single community shared by gods and men: for the long pedigree of this idea see Pease on *De Natura Deorum* 2. 154.

blood-relationships: strictly Cicero's term (*agnationes*) refers only to persons under the authority of the same *paterfamilias*, e.g. sons, sons' wives, and unmarried daughters.

sowing the human race: Cicero does not wish to dwell on the origin of human life; so he moves quickly on. The idea of sowing may recall God as the 'seminal' reason of the universe (D.L. 7. 36 on Zeno); cf. Plato, *Timaeus* 41e–42a and 42d.

remembers his place of origin: he recognizes that his soul has come from God. There is no reason to think that Cicero has in mind the idea that an individual soul had an earlier existence (Plato, *Meno* 81–6).

106 *for man's use*: compare 'The Stoics hold that everything produced by the earth is created for the use of men' (*De Officiis* 1. 22, based on Panaetius).

Following Watt (1) 266, we have omitted the phrase *frugibus atque bacis*, 'crops and fruits', as an explanatory gloss on 'what shoots forth from the earth'.

his enjoyment: presumably Cicero is thinking of wool and hides.

By copying her: for example, the Stoic Poseidonius said that clever men devised the rudder by imitating fish (Seneca, *Epistulae* 90. 24).

senses . . . as servants and messengers: cf. Cic. *De Natura Deorum* 2. 140.

man alone erect: cf. *De Natura Deorum* 2. 140 and Pease's note.

The Greeks . . . have no equivalent: the Latin is *vultus* (expression) as distinct from *facies* (face). As Kenter points out, the Greek *prosopon* could denote 'expression'.

speech . . . the promoter of human fellowship: *ratio* (reason) and *oratio* (speech) are said to provide the bond of human society (*De Officiis* 1. 150).

the books which you have read: Cicero dealt with this subject in the lost *R.* 4.

107 *not on opinion, but on nature*: 'nature' here means objective reality—things as they really are.

apparently leads to the dissolution . . .: but only apparently, because the soul is supposed to survive.

108 *those who worship a dog or a cat*: the Egyptians.

nothing human is alien to them: in Terence's *Self-Punisher* (77) Chremes, an old busybody, excuses his inquisitiveness by saying 'I am a man; I consider nothing human to be none of my business' (*homo sum; humani nil a me alienum puto*).

Socrates was right to curse: according to Clement of Alexandria (second century AD), Cleanthes said in his work on *Pleasure*, Book 2, that Socrates uttered this curse (*Stromateis* 2. 131).

that famous saying of Pythagoras: perhaps 'Friends have all things in common' (D.L. 8. 10). There is a gap in the text.

some people: i.e. the Epicureans. Actually, Epicurus said: 'Of all the things that wisdom obtains for the blessedness of the complete life, far the greatest is friendship' (*Principal Doctrines* 21); 'All friendship is desirable in itself, even though it starts from the need of help' (*Frag.* 23). Cicero himself wrote an essay on the subject; see Powell (1).

109 *the older lot*: e.g. the Presocratics and Plato.

philosophical factories: in *De Finibus* 5. 7 the Old Academy (represented by Speusippus, Xenocrates, Polemo, and Crantor) and the early
Peripatos (headed by Aristotle) are called factories, but without any
hint of irony.

110 *that everything right and honourable should be desired for its own
sake*: Cicero distinguishes (*a*) those who accept this thesis, (*b*) those
who reject it (the Epicureans), and (*c*) those who question it (the New
Academy). Within (*a*) he distinguishes (*a1*) the Old Academy (Speusippus, Xenocrates, and Polemo), (*a2*) the Peripatetics (Aristotle and
Theophrastus), (*a3*) the Stoic Zeno, (*a4*) the Stoic Aristo. Cicero claims
that (*a1*) and (*a2*) are virtually in agreement. In 53–5 he goes on to
suggest that the gap between (*a1*) and (*a3*) is not unbridgeable.

the Old Academy: founded by Plato. In the third century BC its character changed under the sceptical Arcesilaus and Carneades. See Long
88–106.

Aristotle: Aristotle's school is often referred to as the Lyceum or the
Peripatos (covered walkway).

their own little gardens: a patronizing reference to the Epicureans, who
held their discussions in a garden in the suburbs of Athens. Cicero was
opposed to the school for several reasons; one of the most important
was that it discouraged its disciples from engaging in public life.

Let us ask it to keep quiet: as Atticus will have to suspend his devotion to Epicurus 'for a little while', so Cicero will have to keep the
troublesome Academy at a distance. See Introd. pp. xiv–xv.

111 *the plays*: e.g. *The Eumenides* of Aeschylus.

by some advantage or benefit: these words suggest that Cicero still has
the Epicureans in mind; for they maintained that ethics was a matter
of pleasure or pain. But the argument also recalls the thesis presented
by Glaucon in Plato, *Republic* 2. 359–61, viz. that injustice, if unde-
tected, is preferable to justice.

the notorious Thirty: in Athens in the spring of 414, at the end of
the Peloponnesian War, the democrats were ousted by the oligarchs.
A committee of thirty was formed which set up a new council filled
with their own supporters, and abolished the lawcourts. At the
same time they instituted a reign of terror in which hundreds were
murdered or driven out. At the end of the year the Thirty were defeated
by a band of exiles under Thrasybulus; and in 403 democracy was
restored.

our interrex: in 82, L. Valerius Flaccus as interrex introduced a bill
which appointed Sulla dictator with unlimited powers—and not just
for the usual six months. Sulla then brought in his constitutional
reforms, designed to re-establish the power of the senatorial oligarchy.
The system lasted little more than a decade. It was finally dismantled
by Pompey and Crassus in 70.

112 *our opponents*: again, the Epicureans. For an exposition, and a cri-
tique, of their theology see Cic. *De Natura Deorum* 1. 18 ff.

justice and injustice are differentiated by nature: this is denied in
Horace's Epicurean satire (1. 3): 'One has to admit that laws were
invented out of the fear of injustice . . . Nor can nature distinguish just
from unjust in the way that she separates good things from their oppo-
sites, things to be sought from things to be shunned' (113–14). By
'good things' Horace means 'beneficial things'; thus nature can distinguish edible from poisonous fungi, but justice is a balance of advantages and disadvantages which is not 'given' but has to be worked
out.

113 *so-called 'virtue'*: Cicero is dissatisfied in translating the Greek *arete*
(excellence) by the Latin *virtus*; for the latter was derived from *vir*
(man) and originally meant 'manliness'.

a tree or a horse: the virtues, or good qualities, of a tree (e.g. its height,
hardness, or straightness) can all be objectively assessed. The same
applies to a horse's strength, speed, or stamina.

the qualities of young men: moral qualities (honesty, generosity,
courage, etc.) are equally objective; i.e. everyone knows what is meant
by those terms.

honourable: that which is honourable is 'a praiseworthy good' (*laud-
abile bonum*). But we have already shown that a good is objectively
good; therefore that which is honourable is objectively honourable.

the variety and incompatibility of men's opinions: Cicero concedes that
the character of an actual person may be controversial. But he points
out (*a*) that conflicting opinions may arise from ill-informed or biased
judgements, and (*b*) that the person under consideration may not be
uniformly or *invariably* honest, generous, courageous, etc. (unless he
is that unlikely creature, a Stoic sage).

114 *duty*: the English word often implies reluctance. But *officium* carried
the idea of kindly service as well as obligation. ·

for its advantages, not for itself: in this section Cicero argues like the
Stoics, whose moral judgements tended to be categorical (either–or).
He does not consider the case where an action performed for someone
else's sake *also* involves an element of self-interest, however small.

if people are not seen to be grateful etc.: this reproduces the general
sense of the passage. The text is corrupt.

that holy thing, friendship: Kenter sees this as a satirical swipe at the
Epicureans—perhaps rightly, in view of the next sentence.

115 *those philosophers who think it is honourable etc.*: I have translated
qui velle iudicium vitare nisi vitio ipso vitato ⟨honestum⟩ putant. So
Watt (2) 242, on the basis of Eussner and Mueller.

the ultimate good: in *Tusculan Disputations* 5. 85 Cicero divides the
opinions of the various schools into simple and composite. The former

are represented by the Stoics (what is honourable—*honestum*), the Epicureans (pleasure—*voluptas*), Hieronymus of Rhodes, a third-century ex-Peripatetic (freedom from pain), and Carneades (the enjoyment of the primary gifts of nature). In *De Finibus* 5. 20 and *Academica* 2. 131 we hear that this was not Carneades' own view; nor, we may add, does it sound like a simple opinion. Composite opinions are represented by the Peripatetics (mental goods, physical goods, external goods), the Old Academy (much the same), Dinomachus and Calliphro (pleasure and what is honourable), Diodorus (what is honourable and freedom from pain).

116 *an arbitrator*: the magistrate could appoint an arbitrator (a professional lawyer) rather than one of the panel of judges, who, though respectable citizens, were not necessarily expert in questions of law. See Crook 80.

the Old Academy: see note on 37–9 above; and cf. *De Finibus* 5. 7, where we hear that Antiochus used to group Aristotle with the Old Academy. In *De Natura Deorum* 1. 16 we are told that Antiochus held that the Stoics agreed in substance with the Peripatetics, differing from them only in terminology. When Cicero minimizes the differences between some of the schools, he is following Antiochus' line; cf. 54 below.

Antiochus: for an account of Antiochus see Barnes and Glucker (1).

117 *advantageous things*: the others thought of such things as lesser goods. Zeno acknowledged their value, but (since he allowed only one 'good') he called them 'advantageous'. Therefore, says Cicero, the dispute is a matter of terminology.

ultimate ends: the Latin *fines* meant both 'ethical ends' and 'local boundaries'. Cicero proceeds to play on the two senses.

rights of possessors: Zeno is said to claim certain *fines* belonging to the Academy. Marcus, Quintus, and Atticus will act as arbitrators as laid down for disputes over *fines* in the Twelve Tables. Ownership as a result of uninterrupted possession (*usucapio*), as distinct from strict legal title, was recognized by Roman law. See the Twelve Tables, 6. 3; *ROL* iv. 461; Crook 141–2.

within five feet: a strip of land five feet wide ran between one property and another. The strip could be used for turning the plough, but possession could not be acquired on the strip itself.

the Mamilian Law: in 109 a tribune called Mamilius set up a court to try those who had accepted bribes from Jugurtha. Sallust (*Jugurtha* 40) gives his name as Gaius Mamilius Limetanus ('the boundary man'). So it is probable that he was the man mentioned by Cicero, and that at this time he also brought in his law reducing the three arbitrators to one in disputes over boundaries.

the markers laid down by Socrates: as the views of Socrates were represented (whether faithfully or not) by Plato, this indicates that the decision has gone in favour of the Old Academy. Zeno receives rougher treatment in *De Finibus* 4. 19 ff.

the highest good: by presenting the alternatives in these terms Quintus seems to be suggesting that the distinction between the two positions is so subtle that a final decision cannot be made.

means the same as this: reading *idem ac hoc valet* on the suggestion of Watt (in a letter).

118 *a good man . . . a happy one*: the realization is said to come as a result of wisdom or philosophy in general. But it was open to question, as we see from *De Finibus* 5. 12, 70, 79, 84. As so often, the dispute turns out to be a matter of terminology (and perhaps a certain amount of self-deception).

119 *a citizen of the whole world*: 'Although the idea of world citizenship may be ascribed to Socrates (*Tusc.* V. 108), it owes its dissemination to the Stoa.' So Kenter. He cites, *inter alia*, *De Finibus* 3. 64, 4. 7; Seneca, *Epistulae* 28. 4.

disdain, despise, and count as nothing: cf. *R.* 6. 16.

a kind of stockade: according to D.L. 7. 40, this was a Stoic image.

a more expansive . . . style: i.e. rhetoric. See *De Finibus* 2. 17, where dialectic is contrasted with rhetoric. Cicero now goes on to embrace the three types of rhetoric: deliberative, judicial, and demonstrative (i.e. the rhetoric of display).

BOOK 2

121 *Euripuses*: the Euripus was the strait between Euboea and the Greek mainland.

nothing here except rocks: such wild scenery, which thrills the romantic, would not have given pleasure to Atticus. He was happy to find a gentler place with features to which a human being could relate.

122 *that eminently sensible man*: Ulysses, who refused the immortality offered by Calypso so that he might return home (*Odyssey* 1. 55–9, 5. 135–6).

Tusculum: 15 miles (24 km.) south-east of Rome, 2,000 feet (nearly 610 m.) above sea level; a fashionable resort where several important Romans (including Cicero) had villas.

123 The last seven words in the text of section 5 have been deleted as a gloss.

her two saviours: Marius and Cicero.

Plato's Phaedrus: in *Phaedrus* 230b Socrates dips his feet in the Ilissus.

Tyamis: the river Tyamis flows into the sea opposite to Corcyra (Corfu).

Amaltheum: a shrine to Amalthea (see Index of Names). Cicero built one for himself at Arpinum (*Att.* 1. 16. 15).

my version of Aratus' poem: for fragments of Cicero's version see Traglia, 65–111.

124 *the best authorities*: in particular the Stoics.

an eternal force etc.: cf. *L.* 1. 21 and 33.

If [plaintiff] summon [defendant] to court: Twelve Tables 1. 1 (*ROL* iv. 425). The defendant was summoned to a preliminary hearing before the praetor, which is what Cicero has in mind here. If the issue was not resolved there, the case went to trial. See Crook 75–7.

125 *the idea of choosing*: see *L.* 1. 19.

those gentlemen: philosophers using Socrates' method of interrogation.

127 *a measure of consent*: see Plato, *Laws*, 4. 720–3.

the procession of the stars etc.: this recalls the eloquent passage in *De Natura Deorum* 2. 87–119, which contains a translation of Aristotle's *De Philosophia* (95); see Pease's notes.

it has to be admitted etc.: the reasoning is fallacious. This becomes clear when 'superior' (*praestare*) is taken to mean 'superior in intelligence' and one attempts to set out the propositions in the form of a syllogism. Cf. *De Natura Deorum* 3. 22–3.

128 *the preamble to the legal code*: see Plato, *Laws* 4. 722–3.

although our discussion and its setting are private: reading *quamquam* for *quoniam* with Watt (1) 266, following Rath.

Sacred Laws: the *leges sacratae*, which went back to the early fifth century BC, were collective resolutions of the plebs, reinforced by an oath (Cornell 262). An important example was the proclamation that the tribunes of the plebs should be immune from violence. Anyone who contravened this law was pronounced accursed (*sacer*); i.e. he was dedicated as a sacrifice to one of the gods, along with his family and property. Later, the condemned man, instead of being killed, was declared an outlaw; see Greenidge (1) 55.

129 *Liber*: 'The Free', i.e. Bacchus. Cf. *De Natura Deorum* 2. 62.

in the company of: reading *cum* with Watt (1) 266.

flamines: a *flamen* was a priest assigned to carry out the ritual of a particular deity.

patches of withies: flexible twigs would be used for the lictors' rods and also for baskets and fences.

the safety of the people: a reference to the *augurium salutis*, in which the augur tested whether the gods would permit prayers to be offered for the safety of Rome. See Dio 37. 24 and Cic. *De Divinatione* 1. 105 with Pease's note.

130 *fixed quarters of the sky*: the sky was divided into sixteen sections, assigned to various deities. So the observer was supposed to know from what god any particular sign came; see Pallottino 145, fig. 5.

The fetial priests: for references see section 34 below (the law governing war).

in the name of the people: reading *iudices populi nomine sunto* with Watt (2) 242.

Etruscan soothsayers: their divination involved the inspection of animal entrails (*haruspicium*). This, and the interpretation of lightning, were important features of the Etruscan *disciplina* (art or training): see Pallottino 143–7.

except those . . . on behalf of the people: Cicero is thinking of the nocturnal rites of the Bona Dea, a fertility goddess from whose festival on 1 May men were strictly excluded. At her ritual, sacrifice was offered 'On behalf of the people' (Cicero, *De Haruspicum Responso* 37; Seneca, *Epistulae* 97. 2). See further section 36 below.

except those of Ceres etc.: the mysteries of Eleusis in Attica included an enactment of the story of Demeter (Ceres) and Persephone (Proserpina), a myth which 'explained' why corn remained under the earth for part of the year and above it for the rest. To the initiate the perennial rebirth of the crops gave promise of survival. The worship of Ceres had been imported into Rome as early as 493. She had a temple on the Aventine, and special games were held in her honour.

An act of sacrilege: a couple of examples are given in section 41. For the penalty, see on parricide below.

that which can be expiated: if the act was accidental or insignificant, it could be expiated. An early instance was the law which decreed that if a man's mistress touched the altar of Juno (goddess of marriage) she should offer a ewe lamb by way of atonement; see Aulus Gellius 4. 3. 3.

they shall make provision: Cicero means to include theatrical performances here; see section 38.

they shall observe the best: an unhelpful rule, not greatly clarified in section 40 below.

the Idaean Mother: see Cybele in the Index of Names, and the note on section 40 below.

a parricide: a murderer, whether of parent, relative, or fellow-citizen. The penalty was death or exile.

perjury: we confine the offence to false statements about facts, made under oath in the court-room. The Romans interpreted it more widely. The Twelve Tables had, indeed, prescribed the death penalty for *falsum testimonium* (8. 23), though this had ceased to be applied long before Cicero's day. But failure to fulfil a solemn promise was also perjury. Had Regulus broken his word he would have been guilty of that offence (see the discussion in *De Officiis* 3. 107–15). Again, the penalty for breaking an oath to a god had been death, but after the early period the guilty man had been outlawed. Unfortunately Cicero's wording is very condensed, and he declines to elaborate on the matter further in 41. Does he mean to reintroduce capital punishment for perjury? If so, how are cases for 'divine punishment' distinguished from those liable to 'human punishment'? And what does Cicero mean by disgrace? Is the guilty man to be removed from his tribe by the censor and so forfeit his voting rights? Or is he merely to suffer the social effects of a bad reputation?

incest: it is unclear whether Cicero has in mind the general ban on sexual intercourse within certain degrees of consanguinity, or, more particularly, religious offences, e.g. against the chastity of vestal virgins (the charge against Clodius was also one of incest; see note on '*that fellow*', p. 212 below). The penalty for the former, in the early days of the Republic, was to be thrown from the Tarpeian Rock; for the latter, the man was scourged to death and the vestal was buried alive. One hesitates to believe that Cicero would have countenanced such primitive barbarities. See Greenidge (2) 376–80.

131   *No one shall consecrate a field*: see section 45 below.

Let there be moderation: see section 45.

Private religious observances: see section 48 below.

The money . . . and the mourning: see sections 59–66 below.

'*as you propose*': the formula employed by the people when agreeing to a proposal put to them by a magistrate.

On smaller matters: this sentence is given to Marcus by Watt (1) 267.

I shall let you off etc.: see Watt (1) 267.

132   *gods whether new or foreign*: Cumont (1) is still of value here, though it is mainly concerned with the imperial epoch.

the Persian priests: cf. *R.* 3. 14. In Herodotus the Persians are said to worship their gods in the open air (1. 131); Themistocles condemns Xerxes for burning and destroying the statues of the gods (8. 109).

Pythagoras . . . said: 'We are at our best when we approach the gods' (Plutarch, *De Superstitione* 9. 169 E).

Thales . . . said: according to D.L. 1. 1. 27, Thales said that the world was animate and full of divinities.

common opinion: the translation adopts Watt's suggestion (1) 267.

groves in the countryside: clumps of trees were commonly regarded as the dwelling-places of spirits.

Lares: the context shows that Cicero is talking, not of the household Lares, but of those which were worshipped at cross-road shrines, where properties met. According to Festus under *Laneae* (108 Lindsay) and under *Pilae et effigies* (273 Lindsay), Lares were the souls of the deified dead. They could be beneficial to the crops, but could also be malevolent if not propitiated. The discussion in Frazer, 2. 453–80 is still worth reading.

133　*immortal . . . divine*: the virtuous are admitted to heaven *(R. 2.* 17, 6. 13, 6. 16); the wicked are confined near the earth until they are purged (*R.* 6. 29). Both forms of belief are amply discussed in Cumont (2).

Good Sense: a temple to Good Sense (*Mens*) on the Capitol was vowed by T. Otacilius Crassus in 217 (P–A 339).

Devotion: there was a temple to Devotion (*Pietas*) in the Circus Flaminius (P–A 389–90).

Moral Excellence: a shrine to *Virtus* was built by Scipio Aemilianus after the capture of Numantia in 133 (P–A 382).

Good Faith: there was a temple of *Fides* on the Palatine (P–A 209).

have long been . . . dedicated: reading *iamdiuque harum* with Davies and Watt.

a shrine to Insult and Shamelessness: Cicero may have found this piece of information in Theophrastus, who is quoted by Zenobius 4. 6 (*Paroemiographi Graeci*).

Fever: in addition to an altar, three temples were erected to this deity (P–A 206).

Evil Fortune: for the ancient altar of *Mala Fortuna* see P–A 216.

the Stopper: Jupiter was originally called 'the Stopper' because he had 'stopped' the flight of Romulus' soldiers (Livy 1. 12. 6). Later, the cult-title was given a political interpretation, representing Jupiter as the 'establisher' of Roman power.

Hope: the temple of *Spes* in the Forum Holitorium (Vegetable Market) was dedicated by A. Atilius Calatinus during the first Punic war (P–A 493).

Today's Fortune: there was a shrine to this deity on the Palatine (P–A 216).

Fortune the Heedful: there was a temple of *Fortuna Respiciens* on the Palatine (P–A 218).

Chance Fortune: there were three temples of *Fors Fortuna* in the first century BC (P–A 212–13).

First-born Fortune: the first-born daughter of Jupiter (*Fortuna Primigenia*) had a temple on the Capitol (P–A 217–18). For further topographical information, and photographs, see Nash.

intercalation: the insertion of days or months to keep the calendar in line with the movements of the sun and moon. For a detailed account of the problems involved, see Michels, Index.

134　*Vesta*: Vesta and the Greek Hestia had a common root. The shrine of Vesta was the symbolic hearth of Rome. The ever-burning fire ensured the continuing life of the city.

The classification of priests: see Appendix.

I'm an augur myself: Cicero became an augur in 53. The political powers summarized by Cicero here can be seen in their context in Taylor, ch. 6, 'Manipulating the State Religion'. Her criticisms are qualified, but not removed, by Liebeschuetz 15–22.

the Titian Law: see Titius in the Index of Names, and cf. section 14 above.

the Livian Laws: see Livius in the Index of Names, and cf. section 14 above.

135 *a serious disagreement*: later, in *De Divinatione* (On Divination), finished soon after Caesar's death (March 44), Cicero has his brother Quintus advance arguments in support of divination (Book 1), while he himself puts counter-arguments in Book 2. As Cicero, in the present passage, states his belief that divination is a genuine, though obsolete, art, the discrepancy calls for comment. See Introd. pp. xv and xxv.

I do not agree: this is an unsatisfactory compromise. For if in the past augurs were able to inspect signs so as to exert a wise influence on political decisions, why should the art have been allowed to die out? And why should the authorities not have taken steps to revive it? It is clear that in the present context, because of his love of ancestral traditions and because of his acceptance of divination as an effective political instrument, Cicero is in favour of retaining the institution in his ideal state. But that, of course, is not a philosophically defensible position.

I absolutely agree: as an Epicurean, Atticus might have accepted the last two sentences without granting that there was any truth in divination. But he could not have agreed with Cicero's compromise as outlined in section 33. One has to conclude that Cicero has pushed the convention of the complaisant interlocutor rather too far.

136 *the law governing war*: to judge from section 21 above, Cicero is thinking mainly of the duties of the fetial priests, a college of twenty that was concerned with making treaties and declaring war. The procedure is described by Livy 1. 24. 3–9 and 32. 5–14. For a summary see *OCD* under Fetiales; for a detailed discussion see Ogilvie 110–12 and 127–36. In spite of these rituals no independent observer could claim that Rome's declarations of war were always just, or that her conduct of war was always characterized by good faith. See Brunt (1) 175–8, Rich, ch. 3.

Eumolpidae: in a letter of 67 BC Atticus is asked for information about the ancestral rites of the Eumolpidae, i.e. the Eleusinian mysteries (*Att.* 1. 9. 2). Cicero himself is addressed as an initiate in his *Tusculan Disputations* 1. 29 (45 BC).

the comic poets: examples: Menander, *Epitrepontes* 451 ff. (the festival of the Tauropolia), and Plautus, *Aulularia* 36 and 794 ff. (the festival of Ceres).

that fellow: Publius Clodius Pulcher. On 4 December 62 the nocturnal rites of the fertility goddess known as the Bona Dea were being
celebrated by a group of aristocratic matrons in the house of Julius
Caesar, who was pontifex maximus. Clodius disguised himself as a
woman and gained access in order to pursue an affair with Caesar's
wife, Pomponia. He was detected and brought to trial. In the event he
was acquitted thanks to heavy bribery on the part of Crassus. Nevertheless, Caesar divorced Pomponia on the grounds that 'Caesar's wife
must be above suspicion' (Plutarch, *Julius Caesar* 10. 9, Suetonius,
Julius Caesar 74. 2). The piquancy of this was appreciated by all, for
Pompey had just divorced his wife, Mucia, for adultery with Caesar
(Cic. *Att.* 1. 12. 3, Suetonius, *Julius Caesar* 50. 1). In the course of
Clodius' trial Cicero incurred his bitter hatred by demolishing his alibi.
Three years later, Clodius gained his revenge by engineering Cicero's
banishment.

137 *Bacchanalia*: the disorderly rites in honour of Bacchus got out of hand
in 186 and were suppressed by the Senate. For details see Livy 39.
8–18 and Walsh's article.

In his work: Cicero is thought to refer to a scene in the lost *Horai*
(Seasons), of which one fragment reads 'Sabazius, the Phrygian, the
flute-player' (frag. 578, Kassel–Austin). Cf. *Birds* 873–5 and *Wasps* 9.
Sabazius was a Phrygian deity whose cult was widespread in Asia
Minor. His worship was especially popular with women and slaves.
'The other gods' may well have included Adonis; see *Lysistrata* 387–90
and Strabo 10. 3. 18.

I agree with Plato: see Plato, *Republic* 4. 424d.

the laws of music: for the social implications of music see Plato, *Laws*
3. 700–1, Aristotle, *Pol.* 8. 5–7 (Barker), and Horace, *Ars Poetica*
202–19, with Brink's notes.

138 *Pythian Apollo*: in Xenophon, *Memorabilia* 4. 3. 16 the oracle says
'Follow the custom of the state'; cf. 1. 3. 1.

just a few days: the Megalensian festival in honour of Cybele or the
Great Mother (*megale* in Greek meant 'great'), was held during 4–10
April. Lucretius describes how, at the procession, onlookers threw
silver and copper coins into the roadway (*De Rerum Natura* 2. 626–7).
In his fulminations against Cybele Augustine mentions her devotees in
Carthage collecting money 'even from shopkeepers' (*De Civitate Dei*
7. 26). See also Frazer iii. 198–202. Such collections were not for
charity, but for the cult itself.

Alexander: there appears to be no confirmation of this story. Mr E. I.
McQueen points out that while Alexander might have deposited the
200-talent fine paid by the people in a temple during the celebrations
which he organized, he would hardly have left it behind when he
departed, for he was seriously short of money. See Arrian 2. 5. 5–7,
12. 2; Q. Curtius 3. 7. 2.

Cleisthenes: this story is also uncorroborated. There is no record elsewhere of Cleisthenes having daughters.

Plato: a reference to Plato, *Laws* 4. 716–17.

the penalty imposed: again, Cicero is not specific.

139 *On my departure*: on the grounds that he had put Roman citizens to death without trial (namely some of Catiline's accomplices), Cicero was sent into exile in March 58. His house on the Palatine was pulled down, his villas at Tusculum and Formiae were destroyed, and he was forbidden to reside within 400 miles (640 km.) of the capital. The direct agent of all this was Clodius, but Clodius knew he had the backing of Caesar and Pompey. For accounts of this episode see T. N. Mitchell 133–43 and E. Rawson (3) 116.

a temple of Licence: a sardonic distortion. The temple erected by Clodius on the site of Cicero's demolished house on the Palatine was dedicated to Liberty.

the deity who was the guardian of the city: before leaving Rome, Cicero took a statue of Minerva from his house to the temple of Jupiter on the Capitol, where he dedicated it with the inscription 'To Minerva, Guardian of Rome'. Minerva had long been worshipped on the Capitol along with Jupiter and Juno. See T. N. Mitchell 138.

140 *Plato's wishes*: see *Laws* 12. 955–6.

141 *Publius' son*: i.e., Quintus Mucius Scaevola (2).

In the case of heirs: by heir(s) the Romans meant a person or persons who would assume the rights and duties of the deceased, which included settling debts, paying bequests, and attending to the upkeep and rites of the family tomb (see Crook 120 and 135 f.). As these rites, which were performed on the deceased's birthday as well as on the annual festivals of the dead (in February and May), involved much eating and drinking, they might cause considerable expense.

142 *the pontiff*: Scaevola (3).

if no deductions have been stipulated: a testator might stipulate that a deduction be made from the bequests left to legatees; in return the legatees would not be responsible for the rites. Cicero says that if *no* deductions have been made and the legatees have voluntarily accepted less than the sum mentioned in the will, they are absolved from performing the rites. In section 53 Cicero rightly calls this 'a manœuvre'.

In the case of a gift: i.e. a gift made in the event of death (*donatio mortis causa*).

Suppose . . . a man accepted etc.: Y accepts from X the amount of A minus B in order to evade the duty of conducting the rites. Later, Z receives from Y sum A, but then acquires in addition sum B, which Y had decided to forgo. If A + B = half or more of Y's total estate, Z is then obliged to perform the rites himself.

formally declare: a device to escape liability, deprecated in 53 below. By an ancient procedure known as *solutio per aes et libram* ('release through bronze and balance') a debt could be cancelled whether or not the money had been paid (Gaius 3. 173–5; Jolowicz 164–5). Here the legatee releases the heir from the obligation of paying him the legacy. Having ceased to be a legatee he is freed from the burden of the *sacra*. Simultaneously the heir contracts to pay him a sum equal to the former legacy. This sum is then received not as a legacy but as a fulfilment of the contract. See Bruck 7. The procedure *per aes et libram* for the transfer of property is described in Gaius 1. 119.

143 *one hundred nummi*: 100 nummi or sestertii equalled 25 denarii, a sum which from Caesar's time represented one ninth of a legionary's annual pay.

They always used to say: reading *semper* with Watt (1) 267.

the last month of the year: the Roman year once began in March, as the names of our months September to December show. The rites in honour of the dead were performed at the end of the year. Decimus Brutus, a cultivated man and an acquaintance of Sempronius Tuditanus who had made a study of the calendar, apparently took the view that the rites should be performed in December, as that was now the last month of the year. When the change from March to January took place is uncertain. Various theories are listed in Michels, Appendix 4. She herself believes the change was carried out by the Board of Ten in 450 or 451 (127–30). But in any case the people continued to hold the festival (the Parentalia) in February.

144 *whose name is derived from death*: Cicero's etymology is supported by *OLD*, which sees *de nece (piare)* as the origin of the word.

the household god: i.e. the Lar.

the severed bone: before cremation a piece of the body (normally a finger) was cut off and retained for burial 'in deference to the older custom' (Keyes). See Festus under *membrum abscidi mortuo* (Lindsay 135).

according to Xenophon: see *Cyropedia* 8. 7. 15.

Ennius asserts: this, the beginning of a commemorative epigram, is usually combined with words quoted by Seneca, *Epistulae* 108. 33, producing the following: 'Here lies the man to whom no one, neither fellow-citizen nor enemy, will be able to render due reward for his achievements' (*ROL* i. 400).

the pig has been slain: 'Only when a pig had been sacrificed was a grave legally a grave' (Toynbee 50). According to Varro (*De Re Rustica* 2. 4. 9), pigs were the first sacrificial victims, and Frazer's index shows the numerous occasions on which they were killed. As a funeral sacrifice the pig formed part of the funeral feast (*silicernium*).

145 *One of the laws of the Twelve Tables*: Table 10. 1.

the risk of fire: this would explain the ban on cremation. Burial took up space and was thought unhealthy. The mass grave for paupers on the Esquiline, just outside the wall, 'became such a nuisance that in 35 BC it was included in the gardens of Maecenas', Reece 17. Because of this ban, tombs lined the roads leading out of the city.

on account of their valour: see Plutarch, *Quaestiones Romanae* 79.

the temple of Honour: see P–A 258.

146 *Do no more than this*: Table 10. 2.

Women shall not scratch their cheeks etc.: Table 10. 4.

as the word itself suggests: it is not clear what etymology Cicero has in mind.

Solon's law forbids: see Plutarch, *Solon* 21.

One shall not gather etc.: Table 10. 5.

drinking bout: the word *circumpotatio* shows that the cup was passed round.

festoons: the Latin is *longae coronae*. As a *corona* was a chaplet (i.e. a wreath or garland worn on the head), a *longa corona* was presumably a chaplet with flowers and greenery hanging down the back and sides.

a chaplet earned by courage: six types of *corona* are described and illustrated in Maxfield, ch. 4.

fastened by gold: i.e. by gold wire.

147 *mournful songs in Greece*: the word *nenia* is not recorded in Greek.

the cost of tombs: for extravagance in later times see Friedländer ii. 210–18. Cicero himself was fully aware that dead bodies were devoid of sensation; but he thought that, in regard to burial rites, 'a concession should be made to custom and traditional belief' (*Tusculan Disputations* 1. 109).

their first king: reading *ab illo primo rege* with Müller.

148 *it had to be true*: presumably *suggestio falsi* was forbidden but *suppressio veri* was condoned.

the man of Phalerum: Demetrius.

The clause about the three veils: see section 59 above.

herms: a herm was 'a quadrangular pillar, surmounted by a bust of Hermes, or, later, of other gods', OLD.

149 *Plato . . . says this*: see *Laws* 12. 958d–e.

heroic lines: i.e. hexameters.

between one and five minae: this was the equivalent of between 100 and 500 drachmas. At the height of her power Athens paid her oarsmen 1 drachma a day. (This information, and that given in the note on 53 above, was kindly supplied by Prof. Michael Crawford.)

in one summer day: Plato says 'The present day . . . is in fact pretty well the longest day of summer', *Laws* 3. 683c (Penguin translation).

BOOK 3

150 *our friends*: the Epicureans. Cicero mischievously makes Atticus criticize the narrow-mindedness of his own school.

a speaking law: Simonides (*c.*556–468) had said that painting was silent poetry and poetry speaking painting (Plutarch, *Moralia* 346 f, Loeb edn. iv. 500).

151 *six earlier books*: the *Republic*, where the best constitution was said to be a mixture of monarchy, oligarchy, and democracy (*R.* 1. 45, 69).

Magistrates: see Appendix.

Plato: Plato, *Laws* 3. 701c.

before the people: Cicero has in mind the earlier public trials (*iudicia populi*) rather than the jury courts which had come to replace them. Although by Cicero's time the juries were no longer monopolized by the Senate, he may have been dissatisfied with them because they were cumbersome, time-wasting, and open to bribery (so Jones 3 and 25). In the old system, as revived by Cicero, trials involving the defendant's life or citizen's rights (*caput*) would have been held before the Assembly of Centuries; non-capital cases would have come before the Council of the Plebs.

no appeal: apparently appeals had been granted in the first half of the second century.

152 *watch over public funds*: as quaestors.

ensure the security of prisoners, punish capital offences: Cicero is referring to the Board of Three appointed to supervise prisons and carry out executions (*tresviri capitales*).

coin bronze etc.: the Board of Three which managed the mint (*tresviri monetales*).

judge cases: the Board of Ten for Judging Cases (*Decemviri stlitibus iudicandis*) decided whether a person was free or a slave.

the first step on the ladder: Cicero, it seems, intended that the quaestorship should no longer provide automatic entry to the Senate, as it had done since the time of Sulla. Perhaps he had in mind the state of affairs described by Plutarch, *Cato the Younger* 16, where the civil servants in the treasury had become corrupt and incompetent owing to the 'minister's' uncertain grasp of financial matters.

The censors: whereas Sulla had reduced the censors' powers, Cicero revives and increases them. Instead of resigning after 18 months, they are to hold office for 5 years; and then they are to be succeeded without a break. The supervision of temples, streets, etc. seems to represent extra responsibilities, as does the enforcement of marriage, which foreshadows the Augustan legislation of 18 BC. Moreover, in section 47 below we hear that they are to take on the duties of the Greek Guardians of the Laws (*nomophylakes*), and to prepare retrospective reports on the performance of magistrates.

two with royal power: i.e. the consuls. Originally, in their military capacity, they were called praetors (Leaders); but this title soon passed to the legal officials. The consuls retained the right to exercise jurisdiction, 'but they had a great deal else to do, and so seldom appear in this role in the late Republic' (Crook 68). The etymology of the word 'consul' is disputed.

the year-law: redrafting the Lex Villia Annalis of 180, Sulla enacted that no one should become quaestor before the age of 30, praetor before 39, and consul before 42.

one man: the dictator, whom Cicero calls 'Master of the People' (*magister populi*). The office, which was originally a military one (*populus* representing the people under arms, especially the infantry), had been obsolete since 216. (Sulla's position was very different.) Cicero reintroduces it, perhaps because he regarded the emergency decree of the Senate (the *senatus consultum ultimum*) as unsatisfactory (so Jones 2). Cicero implies that the dictator is to be appointed by the Senate, not, as previously, by the consuls.

an officer to command the cavalry: the dictator's lieutenant was called 'Master of the Cavalry' (*magister equitum*).

the legal official: i.e. the praetor.

153 *a member with the power etc.*: an *interrex* was appointed for 5 days to perform this function.

with . . . imperium: the right to command—a power possessed by the higher magistrates. For details see *OCD*.

just wars in a just manner: see note on *L*. 2. 34 above.

no one shall be appointed ambassador: a reference to 'free embassies' (see note on *L*. 1. 10 above). Cicero complains about the practice in section 18 below. Cf. *De Lege Agraria (Contra Rullum)* 1. 8.

tribunes: see the discussion in section 19 below.

The details shall be disclosed to the aristocracy: Cicero attempts to justify this proposal in sections 38–9 below.

154 *the power to overrule*: he shall have the power to overrule the decision of the assembly.

more than one question at a time: they shall not put composite bills to the vote. This practice had been forbidden by the Lex Caecilia Didia of 98.

laws directed at private individuals: see section 44 below.

a citizen's life: a citizen could lose his *caput* by being executed or deprived of his citizen's rights.

the chief assembly: the Assembly of Centuries.

They shall not accept gifts: bribery was endemic in the system, as it was in that of Walpole's England.

Depart etc.: a formula pronounced by the magistrate when dismissing a popular assembly.

156 *such a man*: an ingenious piece of self-praise on Cicero's part.

a monarch's: a reference to Tarquinius Superbus. The objection to monarchy, of course, is that the faults of one man can wreck the entire system.

ephors: annually elected Spartan magistrates, five in number by the fifth century. They had far-reaching powers, including that of controlling the actions of the kings.

what had happened before: the confrontation between patricians and plebeians. See section 19 below.

157 *an irresponsible tribune*: unidentified.

a time of sedition: in 494 the plebeians seceded and set up their own organization, which included two tribunes, on the Sacred Mount (or on the Aventine). For the struggle of the orders see Cornell, chs. 10 and 13, and the essays collected by Raaflaub.

It was quickly put to death: allegedly by the Board of Ten; see *R.* 2. 62.

hideously deformed children: Table 4. 1. Dionysius of Halicarnassus attributes this practice to Romulus (*Antiquitates Romanae* 2. 15. 2), cf. Seneca, *De Ira* 1. 15. 2.

158 *Publius Scipio*: Scipio (5) in the Index of Names.

Saturninus: see Apuleius in the Index of Names.

ourselves . . . our position: it sounds like Marcus' own voice here.

cause confusion among the clans: in March 59 Clodius had himself transferred to the plebs so that he might become a tribune. This was done through the good offices of the pontifex maximus, Julius Caesar.

destructive power: i.e. the tribunes' veto. They were still allowed to intervene on behalf of plebeians in trouble with the law.

159 *a colleague who was blocking*: i.e. the tribune Marcus Octavius. See Gracchus, Tiberius in the Index of Names.

that power: the power of veto.

ten tribunes: by the middle of the fifth century the number had risen to ten.

The plebs were not incited: perhaps not directly, but in January 58 Clodius won their support by obtaining free distributions of grain.

slaves were stirred up: Clodius had a recent law against clubs repealed. He then organized armed gangs, which included slaves as well as freedmen. These were employed to intimidate voters in the assemblies.

For gangs in Rome see Lintott (1) ch. 6. And, for Clodius' conduct, E. Rawson (3) 113–16, T. N. Mitchell 134–8.

Had I not given way: some scholars, reading *si* without a negative, take the passage as referring to the revolt of Catiline.

what I did for the safety of the country: Cicero represents his departure as an act undertaken in the public interest.

160 *eminent men*: e.g. Aristides and Themistocles. Cf. *R.* 1. 5. A lofty interpretation of their state of mind.

As for Pompey: Pompey's attitude to Clodius soon changed from acquiescence, or even support, to opposition. He began to work for Cicero's recall and eventually persuaded Caesar to agree (T. N. Mitchell 150 ff.). Hence Cicero's mildness.

a cause . . . not intrinsically disastrous: the restoration of the tribunate.

justifiable postponements: if the auspices were pronounced unfavourable, the meeting could not continue.

Often the gods have used the auspices: one would like to think that this sentence carried a hint of irony.

161 *this law may well exhaust*: one of the censor's duties was to watch over the conduct of senators.

no one with any blemishes will even get into that order: wishful thinking, of course.

education and training: these are not described in what survives of the work.

162 *those men beget a host of imitators*: the point is repeated seven times in what follows. Such variations were practised in the rhetorical schools.

the opinion of our friend Plato: Plato, *Republic* 4. 424c. Cf. *L.* 2. 38–9 above.

that other work: the relevant sections of Cicero's *Republic* have not survived.

163 *four ballot laws*: the first was introduced by Gabinius in 139. For him, and the others mentioned, see the Index of Names. For details of voting-procedure see Greenidge (1) 258–9.

164 *a storm in a teacup*: i.e. in local politics. The Latin *simpulum* means a wine ladle.

his son: see Index of Names under Gratidianus.

the Aegean sea: i.e. in national politics.

on his recommendation: 'If Scipio could not count on the senatorial jurors of the extortion court to convict his enemies, he might have better luck with the popular assembly, especially if the ballot was secret' (Gruen 39).

The Marian Law: as tribune in 119, Marius introduced a law which narrowed the gangways along which the voters passed. This was designed to reduce the opportunities for bribery and intimidation.

provided the vote is disclosed: if this is seriously meant (and there is no sign to the contrary) Cicero must be deceiving himself. With exemplary restraint, How calls it 'a futile compromise' (31).

165 *this influence*: another suggested supplement is '⟨Maintaining decorum⟩ is not difficult in the Senate'.

in his proper turn: senators were invited to speak in turn, according to rank. For details see Greenidge (1) 268–71.

One ought never to make a long speech: no doubt Cicero would have claimed that his long speeches were justified by exceptional circumstances as classified below.

to waste the entire day: the filibuster is not a purely modern phenomenon.

He shall have a grasp of public affairs: one wonders how this was to be ensured.

166 *to force through a measure by violence*: there were acts of violence (many being of this kind) in every year between 63 and 53. For details see Lintott (1) Appendix A.

Crassus: i.e. Lucius Licinius Crassus. See Index of Names.

the disorder fomented by Gnaeus Carbo: the exact issue is unknown.

he loses his immunity: the tribune's privilege of *sacrosanctitas*.

167 *legislation directed at private individuals*: in *Pro Sestio* 65 Cicero complains that he was driven out by a law naming him specifically, brought before the Council of the Plebs by the tribune Clodius; cf. *De Domo Sua* 47. Interestingly, Ateius Capito, a lawyer of the early empire, includes among examples of *privilegium* the decree *recalling* Cicero (Aulus Gellius 10. 20. 3). For a discussion of Cicero's arguments see Greenidge (2) 361–5.

no legal action had been taken against me: cf. *Pro Sestio* 73.

the whole of Italy: 'On 8 August [57 BC], when I was in Brundisium, I heard from Quintus that the measure legalizing my recall had been passed at the Assembly of Centuries. This was greeted with extraordinary delight by all ages and classes in an astonishing crowd that had flocked to Rome from all over Italy' (*Att.* 4. 1. 4).

168 *no official record*: the bills are to be filed in the treasury (11 above). This practice had existed since early times (Livy 3. 55. 13); but possibly the system was not working to Cicero's satisfaction. Certainly under Augustus, about 11 BC, reforms were made as a result of officials' carelessness (Dio 54. 36).

The Greeks: probably Cicero's source is Demetrius of Phalerum, who is mentioned on other occasions.

a trial . . . in a court of law: magistrates had always been open to prosecution at the end of their term of office. Cicero's proposal is new in that it requires a report to be made even if the magistrate has done well.

169 *Marcus Junius*: see Index of Names under Junius.

INDEX OF NAMES

Each person's names are listed in the order used by Cicero.

ACCIUS, LUCIUS: b. 170, a prolific playwright, he was most famous for his versions of Greek tragedy, but he also handled subjects from Roman history. He died some time after 90. *L.* 2. 54.

ACHILLES: the hero of Homer's *Iliad*. *R.* 1. 30.

ACILIUS, LUCIUS: an authority on law, contemporary with Cato the Censor. *L.* 2. 59.

AELIUS STILO, LUCIUS: the first great Roman scholar. Born *c.*150, he had some famous pupils, including Varro and Cicero. He produced editions of Ennius and Lucilius. *L.* 2. 59.

AELIUS PAETUS CATUS, SEXTUS: consul 198, famous for his knowledge of the law. *R.* 1. 30, 2. 59.

AENIANES: a people living in the upper Spercheus valley in north-central Greece. *R.* 2. 8.

AEQUI: a mountain tribe north-east of Rome. They fought against Rome in the fifth century, but were conquered and eventually absorbed. *R.* 2. 36.

AESCHINES: *c.*397–*c.*322. Famous Athenian orator, opponent of Demosthenes. *R.* 4. 13.

AESCULAPIUS: Latinized form of Asclepius the Greek god of healing. The cult was brought to Rome in 293, and a temple was dedicated in 291. *L.* 2. 19.

AETOLIANS: a people of north-central Greece. *R.* 3. 15.

AHALA, GAIUS SERVILIUS: he was exiled by his ungrateful countrymen after killing Spurius Maelius, a would-be tyrant, in 439. *R.* 1. 6.

ALEXANDER THE GREAT: 356–323. *R.* 3. 15; *L.* 2. 41.

AMALTHEA: nurse of Zeus, variously described as a nymph and a she-goat. *L.* 2. 7.

AMPHIARAUS: a prophet who foresaw that the expedition of the seven Argive chiefs against Thebes was doomed to fail, but nevertheless took part in it at the behest of his wife, Eriphyle, who had been bribed with a necklace by Polynices. *L.* 2. 33.

AMPIUS BALBUS, TITUS: tribune in 63, Balbus was a staunch supporter of Pompey. Exiled by Julius Caesar, he was recalled in 46 through Cicero's influence. *L.* 2. 6.

AMULIUS: deposed his brother Numitor from the throne of Alba Longa, and made Numitor's daughter, Silvia, a Vestal Virgin. She, however, was violated by Mars and became the mother of Romulus and Remus. *R.* 2. 4.

ANAXAGORAS: 500–428. After coming to Athens in 480, he taught that in the beginning the seeds of everything existed in an undifferentiated mixture. Thanks to a rotatory motion initiated by mind, the various seeds separated out, and our world was formed. *R.* 1. 25.

ANCUS MARCIUS: fourth king of Rome (641–617). He built the first bridge over the Tiber and extended Roman territory to the coast, where he founded Ostia. *R.* 2. 5, 33, 35, 38.

ANTIOCHUS OF ASCALON: *c.*125–*c.*68. He broke away from the scepticism of the New Academy and developed an eclectic system embodying elements of the Old Academy, Aristotle, and the Stoics. *L.* 1. 54.

APIS: the sacred bull worshipped by the Egyptians in Memphis. The cult is believed to have given rise to the worship of Sarapis, a Hellenized Egyptian religion which became widespread in the third century. *R.* 3. 14.

APOLLO: a Greek deity with many functions, including music, archery, medicine, and the care of flocks and herds. From early times he was a god of prophecy, and had a number of oracular shrines of which Delphi was the most famous. *R.* 2. 44.

APPIUS: see Claudius.

APULEIUS SATURNINUS, LUCIUS: as tribune in 103 he secured grants of land for the veterans of Marius' campaign against Jugurtha. In 100 he proposed similar grants for the veterans of the campaigns against the Teutones and Cimbri. In addition, against the will of the Senate, he proposed a bill providing cheap corn for the people. Eventually he alienated Marius and was put to death. *L.* 2. 14; 3. 20, 26.

AQUILIUS, MANIUS: consul in 129. With a senatorial commission he organized the province of Asia. *R.* 1. 14.

AQUILO: the north wind (the Greek Boreas). *L.* 1. 3.

ARATUS: (of Soli in Cilicia), *c.*315–240. Author of an astronomical poem entitled *Phaenomena*, which was long admired. Cicero translated it in his youth. *R.* 1. 22, 56; *L.* 2. 7.

ARCESILAUS: 316–242. As Head of the Academy, he gave the school the sceptical direction which it followed until the time of Antiochus. *L.* 1. 39.

ARCHIMEDES OF SYRACUSE: *c.*287–212. Famous as a mathematician and as an inventor of ingenious devices, e.g. a screw for raising water. *R.* 1. 21, 22, 28.

ARCHYTAS: (of Tarentum in southern Italy), flourished in the first half of the fourth century. Famous for the advances he made in mathematics and musical theory. In philosophy he was a Pythagorean. *R.* 1. 16, 60.

ARISTO OF CHIOS: a pupil of Zeno, he founded a branch of Stoicism about 250. Contrary to Zeno, he maintained that, among things neither good nor bad, no distinction could be drawn between 'preferable' and 'non-preferable'. *L.* 1. 38, 55.

ARISTODEMUS: a tragic actor at Athens in the early fourth century. *R.* 4. 13.

ARISTOPHANES: *c.*450–*c.*385. The most famous representative of the Greek Old Comedy, which was remarkable for its outspokenness. *L.* 2. 37.

ARISTOTLE: 384–322. Only a few of Aristotle's voluminous writings seem to have been available to Cicero; but some of the main features of his thinking were to be found in the works of his successors, e.g. Theophrastus and later Demetrius of Phalerum. *L.* 1. 38, 55; 3. 14.

ASELLIO, SEMPRONIUS: he served under Scipio at Numantia (134–3). He wrote a history of his own time in at least fourteen books down to the age of Sulla, in which he consciously improved on the annalistic tradition by dealing with cause and purpose and conveying a patriotic feeling. *L.* 1. 6.

ATILIUS CALATINUS, AULUS: consul 258 and 254, dictator 249, he was a famous general in the first Punic war (264–41). *R.* 1. 1; *L.* 2. 28.

ATTICUS, TITUS POMPONIUS: see Introd. p. xxiv.

ATTUS NAVIUS: a famous augur in the time of Tarquinius Priscus; see Livy 1. 36 with Ogilvie's note. *R.* 2. 36; *L.* 2. 33.

AULUS ATERNIUS: in about 454, with his fellow consul, Spurius Tarpeius, he brought in a law regulating fines and deposits. *R.* 2. 60.

BRUTUS, DECIMUS JUNIUS: consul 138 with Scipio. For his opposition to the tribunes see Curiatius, below. He campaigned successfully in Spain and used the spoils to erect public buildings. Later, in 129, he was responsible for Tuditanus' victory in Illyria. Patron of the poet Accius. *L.* 2. 54; 3, 20.

BRUTUS, LUCIUS JUNIUS: consul in 509 after the expulsion of King Tarquinius Superbus (Livy 1. 56–60). *R.* 2. 46.

BUSIRIS: mythical king of Egypt who slaughtered all foreigners entering the country. *R.* 3. 15.

CAECILIUS STATIUS: came to Italy as a prisoner of war from northern Italy in 223. Wrote over forty Roman comedies which brought him great prestige. Died in 168. *R.* 4. 11.

CALATINUS: see Atilius.

CALCHAS: mythical Greek seer in the period of the Trojan war. *L.* 2. 33.

CAMILLUS, MARCUS FURIUS: he subdued the Etruscan town of Veii in 396, but incurred the hostility of the plebs for his disposition of the spoils and was later sent into exile. He raised an army, however, and defeated the Gauls, who were departing after sacking Rome in 390. He then recovered the gold with which the Romans had bought off the invaders. *R.* 1. 6.

CANULEIUS, GAIUS: as tribune in 445, he introduced a bill allowing intermarriage between patricians and plebeians. *R.* 2. 63.

CARBO, GAIUS PAPIRIUS: a pro-Gracchan tribune in 131, he carried a law extending the secret ballot to legislative assemblies. An energetic opponent of Scipio. *L.* 3. 35.

aerarii). He supported Cicero against Catiline and during his exile. *L*. 3. 45.

CRASSUS, LUCIUS LICINIUS: b. 140, he was a famous orator, admired by Cicero, who made him the chief speaker in his *De Oratore*. As censor in 92, he had the teaching of rhetoric by Latin instructors banned—an act of political conservatism. *L*. 3. 42.

CRASSUS, PUBLIUS LICINIUS: father-in-law of Gaius Gracchus. He was an important member of the group that opposed Scipio and supported the Gracchi. *R*. 1. 31; his wealth is mentioned in 3. 17.

CURIATIUS, GAIUS: tribune in 138, during a food shortage he tried in vain to persuade the authorities to buy corn. When troops were being levied for service in Spain, he demanded that each tribune be allowed to exempt ten men. When the consuls Decimus Brutus and Scipio Nasica refused, he imposed a fine and had them put in prison. *L*. 3. 20.

CURIUS DENTATUS, MANIUS: a much revered figure in the austere old Roman mould. He was consul four times. As a general, he led armies to victory over the Senones in the north, the Samnites, Pyrrhus, and the Lucanians in the south. He died in 270. *R*. 3. 6, 40; *L*. 2. 3.

CYBELE: the Phrygian mother-goddess associated with Mt. Ida, who presided over crops, medicine, prophecy, and war. In consequence of a prophecy that, if brought to Rome, she would rid the country of the Carthaginians, her cult was imported from Asia Minor in 204; she was given a temple on the Palatine and was served by oriental priests. *L*. 2. 22.

CYLON: an Athenian aristocrat who tried to seize power (632?). When he and his followers were besieged on the Acropolis, he escaped, but his friends were killed, although they had taken refuge at an altar. The guilt for this crime was laid on Megacles and his family, the Alcmaeonidae. *L*. 2. 28.

CYPSELUS: tyrant of Corinth in the seventh century. His rule is represented as mild or severe, depending on the sources. Herodotus speaks of him banishing his opponents (5. 92). He promoted trade by founding colonies. *R*. 2. 34.

CYRUS THE GREAT: overthrew Astyages, king of Media, in 549. He then extended his empire to embrace Asia Minor, Babylonia, Assyria, Syria, and Palestine. In spite of his vast power, he had a reputation for wisdom and magnanimity. Best known to the Romans from Xenophon's biographical novel, the *Cyropedia*. *R*. 1. 43, 44; *L*. 2. 56.

DECIMUS VERGINIUS: (Lucius Verginius, according to Livy in his account of the episode in 3. 44–6). His uncompromising defence of his daughter's honour led to the second secession of the plebs. *R*. 2. 63.

DEMARATUS: a Corinthian aristocrat who migrated to Tarquinii, north of Rome, to escape the tyranny of Cypselus. According to tradition he was the father of Tarquinius Priscus. For discussion see Cornell, 124. *R*. 2. 34.

DEMETRIUS OF PHALERUM: b. *c*.350, a Peripatetic philosopher who ruled Athens for ten years. Among other measures, he appointed officials to supervise the observance of the laws. He was later librarian in Alexandria. *R.* 2. 2; *L.* 2. 64, 66; 3. 14.

DIAGONDAS: an obscure Theban lawgiver. *L.* 2. 37.

DICAEARCHUS: fl. 326–296. A pupil of Aristotle, he wrote voluminously on history, constitutions, literature, philosophy, and geography. *L.* 3. 14.

DIOGENES OF BABYLON: *c*.240–152. Pupil of Chrysippus and teacher of Panaetius, he visited Rome in 155, where he did much to develop interest in Stoicism. *L.* 3. 13.

DIONYSIUS: *c*.430–367. Tyrant of Syracuse. With Spartan help he held western Sicily against the Carthaginians and extended his influence to southern Italy. His immense power, however precarious (one recalls the sword of Damocles), brought prosperity to Syracuse. *R.* 1. 28; 3. 43.

DOLOPES: a people of Thessaly in the centre of northern Greece. *R.* 2. 8.

DORIS: a district in central Greece to the east of Aetolia. *R.* 2. 8.

DRACO: a legislator who, *c*.620, gave Athens its first written code. Such was his severity, however, that his laws were said to have been written in blood. *R.* 2. 2.

DUILIUS, GAIUS: consul 260. As commander of Rome's fleet, he defeated the Carthaginians off Mylae in north-east Sicily in the first Punic war. *R.* 1. 1.

EGERIA: a water nymph, worshipped with the Camenae (or Muses) at a spring within a grove outside the Porta Capena. She was said to have given advice to King Numa. *L.* 1. 4.

EMPEDOCLES: *c*.493–*c*.433. A Sicilian noble who won fame for his writings (in verse) on natural philosophy and religion. *R.* 3. 14.

ENNIUS, QUINTUS: 239–169. Most famous for his versions of Greek tragedy and for his *Annals*—a year-by-year account of the foundation and growth of Roman power. He was the acknowledged father of Latin poetry. *R.* 1. 3, 25, 30, 49, 64; 3. 6; 5. 1; 6. 10; *L.* 2. 57, 68.

EPICUREANS: see Epicurus.

EPICURUS: 341–270. He took over and developed Democritus' idea that the world consisted of atoms and void; that, although gods existed, they did not concern themselves with the world; that man's chief end was pleasure (or, rather, freedom from pain); and that the soul was mortal. *R.* 6. 3; *L.* 1. 21.

EPIMENIDES: a semi-legendary Cretan of the late sixth century, who is supposed to have purified Athens from the Cylonian pollution. He is credited with much epic verse and a prose work on *Sacrifice and the Cretan Constitution*. The stories of his life are nearly all miraculous. *L.* 2. 28.

EUDOXUS OF CNIDUS: (in south-west Asia Minor) *c*.390–*c*.340. A mathematician, geographer, and astronomer of the first importance. One of his works was the basis of Aratus' popular poem on stars and weather-signs. *R.* 1. 22.

EUMOLPIDAE: an Attic clan which provided priests for the Eleusinian mysteries. *L.* 2. 35.

FABIUS MAXIMUS, QUINTUS: after the crushing defeats of 218, 217, and 216, Fabius (nicknamed Cunctator, 'The Delayer') refused to risk a further engagement with Hannibal. Instead, he wore him down by guerilla tactics. Eventually, cut off from assistance, Hannibal had to leave Italy to defend Carthage. *R.* 1. 1.

FABIUS PICTOR, QUINTUS: a senator who served in the second Punic war (218–201). He wrote a history of Rome in Greek. *L.* 1. 6.

FABRICIUS LUSCINUS, GAIUS: consul 282 and 278, censor 275. Another example of early Roman austerity and integrity. His campaigns in southern Italy played a major part in the defeat of Pyrrhus. *R.* 3. 40; *L.* 2. 58.

FANNIUS, GAIUS: consul 122, son-in-law of Laelius. It is uncertain whether he or another Gaius Fannius wrote a history of his own times. *R.* 1. 18; *L.* 1. 6.

FIGULUS, GAIUS MARCUS: consul 64, a supporter of Cicero's. His monument was notably extravagant. *L.* 2. 62.

FURIUS PHILUS, LUCIUS: consul 136. As a young man he, like Scipio, was a supporter of Terence.

FLAMINIUS, GAIUS: as tribune in 232, he carried, against senatorial opposition, a bill distributing land confiscated from the Senones in north-east Italy to the Roman poor. He was the first of his family to reach the consulship (223); he died in the defeat at Lake Trasimene (217). *L.* 3. 20.

GABINIUS, AULUS: grandson of a slave. As tribune in 139 he introduced the secret ballot at elections. *L.* 3. 35.

GAIUS JULIUS: a member of the second, unpopular, Board of Ten in 449. *R.* 2. 61.

GAIUS JULIUS IULLUS: consul 430, carried a law commuting fines in livestock to cash (Livy 4. 30). Livy gives his name as Lucius. *R.* 2. 60.

GAULS: they sacked Rome in 390, taking away whatever they could carry, but (it seems) leaving most of the monuments and buildings alone (Cornell 317–18). *R.* 2. 11; 3. 15.

GELLIUS, GNAEUS: an annalist who, *c.*130, wrote a history of Rome down to 146, at least. The work was characterized by its verbosity. See Raaflaub 3 and his references. *L.* 1. 6.

GELLIUS PUBLICOLA, LUCIUS: praetor, then governor of an eastern province. At Athens on his way home he offered to help the philosophers to reach a consensus. He was an adherent of Pompey, and supported Cicero in 63. *L.* 1. 53.

GRACCHUS, GAIUS SEMPRONIUS: younger brother of Tiberius. Tribune in 123, he carried some radical measures, continuing the programme of

Tiberius. In 122 he tried to obtain citizenship for the Latins, but was defeated. When his policies were attacked in 121, he resorted to violence, and, like his brother, was killed in a riot. *L.* 3. 20, 24, 26.

GRACCHUS, TIBERIUS SEMPRONIUS: father of the Gracchi; censor 169, when he opposed the syndicates of tax-collectors in Asia Minor. Distinguished as a general and as a statesman. See Livy 43. 16. *R.* 6. 2.

GRACCHUS, TIBERIUS SEMPRONIUS: cousin and brother-in-law of Scipio. As Tribune in 133 he proposed to the people (by-passing the Senate) an agrarian law assigning public land to the Roman poor. It was vetoed by another tribune, Marcus Octavius, who was then illegally deposed. Gracchus (again ignoring the Senate) proposed that the legacy left to Rome by Attalus of Pergamum should be used to equip the new allotment holders. Scipio Nasica then led a mob of senators against Gracchus, who was killed in the ensuing riot. *R.* 1. 31; 2. 49 (?); 3. 41; *L.* 3. 20, 24.

GRATIDIUS, MARCUS GAIUS: attempted to bring in a ballot law in Arpinum. *L.* 3. 36.

GRATIDIANUS, MARIUS: son of Marcus Gratidius and nephew of Gaius Marius. When he was praetor (probably in 85 or 84) he announced an edict to fix the value of the currency, thus obtaining personal credit for what had been a committee's decision. *L.* 3. 36.

HELENUS: son of Priam, he prophesied the fall of Troy and, later, the course of Aeneas' wanderings. *L.* 2. 33.

HERACLIDES OF PONTUS: a fourth-century academic philosopher who wrote on a wide range of subjects. Among his ethical works were dialogues on government and laws, in which philosophers, generals, and statesmen conversed. *L.* 3. 14.

HERCULES: i.e. Heracles, the most popular of all Greek heroes. At a very early stage his cult came to Rome, where he was worshipped at the *Ara Maxima* (Greatest Altar) and several other places. *R.* 1. 37; 2. 34; *L.* 2. 19, 27.

HERODOTUS: 'the father of history'. Born in Halicarnassus in Caria (Asia Minor) probably in the 490s, he lived until the 420s. He travelled extensively, gathering information of all kinds, which he used in his history of the Persian wars. *L.* 1. 5.

HOMER: accepted in antiquity as the author of the *Iliad* and the *Odyssey*. The date and place of his birth are unknown. Modern opinion puts him in the late eighth century. *R.* 1. 56; 2. 18, 19; 4. 5; 6. 10; *L.* 1. 2.

HORATIUS BARBATUS, MARCUS: consul 449. Following the secession of the plebs and the resignation of the second Board of Ten, he and his colleague passed laws which made important concessions to the plebs in connection with their resolutions, the right of appeal, and the inviolability of the tribunes. *R.* 2. 54.

LUCRETIA: wife of Tarquinius Collatinus. She was violated by Sextus, son of Tarquinius Superbus. This resulted in the expulsion of the Tarquins. See Livy 1. 57–60. *R.* 2. 46; *L.* 2. 10.

LUCRETIUS TRICIPITINUS, SPURIUS: father of Lucretia; consul 509. The family is supposed to have worshipped a three-headed deity, hence Tricipitinus (Ogilvie 228). *R.* 2. 46, 55.

LUCULLUS PONTICUS, LUCIUS LICINIUS: as consul in 74 he obtained a military command against Mithridates of Pontus, but failed to bring the campaign to a successful conclusion. After 59 he lived in luxurious retirement. *L.* 3. 30.

LUCUMO: said to be an Etruscan king who supported Romulus, but the origin of the name Luceres is far from clear (Ogilvie 81; Cornell 139–40). Later, in Livy 1. 34, Lucumo is said to have been the original name of Tarquinius Priscus, who was born in Etruria. *R.* 2. 14.

LYCAONIANS: they lived in Asia Minor, north of Cilicia, east of Phrygia and Pisidia. *R.* 2. 33.

LYCURGUS: according to tradition, he was the founder of the Spartan constitution. *R.* 2. 2, 15, 18, 42, 43, 50, 58; 3. 16; 4. 5; *L.* 1. 57.

MACER, GAIUS LICINIUS: father of Catullus' friend, Calvus. In 73 he campaigned for the restoration of the tribunes' powers. After serving as praetor in 68, he was convicted of extortion in 66 and took his own life. His history of Rome in at least 16 books was used by Livy. *L.* 1. 7.

MAELIUS, SPURIUS: a rich man who in 440 bought corn in Etruria and began to distribute it free to the Roman plebs. He was accused of aiming at the kingship. When he resisted arrest he was killed by Servilius Ahala, Master of the Cavalry (Livy 4. 13–14). *R.* 2. 49.

MAMILIUS LIMETANUS, GAIUS: as tribune in 109, he reduced the three arbitrators on boundaries required by the Twelve Tables to one. Hence his name Limetanus, 'the boundary man'. *L.* 1. 55.

MANCINUS, GAIUS HOSTILIUS: as consul in 137 he was defeated by the people of Numantia in Spain. His quaestor, Ti. Gracchus, managed to make an agreement which saved the Roman army, but it was repudiated by the Senate at the instigation of Scipio. Mancinus was handed over to the Numantines, but they, magnificently, refused to accept him. Mancinus then resumed his career. *R.* 3. 28.

MANILIUS, MANIUS: consul 149; a prominent orator and jurist. *R.* 1. 18, 20, 34; 2. 28, 29; 3. 17; 5. 3(?); 6. 9.

MANLIUS CAPITOLINUS, MARCUS: in 390, alerted by the sacred geese, he held the Capitol against the Gauls (Livy 5. 47). Subsequently he tried to use the gold recovered by Camillus to relieve the conditions of the plebs. He was therefore condemned for treason and put to death (Livy 6. 11–20). *R.* 2. 49.

MARCELLUS, GAIUS CLAUDIUS: served with Cicero in the college of augurs, though he seems to have been entirely sceptical about the institution. *L.* 2. 32, (33).

MARCELLUS, MARCUS CLAUDIUS: consul for the first time in 222, he was a famous general who had several successes in northern Italy, Campania, and Sicily. *R.* 1. 1, 21; 5. 10.

MARCELLUS, MARCUS CLAUDIUS: consul 166 and 155. His policy of conciliation brought peace to nearer Spain from 151 to 143. *R.* 1. 21.

MARIUS, GAIUS: *c.*157–86. Seven times consul. From an equestrian family in Arpinum, he served under Scipio at Numantia (134–3), married into the Julian family, enrolled troops from the Roman poor for his campaigns against Jugurtha in North Africa. After disposing of Jugurtha (104), he defeated the Teutones and Cimbri (German tribes) in 102 and 101. He fought in the Italian war, but fled to Africa when Sulla seized Rome in 88. On Sulla's departure, Marius raised troops and marched on Rome in 87. Sulla was declared an exile, and Marius entered on his seventh consulship in 86. He died early in that year. *R.* 1. 6; *L.* 1. 1, 2, 3, 4; 2. 56; 3. 36.

MARS: whatever his origins may have been, he was identified with the Greek war-god Ares at an early stage. In Roman myth he was the father of Romulus. *R.* 2. 4; 6. 17.

MASINISSA: *c.*240–148. A prince of Numidia in North Africa who helped the Carthaginians against the Romans in Spain before 206. He was then won over by Scipio the elder, and was thereafter a loyal ally of Rome. As such he became master of all Numidia. *R.* 6. 9.

MEGILLUS: a Spartan who figures in Plato's *Laws*. *L.* 1. 15.

MELAMPUS: a legendary Greek prophet who came to understand the speech of birds and animals. *L.* 2. 33.

MERCURY: the Roman equivalent of the Greek Hermes, and one of the seven planets, the others being Venus, Mars, Jupiter, Saturn, the sun, and the moon. The earth was not thought of as a planet. (Uranus, Neptune, and Pluto, being invisible to the naked eye, were unknown in antiquity.) See the index to Manilius, Loeb edn. by G. P. Goold. *R.* 6. 17.

METELLUS, LUCIUS CAECILIUS: consul 251. In Sicily, during the first Punic war, he captured the Carthaginian war elephants at Panormus (250). *R.* 1. 1.

METELLUS MACEDONICUS, QUINTUS CAECILIUS: presided over the annexation of Macedonia in 148, then defeated the Greek forces of Critolaus in 146. This led to the destruction of Corinth and the settlement of Greece. Metellus was consul in 143. He overcame the Celtiberians in Hither Spain, preparing the way for its conquest. He was for many years an opponent of Scipio. For their shifting relations see Astin's index. *R.* 1. 31.

METELLUS NUMIDICUS, QUINTUS CAECILIUS: nephew of Macedonicus. Consul in 109, he fought against Jugurtha with some initial success, but was replaced by Marius in 108. In 100 the tribune Saturninus introduced a bill to obtain land for Marius' veterans in the south of France, and obliged every senator to uphold it on pain of exile. Metellus alone chose exile. He was recalled in 99 or 98. *R.* 1. 6; *L.* 3. 26.

MILTIADES: he persuaded the Greeks to fight at Marathon (490). He then obtained command of an expedition against the island of Paros, which had supported the Persians. He failed to take it, however, and returned home wounded. He was punished with a heavy fine and died soon after. Cicero's is a rather tendentious version of what happened. *R.* 1. 5.

MINOS: prehistoric and semi-legendary king of Crete. His name has been given to the bronze-age civilization of Crete (3000–1000). *R.* 2. 2.

MOPSUS: famous prophet, son of Apollo and Teiresias' daughter. *L.* 2. 33.

MUCIUS: see Scaevola (1).

MUCIUS: see Scaevola (2).

MUMMIUS, SPURIUS: an orator in the Stoic style; he accompanied Scipio to the east in 140–39. *R.* 1. 18, 34; 3. 46–8; 5. 11.

NAEVIUS, GNAEUS: born in Campania *c.*270, he wrote an epic on the struggle with Carthage, tragedies on Greek and Roman themes, and numerous comedies. Though Cicero implies that he did not go far in criticizing politicians, there is a strong tradition that he was jailed for his remarks (Aulus Gellius 3. 3. 15). For his fragments see *ROL* 2. 46–156. *R.* 4. 11; *L.* 2. 39.

NASICA: see under Scipio (5).

NEOPTOLEMUS: son of Achilles. He played a major part in the capture of Troy. He also figured in drama. *R.* 1. 30.

NUMA POMPILIUS: second king of Rome (715–673). He was credited with all the major religious institutions, including the calendar and priesthoods. *R.* 2. 25, 26, 28, 29, 31, 33; 3. 47; 5. 3; *L.* 1. 4; 2. 23, 29, 56.

OPIMIUS, LUCIUS: consul 121, he led the attack on Gaius Gracchus, and was acquitted of the charges subsequently brought against him. Later, probably in 109, he was convicted of incompetence and corruption in dealing with Jugurtha. *R.* 1. 6.

ORITHYIA: daughter of Erechtheus, mythical king of Athens. She was carried off by the north wind while playing by the Ilissus. *L.* 1. 3.

PACUVIUS, MARCUS: 220–*c.*130. Nephew of Ennius. He wrote over a dozen versions of Greek tragedies and was considered one of the best exponents of the genre. *R.* 1. 30; 3. 14.

PANAETIUS: *c.*185–109. Pupil of Diogenes of Babylon. Came to Rome *c.*144 and joined Scipio's group of friends. Head of the Stoa from 129–109. His form of Stoicism suited the practical Roman mind. Cicero drew on him extensively in the *De Officiis*. *R.* 1. 15, 34; *L.* 3. 14.

PAPIRIUS CRASSUS, LUCIUS: censor in 430 according to Cicero. *R.* 2. 60.

PAPIRIUS CRASSUS, PUBLIUS: consul 430. His first name is Lucius in Livy. *R.* 2. 60.

PAULUS MACEDONICUS, LUCIUS AEMILIUS: father of Scipio Aemilianus: consul for the second time in 168, he finished the third Macedonian war by defeating Perseus at Pydna. Of the spoils he is said to have kept only Perseus' library. *R.* 1. 14, 23, 31; 6. 14.

PEISISTRATUS: ruler of Athens; he was expelled on more than one occasion before he finally returned in 546. He kept himself in power by mercenaries and hostages, but retained Solon's constitution. He encouraged mining and agriculture, and his regime saw the beginnings of tragedy and the first recension of Homer. He acquired an Athenian power-base on the Hellespont. *R.* 1. 68.

PERICLES: *c.*495–429. General, orator, and architectural patron, he is the most famous of all Greek statesmen. *R.* 1. 25; 4. 11.

PHAEDRUS: *c.*140–70, An Epicurean whom Cicero heard lecture in Rome before 88 and again ten years later in Athens. *L.* 1. 53.

PHALARIS: tyrant of Agrigentum in Sicily, *c.*570–550. He became a byword for cruelty by roasting his victims alive inside a bronze bull. *R.* 1. 44.

PHIDIAS: b. *c.*490, he was the most famous of all Greek sculptors, known for his huge statue of Athena Promachus (the Foremost Warrior), and the gold and ivory cult statues of Athena in the Parthenon and Zeus in the temple at Olympia. He also supervised the carving of the so-called Elgin Marbles. *R.* 3. 44.

PHILIP: Philip II, King of Macedon, father of Alexander the Great; 382–36. A resourceful general and a shrewd diplomat, who united Macedonia, organized a professional army, and presided over a Greek federation. *R.* 3. 15; 4. 13.

PHILIPPUS, LUCIUS MARCUS: consul 91. He opposed the programme of Livius Drusus and had it rescinded. As censor in 86, however, when Rome was controlled by Cinna, he enrolled the Italians as citizens. After 83 he supported Sulla. *L.* 2. 31.

PHILOLAUS: a Pythagorean of Croton or Tarentum in southern Italy. Born *c.*470. He wrote the first published account of Pythagoras' cosmology. See Freeman 73–7 for his fragments (their authenticity, however, is debated). *R.* 1. 16.

PHILUS, LUCIUS FURIUS: see Furius.

PHLIASIANS: from Phlius in the north-east Peloponnese. *R.* 2. 8.

PHOENICIANS: in modern Lebanon and northern Israel. See Carthaginians.

PHRYGIANS: in central Asia Minor. *L.* 2. 33.

PISIDIANS: in southern Asia Minor. *R.* 2. 33.

PISO FRUGI, LUCIUS CALPURNIUS: tribune in 149, he established a court for cases of extortion. Consul in 133 and censor in 120. His history of Rome from its foundations in 7 volumes was a factual record without any ornaments (Cicero, *De Oratore* 2. 53); but stylistic embellishment could also involve distortion. *L.* 1. 6.

PITTACUS OF MYTILENE (the main city of Lesbos): *c.*650–570. He was legislator between 590 and 580. One of his laws doubled the penalty for all offences committed under the influence of drink. *L.* 2. 66.

PLATO: *c.*429–347. Cicero, in the present works, was mainly interested in his *Republic* and *Laws*; apart from the content, he was influenced by Plato's handling of dialogue. *R.* 1. 16, 22, 29, 65; 2. 3, 22, 51; 4. 4, 5; *L.* 1. 15, 55; 2. 6, 14, 16, 38, 41, 45, 67, 69; 3. 1, 5, 14, 32.

PLAUTUS, TITUS MACCIUS: a prolific and popular writer of Graeco-Roman comedy in the late third and early second centuries. *R.* 4. 11.

POLEMO OF ATHENS: head of the Academy from 314–270. *L.* 1. 38.

POLLUX: see Castor.

POLYBIUS: b. *c.*200, died after 118. A major Greek historian who recorded the rise of Rome in 40 books from 220–146. He ascribed Rome's supremacy to her mixed constitution, her army, and her early development. Though rather dull, he was a scholarly and honest writer. An important source for Livy. *R.* 1. 34; 2. 27; 4. 3.

POLYIDUS: a mythical Corinthian prophet and miracle-worker. *L.* 2. 33.

POMPEIUS, QUINTUS: consul 141; he took over from Metellus in Spain, but failed to subdue the inhabitants of Numantia. He made a treaty with them, but denied having done so. The Senate recognized that the treaty had been made, but refused to honour it. *R.* 3. 28.

POMPEY: Gnaeus Pompeius Magnus, 106–48. He became consul in 70 with Crassus though not legally entitled to that office. They dismantled Sulla's constitution and restored the tribunes' powers. When Pompey returned to Rome in 62 after reorganizing Asia Minor, Cicero hoped that he and the Senate could be induced to work together. This, however, proved impossible. The Senate refused to ratify Pompey's settlement, and so he combined with Crassus and Caesar to overthrow the Senate's authority. This was the so-called First Triumvirate. Though the partnership was renewed in 55, Crassus was killed in 53, and Pompey and Caesar became enemies. This culminated in the civil war (49–45) from which Caesar emerged victorious. (Pompey was defeated at Pharsalus and then murdered in Egypt.) *L.* 1. 8; 2. 6; 3. 22, 26.

POPILLIUS LAENAS, GAIUS: son of Laenas (see above). Following the defeat of the consul L. Cassius' army in the valley of the Garonne (107), Popillius saved the survivors by surrendering half of the baggage and giving hostages to the Tigurini. He was therefore prosecuted for treason by Coelius Caldus. *L.* 3. 36.

PORCII: (1) In 199 the tribune Publius Porcius Laeca gave the right of appeal to Romans in Italy and the provinces.

(2) In 198 or 195 Marcus Porcius Cato prohibited the flogging of citizens without appeal.

(3) In 184 the consul Lucius Porcius Licinus protected them from summary execution when on military service. *R.* 2. 54.

POSTUMUS COMINIUS: consul 493 with Spurius Cassius. *R.* 2. 57.

PROCULUS JULIUS: a farmer from Alba Longa, who had come to Rome for the day, claimed that the ascended Romulus had appeared to him (Livy 1. 16). *R.* 2. 20; *L.* 1. 3.

PUBLICOLA: see Valerius.

PUBLIUS PINARIUS: censor in 430. *R.* 2. 60.

PYTHAGORAS OF SAMOS: emigrated to Croton *c.*531. He believed in the cycle of reincarnation from which the soul might obtain release by ritual purity. He was a pioneer in mathematics and musical theory. *R.* 1. 16; 2. 28, 29; 3. 19.

QUIRINUS: the deified Romulus. For the name, which is linked with the Quirinal hill and with *Quirites* (the formal name of the citizen body), see Ogilvie 84. *R.* 2. 20; *L.* 1. 3; 2. 19.

RAMNES: one of the three tribes of early Rome. The name was supposed to be derived from Romulus. *R.* 2. 36.

REMUS (the *e* is short): brother of Romulus. 'Romulus' and 'Remus' may have been the Etruscan and Greek forms of the same name. So Ogilvie 46. For discussions of the legend, see Ogilvie 46–8; Cornell 57–63. *R.* 2. 4; *L.* 1. 8.

ROMULUS (the *o* is long): mythical founder of Rome. See under Remus, above. *R.* 1. 25, 58, 64; 2. 4, 10, 11, 14, 16, 17, 18, 19, 20, 22, 23, 25, 26, 50, 51, 52, 53; 3. 47; 6. 24; *L.* 1. 3, 8; 2. 33.

ROSCIUS GALLUS, QUINTUS: d. 62. Rome's most famous actor (see Garton's index). Sulla made him a knight—a rank which involved a fortune of at least 400,000 sesterces. *L.* 1. 11.

RUTILIUS RUFUS, PUBLIUS: pupil of Panaetius in philosophy, Publius Scaevola in law, and Servius Sulpicius Galba in oratory. Consul 105. In 94 he offended the knights by his reorganization of the finances of Asia Minor. He was convicted unfairly of extortion in 92, and went into exile in Asia Minor, where he was welcomed with honour. *R.* 1. 13, 17.

RUTULI: an ancient people of Latium, whose capital was Ardea, some 20 miles (32 km.) south of Rome. Ardea was the home of Turnus in the *Aeneid*. *R.* 2. 5.

SABAZIUS: the Phrygian Dionysus or Zeus. His rites, ridiculed by Aristophanes and Demosthenes, were supposed to remove inherited guilt and to guarantee admission to the banquets of the blessed. *L.* 2. 37.

SABINES: a people living in the hills north-east of Rome. They were in inter-mittent conflict with the Romans from regal times down to 449, when they suffered a heavy defeat. They became Roman citizens in 268 and were quickly assimilated. *R.* 2. 12, 13, 14, 25, 36; 3. 7, 40; *L.* 2. 3.

SAMNITES: a hardy people living to the east of Latium. Rome's main Italian rival in the fourth century, they assisted Pyrrhus and Hannibal in the third, and continued to oppose the Romans down to the time of Sulla. *R.* 3. 7, 40.

SATURN: an old god identified by the Romans with the Greek Kronos, who was ousted by Zeus and took refuge in Latium, where he presided over a golden age. One of the seven planets. *R.* 6. 17.

SCAEVOLA (1), PUBLIUS MUCIUS: consul 133; an eminent lawyer; opponent of Scipio; adviser of Ti. Gracchus. *R.* 1. 20, 31; *L.* 2. 47, 50, 52, 57.

SCAEVOLA (2), QUINTUS MUCIUS 'THE AUGUR': son-in-law of Laelius; consul 117; a distinguished lawyer who taught Cicero. *R.* 1. 18, 33; *L.* 1. 13.

SCAEVOLA (3), QUINTUS MUCIUS 'THE PONTIFEX': son of Publius Mucius. He published the first systematic treatise on civil law. Reorganized the province of Asia Minor. Pontifex maximus in 89. Murdered in 82. *L.* 2. 47, 49, 50, 52.

SCAEVOLA (4), QUINTUS MUCIUS: tribune 54; friend of Quintus Cicero; men-tioned as a poet by Pliny the Younger (*Letters* 5. 3. 5). *L.* 1. 1 (?).

SCAURUS, MARCUS AEMILIUS: consul 115, married a Metella and became leader of the Metellus faction. Censor 109. In 100 led the Senate against Saturninus and his supporters. *L.* 3. 36.

SCIPIO (1) CALVUS, GNAEUS CORNELIUS: consul 222. Was sent to Spain to work with his brother (Scipio 2) against the Carthaginian Hasdrubal. They captured Saguntum in 212, but both were defeated and killed in 211. *R.* 1. 1; 4. 11.

SCIPIO (2), PUBLIUS CORNELIUS: consul 218; father of Scipio Africanus Major (3). Defeated by Hannibal in 218, sent to Spain in 217, where he met his death. *R.* 1. 1; 4. 11.

SCIPIO (3) AFRICANUS MAJOR, PUBLIUS CORNELIUS: 236–183; son of Scipio (2). He established Roman power in Spain (210–206); he then invaded Africa and eventually overcame Hannibal at Zama (202). *R.* 1. 1, 27; 6. 10, 15, 17, 20, 26, frag. 3, 4; *L.* 2. 57.

SCIPIO (4) AEMILIANUS AFRICANUS MINOR, PUBLIUS CORNELIUS: see Introd. pp. xviii–xix and the study by Astin.

SCIPIO (5) NASICA SERAPIO, PUBLIUS CORNELIUS: consul 138 (see Curiatius, Gaius). In 133, when Ti. Gracchus agitated for a second tribunate, Nasica led a crowd of senators to the assembly, where they killed Gracchus and large numbers of his followers, thus incurring the odium of the people. *R.* 1. 6; *L.* 3. 20.

SERVIUS SULPICIUS GALBA: consul 144. A famous orator; but as a general he contributed to Rome's reputation for treachery in Spain. *R.* 3. 42.

included an expansion of the Senate, a drastic reduction in the power of the tribunes, and the creation of seven criminal courts with senatorial juries. *L.* 2. 56, 57; 3. 22.

SULPICIUS GALUS, GAIUS: an astronomer who predicted the eclipse of the moon on 21 June 168. Consul 166. *R.* 1. 21, 22, 23.

SULPICIUS RUFUS, PUBLIUS: tribune in 88, he wanted, like Livius Drusus, to distribute the newly-enfranchised Italians over all the thirty-five tribes. When opposed by the Senate, he enlisted the support of Marius and pushed through his programme. Sulla, however, took over the capital, and Sulpicius was hunted down and killed. *L.* 3. 20.

TARQUINIUS PRISCUS, LUCIUS: fifth king of Rome (616–579), said to be the son of Demaratus of Corinth. The story of the eagle snatching off and replacing his cap (an omen of future kingship) is told in Livy 1. 34. 8. For the Tarquin family tree, see Cornell 123. *R.* 2. 35, 37, 38; *L.* 1. 4.

TARQUINIUS, SEXTUS: the most famous rapist in history. His father had made him king in Gabii; but when the inhabitants heard about his violation of Lucretia, they put him to death (Livy 1. 54, 57–8, 60). *L.* 2. 10.

TARQUINIUS SUPERBUS, LUCIUS: last king of Rome (534–509). 'Under his rule Rome became the dominant power in central Italy, and its prosperity was reflected in the monumental development of the city' (Cornell 121). In the tradition, however, he is also a ruthless tyrant. After his son's rape of Lucretia the family was expelled. *R.* 1. 62; 2. 28, 46, 51, 52; *L.* 2. 10.

TATIUS, TITUS: a Sabine king. After the peace brought about by the abducted Sabine women (Livy 1. 13. 5–8, 14. 1–2) he reigned jointly with Romulus until his death. *R.* 2. 13, 14.

TAURIANS: a people living on the mountainous south coast of the Crimea. Their maiden goddess, to whom strangers were sacrificed (Herodotus 4. 103) was identified with the Greek Artemis. *R.* 3. 15.

THALES OF MILETUS: according to tradition, b. 640. He is supposed to have predicted the solar eclipse of 28 May 585. The numerous discoveries and sayings attributed to him are listed in D.L. 1. 1. These include the contention that water is the primary substance underlying everything, and that the world is animate and full of divinities. *R.* 1. 22, 25; *L.* 2. 26.

THEMISTOCLES: *c.*528–462. He used the revenue from the mines at Laurium to build a fleet, which he commanded successfully against the Persians at Salamis (480). Subsequently, however, he lost influence, and *c.*470 was driven into exile by a vote of the people. *R.* 1. 5.

THEOPHRASTUS: *c.*370–*c.*285. He succeeded his teacher, Aristotle, in 323 as Head of the Peripatetic school; he produced a wide range of work on biology, physics, and ethics, and also on politics and law (D.L. 5. 42–50). *L.* 1. 38; 2. 15; 3. 13, 14.

THEOPOMPUS OF CHIOS: *c.*378–300. A pupil of Isocrates and a prolific historian. He continued Thucydides' work from 411 to 394, concentrating on the supremacy of Sparta. He also wrote a universal history in 58 books, starting from the accession of Philip of Macedon in 359. *R.* 2. 58; *L.* 1. 5; 3. 16.

THESEUS: legendary hero of Attica, which he is supposed to have unified into one state with Athens as its capital. For his numerous exploits, of which the most famous is his killing of the Minotaur and his elopement with Ariadne, see Plutarch, *Theseus. R.* 2. 2; *L.* 2. 5.

TIMAEUS: (1) of Locri in S. Italy. A Pythagorean philosopher, chief speaker in Plato's *Timaeus. R.* 1. 16.

(2) of Tauromenium in north-east Sicily: *c*.356–260. Fled to Athens, where he lived for 50 years. He wrote a history of Sicily in 38 books, which was admired by Polybius and Cicero. *R.* 3. 43; *L.* 2. 15.

TIMOTHEUS OF MILETUS: *c*.450–360. He developed the range of the lyre by increasing the number of its strings from seven to twelve, and was criticized for doing so. *L.* 2. 39.

TITANS: children of Heaven and Earth. Their struggle against Zeus is recounted by Hesiod, *Theogony* 664–721. *L.* 3. 5.

TITIUS, SEXTUS: tribune 99, proposed an agrarian law which was subsequently cancelled. In 98 he was convicted of treason, mainly because he kept a portrait of Apuleius Saturninus in his house. *L.* 2. 14, 31.

TITIES: the tribe named after Titus Tatius (see above). *R.* 2. 36.

TORQUATUS, AULUS MANLIUS: consul 244, 241; censor 247. *L.* 2. 55.

TRICIPITINUS: see Lucretius. *R.* 2. 46.

TUBERO, QUINTUS AELIUS: Scipio's nephew; a Stoic jurist. *R.* 1. 14, 17, 23, 26, 29, 31; 2. 64, 65.

TUBERTUS, PUBLIUS POSTUMIUS: consul 505 and 504. He campaigned successfully against the Sabines (Livy 2. 16). *L.* 2. 58.

TUDITANUS, GAIUS SEMPRONIUS: consul 129. He overcame the Iapydes in Illyria thanks to his lieutenant D. Junius Brutus. He wrote extensively about the Roman magistrates. *R.* 1. 14.

TULLUS HOSTILIUS: third king of Rome (674–642). He is supposed to have destroyed Alba Longa and transferred its population to Rome (Livy 1. 29). The senate house *Curia Hostilia* bore his name. *R.* 2. 31, 53; 3. 47.

VALERIUS POTITUS, LUCIUS: consul 449. See Horatius Barbatus. *R.* 2. 54.

VALERIUS PUBLICOLA, PUBLIUS: consul 509–4. A man of popular sympathies; hence the name Publicola or Poplicola (Livy 2. 8. 1). He was so poor that the authorities had to pay for his funeral. The authenticity of the appeal law (*R.* 2. 55) is defended by Cornell 276–7. *R.* 2. 53, 55; *L.* 2. 58.

VENNONIUS: a late second-century historian, used by Dionysius of Halicarnassus (4. 15. 1) and (to his annoyance) not available to Cicero (*Att.* 12. 3. 1). *L.* 1. 6.

VENUS: Roman goddess of love and sex. *R.* 6. 17.

VESTA: the hearth goddess, etymologically connected with the Greek Hestia. The Vestal Virgins had to ensure that the fire in her temple did not go out. *L.* 2. 29.

VICA POTA: an old Roman goddess of Victory, whose festival was on 5 January. She had a temple at the foot of the Velian hill. *L.* 2. 28.

VOLSCIANS: a people in south Latium who were strong opponents of Rome in the fifth and fourth centuries. *R.* 3. 7.

XENOCRATES: (of Chalcedon on the Bosporus), head of the Academy 339–314. He is credited with the division of philosophy into logic, physics, and ethics. *R.* 1. 3; *L.* 1. 38, 55.

XENOPHON OF ATHENS: *c.*428–*c.*354. An aristocrat who was a disciple of Socrates. In his *Anabasis* he described the retreat of the army of Greek mercenaries to the Black Sea in 399. Amongst other works he wrote a novelistic account of the education of Cyrus in 8 books. *L.* 2. 56.

XERXES: king of Persia 486–65. He bridged the Hellespont, dug a canal behind Mt. Athos, and ravaged Attica; but he was defeated at Salamis in 480. *R.* 3. 14; *L.* 2. 26.

ZALEUCUS: a stern lawgiver in the Greek colony of Locri in the toe of Italy in the seventh century. As with Charondas, the material about him is mainly fictitious. *L.* 1. 57; 2. 14, 15.

ZENO: (of Citium in Cyprus), 335–263. Founder of the Stoic school. See D.L. 7. 110–262. *L.* 1. 38, 53, 54, 55.

ZETHUS: son of Zeus and Antiope. He was a warrior, twin brother of the musician Amphion, with whom, according to one version, he founded Thebes. Here a character in a play by Pacuvius, doubtless his *Antiopa*. *R.* 1. 30.

The Oxford World's Classics Website

www.worldsclassics.co.uk

- Information about new titles
- Explore the full range of Oxford World's Classics
- Links to other literary sites and the main OUP webpage
- Imaginative competitions, with bookish prizes
- Peruse the Oxford World's Classics Magazine
- Articles by editors
- Extracts from Introductions
- A forum for discussion and feedback on the series
- Special information for teachers and lecturers

www.worldsclassics.co.uk

American Literature

British and Irish Literature

Children's Literature

Classics and Ancient Literature

Colonial Literature

Eastern Literature

European Literature

History

Medieval Literature

Oxford English Drama

Poetry

Philosophy

Politics

Religion

The Oxford Shakespeare

A complete list of Oxford Paperbacks, including Oxford World's Classics, Oxford Shakespeare, Oxford Drama, and Oxford Paperback Reference, is available in the UK from the Academic Division Publicity Department, Oxford University Press, Great Clarendon Street, Oxford OX2 6DP.

In the USA, complete lists are available from the Paperbacks Marketing Manager, Oxford University Press, 198 Madison Avenue, New York, NY 10016.

Oxford Paperbacks are available from all good bookshops. In case of difficulty, customers in the UK can order direct from Oxford University Press Bookshop, Freepost, 116 High Street, Oxford OX1 4BR, enclosing full payment. Please add 10 per cent of published price for postage and packing.